Dragonflies
of the world

Jill Silsby

Smithsonian Institution Press
Washington, D. C.

Published in 2001 in the United States of America
by the Smithsonian Institution Press
750 Ninth Street NW, Suite 4300
Washington, DC 20560–0950

in association with CSIRO PUBLISHING
150 Oxford Street (PO Box 1139)
Collingwood VIC 3066
Australia

Library of Congress Cataloging-in-Publication Data
Silsby, Jill.
    Dragonflies of the world / Jill Silsby.
        p.   cm.
    Includes bibliographical references (p.).
    ISBN 1-56098-959-9 (alk. paper)
        1. Dragonflies. I. Title.
    QL520.S56   2001
    595.7′33—dc21   2001020891

National Library of Australia Cataloguing-in-Publication Data available

Printed in Singapore by Craft Print International, not at government expense
08 07 06 05 04 03 02 01   5 4 3 2 1

Foreword

The publication of this book has come at a highly opportune time when the large numbers of people around the world showing an active interest in dragonflies are, through international travel, seeing many unfamiliar species. In her Preface, Jill says that her book 'is aimed at interested amateurs as well as experienced zoologists', and indeed, there is a wealth of beautifully presented important information in this work for anyone with an interest in the Odonata.

When I first became fascinated by dragonflies as a boy, my progress was painfully slow because the sole text to which I had access was Cynthia Longfield's *The Dragonflies of the British Isles* in Warne's *The Wayside and Woodland Series*. What a long way we have come since that wonderful pioneering effort of 1937! We now have many excellent, well illustrated books on the dragonflies of different countries and various parts of the world. The increasingly accessible information on odonates in books has gone hand-in-hand with a tremendous spurt in global research output on the group in recent years.

However, until the present time, a large void has existed in the dragonfly literature — no text existed which covered 'dragonflies of the world'. Earlier workers dealt with the general biology of the group, without attempting to describe the range of species in a taxonomic sense. Until Jill set out to portray at least one species from each of the 73 subfamilies of dragonflies, and to relate the overall classification to their evolution, ecology, behaviour and physiology, it was difficult to gain an integrated understanding of the Order Odonata.

There is no doubt that this book will intrigue and stimulate many readers who, while interested in natural history and in dragonflies particularly, had no general text to help them identify, at least to the family and subfamily levels, odonates seen anywhere in the world. Furthermore, having determined the type of dragonfly being observed, the book ensures that information is readily available on many aspects of their biology.

Dragonflies of the World is a really superb contribution to odonatology and complements magnificently Philip Corbet's monumental and much more specialised academic work *Dragonflies: Behaviour and Ecology of Odonata*.

May Jill Silsby's enthusiasm and skill — aided by the contributions of several other eminent odonatologists — in producing this fine work be reflected in an even greater interest in this ancient and beautiful group of insects.

Michael J. Parr
President, Worldwide Dragonfly Association

Contents

Opposite: *Libellula pulchella.*

Preface and acknowledgements

The beauty of dragonflies and their mastery of the air is fascinating to watch. I have long felt that we deserve to be given a greater knowledge of the dragonflies found in parts of the world other than those in which we live. A book describing the unique attributes of dragonflies in general, the distinctive features of individual families and subfamilies, and showing the incredible variety of these lovely, ubiquitous insects is long overdue.

Dragonflies of the World is aimed at interested amateurs as well as experienced zoologists and I have therefore refrained from using too much technical jargon. Taxonomic and physiological details are kept to a minimum and I have concentrated on describing general appearance and behaviour. English names, in addition to the scientific ones, are given where possible since I think many people find it easier to identify with a vernacular name. Where a genus is known in Britain as, for example, a chaser and in the United States of America as a skimmer, I have used the British version.

One of the problems presented by attempting to write a book on dragonflies is that of deciding how to refer to them. They belong in an Order called Odonata and it is common practice to refer to them all, loosely, as 'dragonflies' — hence *Dragonflies of the World*!

Complications arise because of the fact that the Order is divided into two principle suborders: Anisoptera and Zygoptera. Anisopterans are known as 'dragonflies' and zygopterans as 'damselflies'. In order to distinguish between the two meanings, I shall use the words 'dragonfly' and 'damselfly' respectively for anisopterans and zygopterans but, from this point onwards, 'Odonata' or 'odonates' when writing of them generally as members of the Order.

There are well over 5000 species of odonates known in the world and it is clearly impossible to illustrate or to describe them all. They are classified into suborders, superfamilies, families, subfamilies, genera and species. My object has been to classify down to subfamilies and tribes and to portray at least one species from each. Although I have travelled fairly extensively in all six continents, I have not been able to see representatives of all the subfamilies and I am grateful to experts from all over the world for photographs and information (including some major and very important contributions to the text), where I could not provide them myself.

In the past few years various alternative classifications have been proposed by a number of eminent odonatologists (Carle, Louton, Bechly, Nel, Pfau, Rehn and Trueman, to name some of the chief ones). In each of these, innovative ideas are put forward and many valuable points are made, but agreement is far from being reached. Major classification changes need plenty of time to be absorbed before they can be generally accepted but this book is not the vehicle to cover them. No one denies that there are anomalies in the well-tried Davies & Tobin system — interesting anomalies that present challenges and that include many that are accepted by Allen Davies himself. After much thought and discussion, we have decided to follow the Davies & Tobin classification in all but a few instances. This, which owes much to the earlier Fraser & Tillyard arrangement, is largely based on wing venation and venational changes that have been traced back through the millennia to our odonates' earliest ancestors.

In a book like this, formal references are out of place and I would like to acknowledge here the information I have gleaned from the published works of many eminent odonatologists from around the world, in particular: Dr Richard Askew, Professor Philip Corbet, Dr Henri Dumont, Dr Sidney Dunkle, Lt Col. F. C. Fraser, Dr Peter Miller, Dr Norman Moore, Dr Elliot Pinhey, Dr Richard Rowe, Professor Hidenori Ubukata, Dr Tony Watson and Mr Keith Wilson into whose works I have delved deeply. Papers printed in back numbers of Pantala and Odonatologica have been invaluable, as have articles in Kimminsia and WDA's AGRION.

The work would not have been possible without the support and technical expertise of many fellow members of the Worldwide Dragonfly Association (WDA), the British Dragonfly Society (BDS), the Dragonfly Society of the Americas (DSA), and the ex-Societas Internationalis Odonatologica (SIO). In particular, my thanks and appreciation go to Dr Allen Davies who has provided me with innumerable pieces of information by telephone, letter and while sitting in pubs over glasses of liquid refreshment, and who has let me photograph the priceless and, in many cases, unique specimens in his comprehensive collection. Drs Michael Parr, Matti Hämäläinen and Edmund Jarzembowski deserve special thanks for volunteering to check the text, for picking up mistakes and making many valuable suggestions.

Throughout the project I received help and encouragement from many people and am grateful to every one of them but the names of four must be specially mentioned. Ray Andress, Sidney Dunkle, Georg Rüppell and John Trueman were the first to come forward with something really concrete and it was their kindness and optimism that made me believe *Dragonflies of the World* would eventually materialise. The fact that it has, after so many vicissitudes, appeared in print is due to the patience and encouragement I have received from the CSIRO Publishing team who have worked so hard to bring my dream to fruition. Finally, my husband Ronnie, who has put up with so much and given me such endless support, deserves the biggest thanks of all!

Any piece of text that has not been written by me has the name of the author below its heading; any photograph that has not been taken by me has been credited.

Jill Silsby
January 2001

Contributors

Text: Stephen Butler, Nick Donnelly, Sidney Dunkle, Rosser Garrison, Vicky McMillan, Ivan Meskin, Norman Moore, Georg Rüppell, Michael Samways, John Trueman, Graham Vick and Keith Wilson.

Photographs: Cindy Allen, Matjaz Bedjamic, David Chelmick, Viola Clausnitzer, Allen Davies, Sidney Dunkle, Ian Endersby, Rosser Garrison, Kiyoshi Inoue, Ed Jarzembowski, Gerhard Jurzitza, Bob Kemp, John Mason, Norman Moore, Bert Orr, Kazuo Ozaki, Amnuay Pinratana, David Pryce, Steve Richards, Michael Samways, Atsushi Sugitani, Kay Thompson, Robert Thompson, Carlo Utzeri, Graham Vick, Keith Wilson and Neville Yates.

Drawings: Rob Arnold, Steve Price, Georg Rüppell and John Trueman.

Lestes virgatus.

1
Introduction

The reaction of most people, when an insect approaches them, is to make an involuntary exclamation and swiftly swipe it away. We have learnt, often to our cost, that bees and wasps have stings, mosquitoes and midges bite and that the sooner such creatures leave our vicinity the happier we will feel. The fact that the majority of insects neither sting nor bite leaves us supremely unmoved and many totally innocuous creatures are swatted by nervous humans as they buzz harmlessly by.

Dragonflies, in particular, seem to inspire fear and, indeed, they could be said to have a somewhat ferocious appearance. Many have an inquisitive nature and their large size, together with the audible clatter of their wings, can understandably cause alarm. In the past dragonflies were known as 'Horse-stingers' and 'Devil's Darning Needles'. However, all fears where these insects are concerned are groundless: they have no sting and their powerful jaws are incapable of doing us — or horses! — any harm. On the contrary, in more ways than one, they are beneficial to humans: their presence at a piece of water indicates that the water is not polluted; they have voracious appetites and, since they are solely carnivorous, they consume vast quantities of insects that can cause us annoyance or, even, actual harm. There have even been projects where dragonfly larvae were released into domestic water-storage containers in order to suppress the pre-adult stages of disease-carrying mosquitoes.

Dragonflies and damselflies — the Order Odonata — are among the most beautiful and interesting insects on earth and the purpose of

Libellula incesta (Slaty Chaser).

this book is to show how valid that claim is. As the pages are turned, so their beauty will become evident and the variety of their often intriguing behavioural patterns will unfold.

Odonates are also among the most ancient of Earth's living fauna and, before looking in detail at the families flying today, we should attempt to get some idea of just how long they and their ancestors have been around. It will help first to put them in context with other creatures and to take a brief look at the planet on which they all evolved. We will examine the divisions of geological time and see what was about in the relatively recent periods.

Serious questions regarding the age of our planet have exercised enquiring minds for the past three or more centuries. One of the first calculations made was that of James Ussher in 1654. He came up with the date 4004 BC. His conclusion, which commanded great respect, was reached by studying the genealogical verses in the Book of Genesis and the date was accepted without question by the majority of those living at the time and, indeed, by their

The divisions of geological time.

descendants for well over 100 years to come. There were, however, people who studied the earth, its mountains and valleys, its rocks and rivers, its plateaux and its oceans. Seashells were found on the tops of mountains which seemed to prove that high land had once been the sea floor; bones were discovered that had clearly belonged to creatures that were no longer found on Earth. Such discoveries, and many others, gradually forced scientists to reject Ussher's date in favour of a very much earlier one. Suggestions as to the real age of the earth varied enormously and ranged from hundreds of thousands of years to thousands of millions. Today it is reckoned that Earth is around 4600 million years old.

Life existing during in *Precambrian* times was, generally speaking, unicellular and fossils have only rarely been found in the sedimentary rocks laid prior to the Phanerozoic. In 1946, however, the fossilised remains of some extra-ordinary multicellular jellyfish-like creatures were discovered in the 550–600 million-year-old Precambrian rocks of the Flinders Ranges in

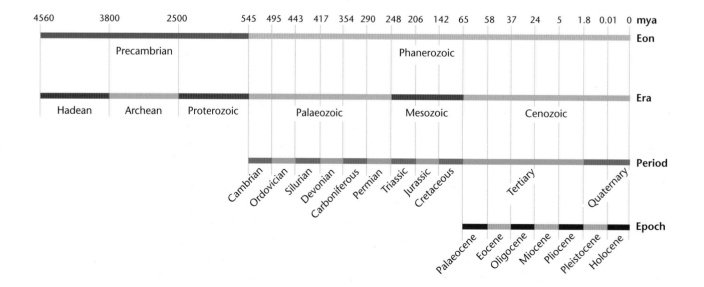

South Australia and were named Ediacara fauna, after the mine in which they were excavated. More ediacaran fossils have since been found in rocks of similar age in other parts of the world and recent scientific work hints at even earlier multicellular forms. The origins of life are continually being pushed further and further into the dim and distant past.

Phanerozoic time extends from the end of the Precambrian until the present day and is represented by rock strata that contain clearly recognisable fossils. It is divided into three Eras: *Palaeozoic*, meaning 'Ancient Life'; *Mesozoic*, 'Middle Life' and *Cenozoic*, 'Recent Life'.

Palaeozoic era

The *Cambrian* period covered the first part of the Palaeozoic era and during that time several marine invertebrates, particularly trilobites, flourished. A trilobite is a very early arthropod (a creature possessing a segmented external skeleton that is divided into three parts). Modern representatives of the phyla which started to appear in the fossil record of this period include worms, corals, crabs, shellfish, sponges and centipedes.

The *Ordovician* period, lasting 50 million years, saw the proliferation of marine invertebrates and the appearance of the earliest fish.

During the *Silurian* period, which lasted for 40 million years, marine life (with the exception of mammals and amphibians) was partly as we know it today.

In the lower *Devonian* strata the first amphibians appear and the upper strata contain evidence of the 'conquest of land'. A few fossil (wingless) insects are also present in these strata.

Fossils of the Order Protodonata (Chapter 12) first appear in rocks of the *Carboniferous*, the period that saw Earth's coal deposits laid. Among these are members of the family Meganeuridae which included the giant *Meganeura monyi*. It is probable that from one of these 300+ million-year-old insects are descended all the odonates that fly today. Fossil remains of primitive cockroaches and mayflies are also present, although the latter are very rare.

In the *Permian* deposits, which were laid some 285 to 245 million years ago (mya), fossils of the Order Protozygoptera have been found.

Mesozoic era

This, the 'Middle Life', began some 245 mya and is known as the 'Age of the Dinosaurs'. In Britain, Jarzembowski has found fossil remains of modern Anisoptera, Zygoptera and Mesozoic 'Anisozygoptera' dating from this era.

During the *Triassic*, the first of the Mesozoic periods, reptiles flourished (including a few small carnivorous types of dinosaur). The first 'modern' dragonflies (of the suborder Anisozygoptera) appear.

The *Jurassic* saw the supremacy of the dinosaurs. There were pterosaurs, not birds, in the air. It is in the strata of this period that fossil ammonites are found and also, in addition to the earliest mammals, the first Hymenoptera (solitary bees and wasps but, according to Jarzembowski, no social species) and Lepidoptera (moths but, according to the same source, no butterflies). Fossils of Aeshnidae, Gomphidae and Petaluridae make their first appearance in these layers.

During the *Cretaceous* period chalk deposits were formed, flowering plants first evolved and birds flew. The broad-winged damselflies (Calopterygoidea) appear here. The larger and best-known dinosaurs did not survive the end of this period but a number of other groups did, for example crocodiles, turtles and birds. The boundary between the end of the Mesozoic era and the beginning of the Cenozoic was marked by what is known as a 'mass extinction' and is known as the K/T line.

Cenozoic era

The last of the three eras (Recent Life) is also known as the Age of the Mammals. Rocks deposited at the commencement of the Cenozoic show evidence of dynamic change to the planet. During the earlier Cenozoic periods there is evidence of tropical palms in southern England but the end of the era heralded a much cooler climate. It was not until the Cenozoic, which began just 65 mya and takes us up to the present day, that mammals gradually became dominant. During the deposition of Cenozoic strata, many older forms of life became extinct and recent species of both animals and plants took their place. Hoofed mammals appeared some 39 mya and by 7 mya many of our modern animals were flourishing. As in the case of the previous two eras this one is also divided, this time into just two periods:

The *Tertiary* period began 65 mya and lasted for around 63 million years. The period is divided into five further rock series that are known as epochs and, since they are often used when referring to fossil deposits, it will be useful to note their names. The *Palaeocene* was characterised by the appearance of placental mammals and, by the end of the epoch, primates had evolved.

A model built from a reconstruction (drawn by Wolfgang Zessin) of *Namurotypus sippelli* (wingspan 32 cm). The fossil was recovered from strata laid 325 mya in Germany.

Fuhlrott Museum, Wupertal

The *Eocene* rock strata show the rise of the mammals; rodents and whales were among the groups to make their first appearance, and the first monkeys. It was not until this epoch that libelluloid dragonflies appeared. *Oligocene* strata began to be laid about 35 mya and the Epoch was characterised by the continued rise of the mammals; pigs, rhinoceroses and tapirs, for example, made their appearance, and the first apes. *Miocene* strata are characterised by the appearance of fossilised grazing animals and Afropithecines (early hominoids).

The spread of grasses was responsible for many important ecological changes. The *Pliocene* is the last of the sedimentary deposits laid down in the Tertiary period. It is characterised by the appearance of modern plants and animals, and the first Australopithecine (early hominid).

The *Quaternary* period began approximately 1.8 mya and is made up of two epochs, the *Pleistocene* and the *Holocene*. The former is the earlier and is characterised by the alternate procession and recession of northern glaciers (Ice Ages) and, the first appearance of *Homo sapiens* and the Neanderthals, although the advent of hominoids has been traced much earlier, to the Tertiary. Holocene strata are still being laid today.

Odonates lived alongside the Jurassic dinosaurs some 200 million years ago; and insects not so very different from them were flying 100 million years before that, when the ancestor of all the dinosaurs was just a small, reptile-like creature somewhere in a Carboniferous rainforest. Odonates were here before some of our ancient mountains arose and before the continents separated into the landmasses we know today. They witnessed the appearance and disappearance of the dinosaurs, the arrival of the birds and the evolution, just yesterday, of the human race.

SURVIVAL

The question is often asked, 'Why did dinosaurs disappear?'. It is an interesting question and many answers have been put forward to account for their extinction. One is that a gigantic meteorite crashed into Earth with dire consequences for much of the animal life on the planet. Another suggests that a series of explosive eruptions on the earth's surface had similar consequences. Others suggest that all but a few species were unable to adapt to, or escape from, periods of global warming, or of advancing glaciation. It has even been mooted that dinosaurs failed to survive the Flood because they were too big to get into the Ark! Present research indicates that one or other of the first two answers is the right one.

An equally interesting question is, 'Why did odonates survive?'. That can be answered by posing another question, 'Why does anything survive?'. Darwin provided an answer to that when he published his well known theory regarding 'the survival of the fittest'. Creatures survive because they adapt to make the best use of a changing environment. As we have seen, the end of the Mesozoic era was marked by a mass extinction that only a very few creatures managed to outlive. Dinosaurs (apart from birds) were among the many groups that succumbed but odonates were one of a few that survived and their 'fitness' to do so (in the context of Darwin's theory) is largely due to a couple of very different factors.

First, during their lifetime odonates experience two totally different life styles. In almost all cases, the egg and larval stages are spent in water whilst the adult stage is an aerial one. Following emergence from their larval casings, the newly winged insects instinctively fly away from the water, dispersing into the neighbouring countryside and sometimes travelling very considerable distances. This dispersal period has been a vital factor in odonate survival. Over the millennia, should one piece of water have dried up or turned into ice, or should a river have changed its course, odonates were able to find suitable replacements and would soon colonise them.

Sadly this is no longer true and it is becoming increasingly urgent that steps are taken to halt the decline in the number of suitable breeding places: we can no longer 'leave it to nature'. Despite a growing awareness of the plight of odonates, the number of habitats that are disappearing due to deforestation, drainage, pollution etc., far exceeds the number of habitats being created and, until this trend is reversed, there must be continuing cause for concern. Chapter 10, written by one of the world's best known conservationists Norman Moore) provides an important, worldwide insight into the problems of dragonfly conservation, together with an account of how some of the problems are being addressed.

The second factor leading to the survival of Odonata is the extreme efficiency of the basic body design, a design that has proved capable

Pantala flavescens (Globe Skimmer) is a compulsive migrant and can fly thousands of miles, even over oceans.

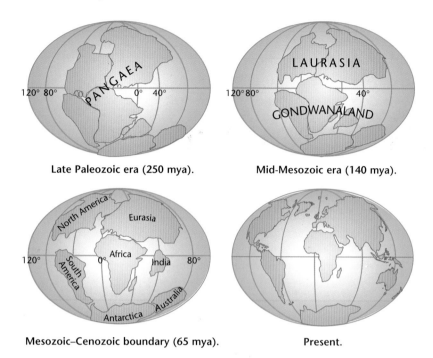

Late Paleozoic era (250 mya).

Mid-Mesozoic era (140 mya).

Mesozoic–Cenozoic boundary (65 mya).

Present.

Earth's zoogeographical regions.

aerial hunters par excellence and have occupied a niche in the environment which, over the millennia, no other creature has managed to usurp.

EARTH'S DRIFTING CONTINENTS

The changes that led to today's arrangement of the oceans and continents have occurred only very recently in the 4.5 billion years of earth's history. It has been calculated that 250 million years ago, fragments of land (both large and small) had drifted together to form a huge single landmass (Pangaea) which was surrounded by a 'super-ocean' (Panthalassa). By 135 mya, Pangaea had split into Laurasia and Gondwanaland; and by 65 mya Gondwana has split up into four separate continents.

However, fossil remains of the ancestors of today's Odonata have been found in rocks laid well over 300 mya and, by 135 mya, many 'modern' species had already evolved. These facts explain some of the very strange distribution patterns and it is not surprising that, for example, one part of the small extant zygopteran subfamily Rimanellinae occurs in Venezuela and the other in West Africa. And, when a presentation of the world map is shown with the Pacific in the centre, the distribution of the anisopteran Petaluridae becomes easily understood.

Today the earth can be divided into five major zoogeographical regions separated by natural barriers such as oceans, deserts and mountain ranges: the Holarctic (subdivided into the Nearctic and Palaearctic); the Neotropical; the Ethiopian; the Oriental; and the Australasian. It is probable that the broad character of the fauna of each region depends on the process of continental drift and the stage of evolution that had been reached when the various landmasses became isolated.

of adapting to the many fundamental changes that have occurred on Earth during the past 300 million years. Darwin also contended that each species must find itself a niche that suits it — and keep it, or else die out. As we will see in Chapter 4, the combination of large compound eyes, wings that can move independently of one another and a unique body shape has made odonates superb hunting machines: they are

2
Today's Odonata

Dragonflies living today are divided into three suborders: Zygoptera, Anisozygoptera and Anisoptera.

Zygoptera (damselflies)

Generally speaking, zygopterans are of slight built and have a weak, fluttery flight. Other features include:

- eyes are separated by more than the width of an eye
- the two pairs of wings are of similar shape and at rest are usually held closed/nearly closed, over or alongside the abdomen
- the discoidal cell (the 'quadrilateral') is not divided as it is in anisopterans
- males have two pairs of anal appendages
- females have complete (functional) ovipositors
- larvae are long and narrow and breathe through three caudal gills situated at the tip of the abdomen

Anisozygoptera

Anisozygopterans show zygopterous and anisopterous characters in various proportions and could be said to provide the link between broad-winged damselflies and dragonflies, although they are closer to the latter. The unique suborder dates from the Mesozoic era and contains 10 or so fossil families and one that still flies today. Their flight is weak but very direct and they show the following features:

- eyes are separated but by less than the width of an eye
- fore- and hindwings are of zygopteran shape
- the tip of the male's abdomen bears a pair of superior anal appendages and a single inferior one
- females have complete (functional) ovipositors
- larvae are broad-bodied and breathe through rectal tracheal gills though they are unable to benefit from jet propulsion

Anisoptera (dragonflies)

Although, as always, there are exceptions, anisopterans are generally more robust than zygopterans and are capable of stronger and more sustained flight. Other features include:

- eyes touch to a greater or lesser extent at the top of the head (except Petaluridae and Gomphidae)

THE ORDER ODONATA

Zygoptera (damselflies)

Hetaerina americana shows typical zygopteran features: slight build, separated eyes, fore- and hind-wings of similar shape.

Anisozygoptera

Epiophlebia superstes shows a mixture of characters: zygopterous wings and anisopterous head and thorax.

Allen Davies

Anisoptera (dragonflies)

Brachytron pratense shows typical anisopteran features: robust build, eyes touching, fore- and hindwings of dissimilar shape and held horizontally away from the body.

- the two pairs of wings are of dissimilar shape, the hind pair being considerably broader at the base; at rest they are held horizontally outwards or even drooping downwards but almost never closed as in the case of damselflies (Cordulephyinae is an exception)
- the discoidal cell is divided into 'triangle' and 'hypertriangle' and, in some species, there may be a 'subtriangle'
- the tip of the male's abdomen bears a pair of superior anal appendages and a single inferior one (which in some species may be so deeply cleft that it appears as two);
- females, with a few exceptions (e.g. aeshnids, petalurids), have non-functional or vestigial ovipositors
- larvae are broad-bodied, breathe through rectal tracheal gills and can propel themselves forward by expelling water through the rectum

STRUCTURE OF THE ADULT DRAGONFLY

Insects are invertebrate which means they lack a backbone. In order to give them rigidity they possess an external skeleton or 'exoskeleton', which consists of hardened, sclerotised plates (sclerites), separated by narrow areas of flexible membranes. The outer layer of an insect's skin (the epidermis) is just one cell thick and is covered by an impermeable cuticle which takes the form of a layer of horny non-cellular material called chitin. It is this chitinised cuticle that forms the exoskeleton. The hardness of the cuticle depends on the proportion of the protein 'sclerotin' present and, where hard structures are needed (to give rigidity), the proportion is high. On the other hand, the very soft, flexible cuticle that forms the membranes between abdominal segments contains a very low proportion of sclerotin.

Like all insects, the bodies of odonates are divided into three parts: the head, the thorax and the abdomen.

Head

Apart from the strong mouthparts used for chewing food, the parts of the head that concern us are the frons or forehead (bearing a pair of small antennae), a pair of large compound eyes and three simple eyes (ocelli), the purpose of which is debatable. A few species of zygopterans (some Coenagrionidae for example) have a pair of brightly coloured post-ocular spots behind the eyes which can be a helpful means of identification. The back of the head is called the occiput and the top of the head, the vertex. The head is joined narrowly to the thorax by what is often referred to as a 'neck', which consists of two chitinous plates (sclerites) that permit great mobility.

Thorax

The thorax is the locomotory centre of most insects. It has three segments, each of which bears a pair of legs and, in addition, each of the two posterior segments carry a pair of wings. The first segment, the prothorax, is covered dorsally by a plate called the pronotum, the shape of which often helps in the separation of female damselflies. In Odonata, the two posterior segments (meso- and metathorax) are fused together to form the synthorax. The frontal surface of the thorax may be adorned with stripes, as can the sides, where they are known as lateral stripes.

The legs are well developed for seizing prey and for perching or roosting but are seldom used for walking. They have three main sections: the femur, the tibia and the tarsus, the last of which ends in a pair of tiny claws.

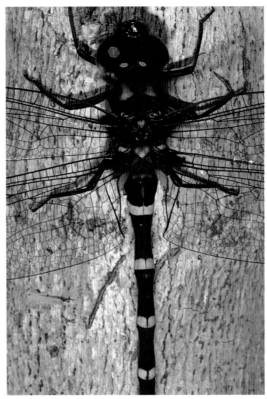

Bert Orr

The thorax is the locomotory centre of an odonate. This male *Indaeschna grubaueri* was photographed in Brunei.

The colour, length and shape of the legs can provide good clues to identification.

The wings are generally hyaline (clear and transparent), sometimes with coloured areas. In some families the male's hindwings are angulated, a feature that presumably evolved to prevent the wings from coming into contact with auricles set on either side of the basal abdominal segments.

The membrane of the wings is strengthened and supported by a series of longitudinal veins which are strut-like thickenings and these are linked by a multitude of crossveins. Together they form characteristic patterns by which families and subfamilies can be identified. Venation is complicated but it really is worth taking a little time to understand the main features so that, when they are mentioned in the following pages, they are not totally incomprehensible.

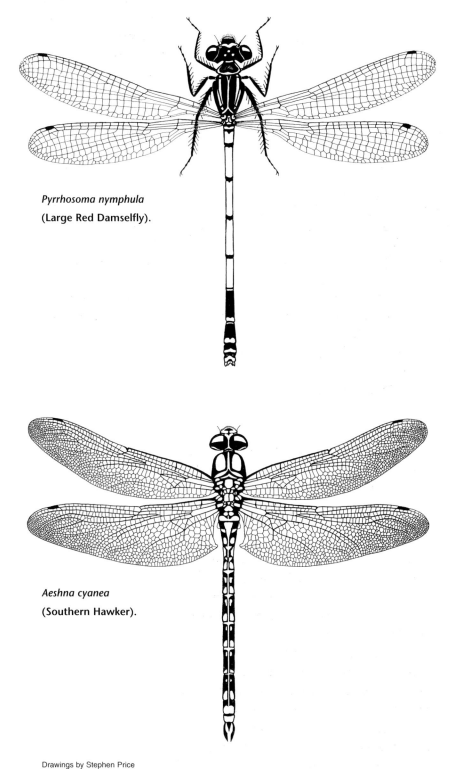

Pyrrhosoma nymphula
(Large Red Damselfly).

Aeshna cyanea
(Southern Hawker).

Drawings by Stephen Price

Five principal veins rise from the base of the wing: *costa, subcosta, radius-*and-*median* (or *medius*), *cubital* (or *cubitus*) and the *anal* vein.

The *costa* runs along the entire anterior (leading) edge of each wing. Somewhere near the centre of the *costa* there is an indentation called the *nodus* which allows the wing to twist. Its exact position on the wing varies quite considerably, being nearer to the base in damselflies, more to the centre in the Aeshnoidea and nearer to the apex (tip) in the Libelluloidea.

The *subcosta* starts at the base of the wing and ends at the *nodus*.

The r*adius* and *median* are fused together at the base of the wing but separate after a short distance. The *radius* (R1) runs in an almost straight line to the apex of the wing, while the *median* branches off via a stout, angled vein called the *arculus*. From here it forms the anterior edge of the *discoidal cell*, and curves down to meet the posterior margin of the wing. Many texts refer to this as the *anterior median* vein — there is no *posterior median* in odonates. The field of cells between the radius and the median is supported by the *radial sector* (RS) and its branches (R2, IR2, R3, IR3, R4). The development of this area of the wing varies across the order and is useful in separating the subfamilies.

The *cubital* vein forms the posterior side of the damselfly's discoidal cell and the basal side of the dragonfly's triangle, after which it wends its way to the posterior wing margin.

The *anal vein* is the last of the veins to arise from the base of the wing. In damselflies, it generally is fused with the wing border until it separates at about the level of the *arculus* when it runs parallel to the *cubital*. In dragonflies the vein runs a more complex course and, from it, is sometimes formed the very variable *anal loop*. This loop encloses a collection of cells that are of different shape to those surrounding them and it can be an important aid to identification.

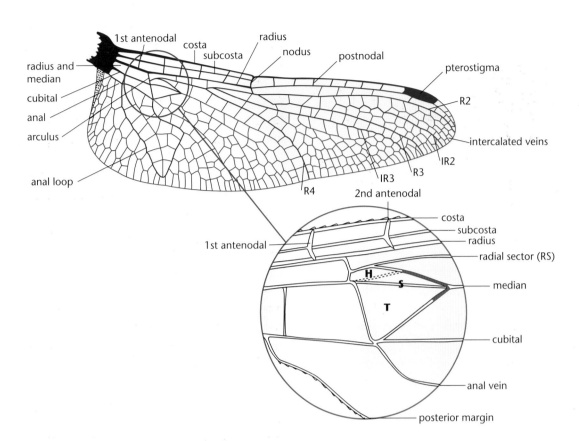

The main features of an anisopteran wing. The discoidal cell is divided by the *strut vein* (S) into the *hypertriangle* (H) and *triangle* (T).
In the enlargement, the dotted line shows the position of the strut vein in Tetrathemistinae (making the *triangle* four-sided) while the darkened portion of the median vein and distal crossvein of the discoidal cell shows the full range of positions of the strut vein found in modern dragonflies.

Several series of crossveins are important. These include the *antenodals* and *postnodals*.

Antenodals lie at the front of the wing in the area bounded by the *costa* and the *radius,* and the wingbase and the *nodus*. In some families the two rows are aligned and in others they are not. Zygoptera, except for the Calopterygidae, have only two such crossveins and these correspond to the two stout primary *antenodals* found in a number of anisopteran families.

In some libellulid subfamilies, the most distal antenodal (i.e. the one immediately before the *nodus*) is said to be 'complete', in that it extends from *costa* to *radius*; in other subfamilies, it is 'incomplete', extending only to the *subcosta*.

Between the *nodus* and the *pterostigma*, the *costa* and *radius* are connected by a single row of *postnodal* veins.

Intercalated veins are found, when present, near the apex of the wing; they are small longitudinal veins inserted between the major ones.

The *discoidal* cells, which are called *quadrilaterals* in damselflies, and *hypertriangles* plus *triangles* in dragonflies, are important features of the wings.

In damselflies, the cell is a simple, four-sided figure made up of the *median* and *cubital* veins at front and back, and two crossveins, one of which forms the lower portion of the arculus and the other which closes the cell distally. In one or two primitive species the *arculus* is only present in its upper portion, thus leaving the *quadrilateral* open at the base. Sometimes (e.g. in Lestidae) the distal crossvein is oblique, causing the quadrilateral to be pointed. In Anisozygoptera the distal crossvein is long which makes the cell quite wide distally.

In dragonflies, the discoidal cell is divided in two by a crossvein forming the *hypertriangle* above and the *triangle* below. In some species there is a *subtriangle* proximal to the triangle. In most cases the hypertriangle and triangle are three-sided, but in a very few subfamilies, including Tetrathemistinae and Neophyinae, the dividing crossvein runs forward onto the *median* vein, thus making the triangle four-sided!

Abdomen

Ten segments (divided by intersegmental membranes) make up the abdomen, the dorsal surface of which is frequently decorated with spots, bands, central lines, and other marks which, when taken together, form a pattern that is unique to the individual species. The segments are numbered I to X, starting at the base (i.e. next to the thorax). The abdomen is long, usually narrow, and flexible. Anisopteran males are often waisted at segment III, while the abdomens of females are almost invariably stouter than those of their male counterparts.

At the tip of the male's abdomen are the anal appendages. In damselflies these consist of a pair of cerci (superior dorsal appendages) and a pair of paraprocts (inferior ventral appendages). In dragonflies they are made up of a pair of cerci and, instead of the pair of paraprocts, a single epiproct. These are used to clasp a female round her prothorax (damselflies) or back of the head (dragonflies) during mating.

As will be seen later, reproduction among odonates is complicated by the fact that, although the male produces sperm from an opening near the tip of his abdomen, he must then transfer it to an accessory organ situated on the underside of segments II and III. The males of some anisopteran families possess an ear-shaped auricle on either side of segment II and, since F. C. Fraser's work in the early 1940s, it has become generally accepted that the purpose of these small protuberances is to guide the female's abdomen into the position required to ensure successful copulation.

Females bear their genitalia on the underside of segments VIII and IX. This takes the form of ovipositor in all zygopterans, anisozygopterans and in three families of Anisoptera (Aeshnidae, Petaluridae and Neopetaliidae). Ovipositors are made up of three pairs of serrated valves and are used first to make slits in plant tissue and then to insert eggs into the slits. The ovipositor of the cordulegasterids is unserrated and of a simpler construction; it could be described as a halfway house to the genitalia associated with the rest of the anisopterans, whose females bear non-functional 'incomplete' ovipositors which are otherwise referred to as vulvar scales. They are all that remains of the anterior part of the ovipositor and are all that is needed by female gomphids, macromiids, synthemistids, corduliids and libellulids, most of which just scatter their eggs onto open water or mud.

3
Life cycle

Odonate females have two basic methods of laying eggs and, although there are exceptions, the shape of the egg depends on the method used.

Those species with a complete (or functioning) ovipositor, i.e. all zygopterans, anisozygopterans and, among anisopterans, the members of the Aeshnidae, Petaluridae and Neopetaliidae, are endophytic. This means that, by using their ovipositors, they insert their eggs into plant material above or below the surface of the water, into floating wood or into moss, slime or mud at the water's edge. Their ovipositors are equipped with saw-like edges and, using these, females can cut slits into the stems of aquatic plants or the underside of their floating leaves, sometimes (particularly in the case of damselflies) completely submerging themselves as they do so. They can even cut into the stems of thick, overhanging branches or into the trunks of trees growing at the waterside, and floating logs.

Females of the remaining anisopteran families (including Gomphidae, Corduliidae and Libellulidae) are exophytic: they have reduced (non-functioning) ovipositors and merely

deposit their accumulated eggs onto the surface of water or surrounding ground or, in a few species, the male, while the pair is still in tandem, will fling the female violently up and down so that her eggs are dislodged.

In a few species (those belonging to the genus *Epitheca* are good examples) the female, after mating, perches on a bank side plant, curves her abdomen upwards and commences to prepare an egg strand. The eggs are emitted

A female *Anax imperator* (Emperor) egg-laying into the stems of aquatic plants.

Kazuo Ozaki

A female *Epitheca bimaculata sibirica* with an accumulated egg mass which will shortly be released.

Members of this genus are called Baskettails in the United States and Canada because, as Sidney Dunkle puts it, 'they hold all their eggs in one basket'.

Most species are careful to select suitable sites into which to deposit their eggs. Among endophytic species, some pick dry stems, some damp moss or waterlogged logs, while others use plant material below the surface of the water. Cordulegastrids possess particularly long (non-functional) ovipositors, which they use to stab eggs into the substrate of shallow rivers, streams and ditches and, as they do so, they hold their bodies almost vertical so that the movement is rather like the needle of a sewing machine going up and down.

little by little until a sticky ball, or 'basket', of some 1000–2000 eggs has amassed. She then flies to the water, dips the tip of her abdomen on to an almost submerged clump of plant material and releases the ball which adheres, by one end, to the plant and unravels into a gelatinous strand that swells on contact with the water.

Among the exophytic species, some need to find running water, some bogs and marshes, others ponds or lakes. A few (the European *Sympetrum sanguineum* and *S. flaveolum* for example) will drop their eggs over dry land, generally into long grasses growing at various distances from the water but which will, almost invariably, become inundated during the following winter. It is fascinating to watch a female *Libellula depressa*: after mating she finds a piece of floating debris or a clump of plants growing in shallow water near the bank and, with each energetic, forward swoop, she knocks the end of her abdomen against it thereby releasing her eggs. Others (*Tetrathemis* for example) deposit their eggs on to the surface of leaves overhanging the water or on the underside of blades of water plants from where the tiny, newly hatched prolarvae will drop into the water below.

Bert Orr

Lyriothemis cleis, in Borneo, Indonesia, will breed in water that has collected in tree holes.

There are a number of interesting variations. The South American tropical genus *Mecistogaster,* whose females have exceptionally elongated abdomens, lay their eggs into the water collected at the base of bromeliads growing on forest trees, flicking their abdomens from some distance away, so that the eggs drop into the right spot. Other species choose the hollow stems of bamboo. M. A. Lieftinck recorded that the South-East Asian species *Lyriothemis magnificata* was known to select a variety of strange sites including crevices in fallen tree trunks. Another member of the same genus, *L. cleis*, from Borneo, breeds in tree holes and, indeed, there are number of species throughout the tropics that choose such sites.

Another group lay their eggs into the dripping moss growing on the rockface at the back of waterfalls and others (members of the genus *Zygonyx* for example) seem to revel in flying through the spray and laying their eggs into the roots of clinging plants. And then there is the small number of species that are totally catholic in their needs, *Pantala flavescens* (Globe Skimmer) being a good example. This ubiquitous species will lay in most types of water: ponds, lakes, swimming pools, temporary puddles and even in running water.

Once a female has completed egg laying, she will leave the breeding site and must wait between one and five days while the next batch of eggs matures and becomes ready to be fertilised. Males, on the other hand, once mature, have a constantly replenished supply of sperm and are thus able to copulate at every opportunity.

THE EGG

The eggs of endophytic species are long and cylindrical whilst those of exophytic species are, almost always, broad and elliptical. There are exceptions to this, particularly among gomphids.

At one end of the egg there are one or more minute holes through which the sperm enters just before the eggs are laid. In some species (particularly among those that lay their eggs into running water such as the majority of gomphids) the eggs are surrounded by a jelly-

A male *Pachydiplax longipennis* (Blue Dasher) in New York State, USA. The female can lay 300–700 eggs in 35 seconds.

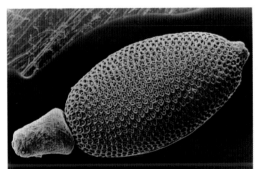

John Trueman

The egg of *Ictinogomphus australis* has a 'coil of yarn' on the rear end that unwinds in water to give a number of sticky threads which tangle in vegetation thus keeping the egg within the water body of the tropical ponds where these dragonflies breed.

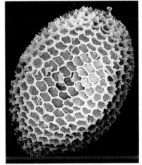

John Trueman

The egg *of Synthemis regina*. The inner egg (egg proper) is smooth and ovoid, as one would expect. The outer envelope is strong and multi-layered, its outer surface raised into walled cells roughly hexagonal in shape.

like substance that enables them to attach themselves to the leaves of plants or to stones and rocks under the water, thus preventing them from sinking into the mud or being swept away by fast flowing water.

The eggs of some species (the Palaearctic *Epitheca bimaculata* is one) are combined in long strands which may float on the surface of the water for several days. Hidenori Ubukata tells us that researchers in Japan examined an egg strand of this species and found it to contain some 1000 eggs.

Mitsutoshi Sugimura tells us that tiny 'parasite bees' insert their eggs into the eggs of *Epiophlebia superstes* that have been laid in the stems of butterburrs and mountain lilies. It takes a month for an *Epiophlebia* egg to hatch and, during this short time, the parasite will, while feeding on its host, progress from egg, through larva and pupa, to imago and, when the month is up, it will emerge from the empty shell and be on the wing. Philip Corbet, in his *Biology of Dragonflies*, quotes similar parasitic behaviour by minute wasps on the eggs of several endophytic odonates. He tells us that the wasps will search the stems of underwater

plants for suitable hosts or will look for them in branches some way above the water. Generally just one wasp egg is laid in each odonate egg, but there is one species (*Prestwichia solitaria*) which lays a single egg in a coenagrionid egg but two or three in that of an aeshnid.

John Trueman has examined many hundreds of libelluloid eggs using a scanning electron microscope (SEM) and has found that the outermost eggshell layer is thin, flexible and loosely surrounds the egg which is free to move inside it. He found that 'all libelluloid-type eggs develop and hatch perfectly well whether the outermost layer is left on or carefully cut off'. Among others, the eggs of *Synthemis regina* were examined by Trueman who considered them very unusual, surmising that they would retain their shape under considerable pressure and that the space between the inner and outer layers would be water-filled even in bottom mud.

While working on the Australian Gomphinae, John Trueman found that the eggs of *Hemigomphus* are long and plain whereas the eggs of *Austrogomphus* are round and covered with unique pillar-shaped structures under a jelly-like outer covering. Such characters will undoubtedly prove helpful in classifying the various groups within the Gomphinae.

Although some species (particularly those breeding in temperate climates) overwinter as eggs, most eggs start to develop soon after they have been laid and, with a few exceptions, the larvae hatch out one to three weeks later. In some instances, the length of time spent as an egg differs even in an individual species: for example, eggs of *Gomphus flavipes* that are laid in summer will hatch after a few weeks, whilst those laid in the autumn will not do so until the following spring. The eggs of some species (particularly tropical ones) can survive a long dry period and will hatch only when the rainy season commences.

Sectioned egg of *Austrogomphus prasinus*.

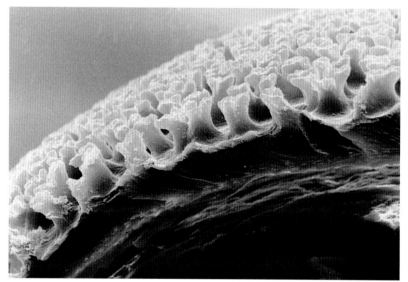

John Trueman

THE LARVA

This is the growth stage of an insect's life. As with all arthropods, odonate larvae must repeatedly shed one outer casing (exoskeleton) in order to grow a new one and the life of a developing larva is thus punctuated by a series of moults, during which it is extremely vulnerable. Put another way, as the larva grows, its hard cuticle becomes too small, like old clothes, and it must change into larger ones; the old exoskeleton cracks open and the larva emerges with a new wrinkled 'skin' that inflates and hardens. Periods between these moults are called 'stadia' or 'instars' and the number necessary to complete development varies between eight and 15.

The first larval stage of an odonate, during which it is known as a prolarva, is quite different in shape and in duration from all those that follow. In some species, the prolarva, which is long, thin and rather fish-like in appearance, will moult into a true larva in a matter of seconds; in others the stage may extend to a couple of hours. The length of time depends on the degree of difficulty encountered in freeing itself from the egg and on the distance it finds itself from the water. During this stage in its life cycle, the insect does not feed and cannot walk — as soon as a prolarva reaches the water, the casing cracks open and a tiny six-legged creature emerges: the larval stage has begun.

Most damselfly larvae have slender, cylindrical bodies, ending in three appendages that vary in shape according to family. These are their gills and they often bear striking patterns.

Dragonfly larvae are robust and lack the damselfly's caudal gills; their shape depends on the type of habitat in which they develop. There are two principal divisions, bottom-dwellers and weed-dwellers.

Bottom-dwellers are often sluggish in behaviour; they have flat, stubby, hairy bodies and short, strong legs (often armed with tibial hooks), that are clearly fashioned for digging. Typically, gomphid larvae bear, in addition, paddle-shaped or club-like four-segmented antennae which help their excavations. One or two gomphid genera provide exceptions (*Heliogomphus* is one). Keith Wilson tells us that these unusual sprawling larvae frequent moderately

Robert Thompson

Larva of *Erythromma najas* (Red-eyed Damselfly). Most damselfly larvae have slender, cylindrical bodies ending in three appendages. These are their gills.

Robert Kemp

The larvae of Anisozygoptera possess anisopterous features. This *Epiophlebia laidlawii* larva was reared by Stephen Butler.

Robert Thompson

Larva of a typical mud-dweller, *Gomphus vulgatissimus*.

Exuvia of *Sieboldius japponicus*, showing the unusual flattened body. Emergence had taken place on a flat rock in a fast-flowing river in southern Thailand.

fast streams; they have flattened bodies, lack burrowing tibial hooks and the third segment of the antenna is extraordinarily expanded to form a fan shape. Another somewhat similar example is the very flat-abdomened species *Sieboldius japponicus*; this species looks rather like a miniature sting ray. The flattened body shape is a useful adaptation to reduce current resistance. Another exception is the sand-burrowing *Progomphus* genus; Sidney Dunkle tells me that, in some of these species, the body is polished and torpedo-shaped, and that the fore and middle legs bear 'sand brushes' which are used to sweep sand to the side, allowing the larva to burrow out of sight in just seconds. These insects reveal their presence by V-shaped grooves in the sand, each of which can be tracked to the busy excavator at its base.

Weed-dwellers are much more active and have long, smooth, streamlined bodies; they can move easily among the aquatic vegetation, and stalk their prey as do the big cats in the African grasslands.

Keith Wilson

Heliogomphus scorpio; note the adapted antennae. **Photographed in Hong Kong, China.**

Robert Thompson

The *Cordulia aenea* larva crawls among sunken leaf litter.

Robert Thompson

Anax imperator is a typical weed-dweller.

A few species are neither one nor the other, spending their time on the surface of the mud or sand base, or amongst sunken leaf litter. These species (the genus *Macromia* is a good example of the first and *Cordulia* of the second) have flat bodies and long, spidery legs.

The larvae of a handful of species are terrestrial or semi-terrestrial: some, such as *Uropetala carovei*, living in 'burrows', others in spring-fed seepages. Some can survive in the beds of dried-up streams (e.g. the Australian *Diphlebia* and the Japanese *Lyriothemis pachygastra*) and a few possess a high freezing tolerance (e.g. the European *Somatochlora alpestris* whose larvae must overwinter several times in frozen river beds).

John Mason

The burrow of *Uropetala carovei*, in New Zealand, shows freshly excavated mud at the lip. The 20 cent coin measures 28 mm in diameter.

John Mason

Uropetala carovei larva, temporarily removed from its burrow.

RESPIRATION

Respiration has two meanings, the first pertains to the chemical breakdown of organic substances in cells during which energy is released and carbon dioxide produced. Respiration is also the process of taking in oxygen from the environment and giving out carbon dioxide. The exchange of oxygen and carbon dioxide takes place in the respiratory organs: lungs in air-breathing vertebrates; tracheae in many insects; gills in fish and aquatic larvae. Most odonate larvae are aquatic and breathe through gills.

In most damselflies, the gills are external and take the form of three leaf-like caudal appendages (lamellae) at the tip of the abdomen, the form and shape of which vary enormously according to habitat and life-style. The Asian calopterygid *Neurobasis chinensis* is a

The tiny larva of *Neurobasis chinensis,* photographed in Hong Kong, China.

mud burrower and possesses an unusual spear-shaped apical appendage held in the manner of a scorpion's sting. The larvae of two zygopteran families (Euphaeidae and Polythoridae) possess, in addition, abdominal gills — soft, finger-like appendages that are found in pairs on segments II–VII and II–VIII respectively.

The gills of dragonflies take the form of projections within the rectum (according to Peter Miller, there are 60–80 of them). As has been said, in some dragonfly species the larval stage is spent almost totally buried in mud at the bottom of a stream; the head, with its feeding apparatus, remains above the surface of the mud but it is important that the tip of the abdomen also does so to enable the gills to function. In *Cordulegaster*, for instance, the abdomen curves upwards in order to protrude and, in some species of tropical Gomphidae, the ninth or tenth abdominal segments are conspicuously elongated to form a respiratory tube (the Chinese *Labrogomphus torvus* is a good example and the deep burrowing African species, *Lestinogomphus africanus* is another. The abdomen in the latter species, carries a long respiratory tube, measuring 60 mm).

Allen Davies suggests it is possible that, as odonates have evolved, the effectiveness of the

Labrogomphus torvus larva showing the long ninth abdominal segment.

Keith Wilson

larval breathing apparatus has improved so that the more recent forms are able to breathe in water with much lower oxygen levels than those required by the more primitive odonates. It will be noticed that many of the oldest relics occur where mountain streams and their waterfalls provide the highest oxygen levels whereas the most recent (the libellulids) are able to benefit from the multitude of watery habitats that have resulted from human activities: reservoirs, rice fields, farm ponds, gravel pits, irrigation systems, water treatment lagoons, lakes for the watering of wildlife reserve animals, and even lakes for the rearing of fish. All these may have contributed to their obvious 'success'.

Both respiratory systems also serve as means of moving around in the water. In damselflies with leaf-like lamellae these are used as rear paddles; those with triquetal or saccoid lamellae are less able to use them in this way, which may partly account for the fact that, for example, calopterygids are poor swimmers. The pump that ventilates the dragonflies' rectal gills provides a useful and spectacular method of jet propulsion — water is sucked in slowly and then ejected forcibly to propel the insect forward.

The gills of the two species within the suborder Anisozygoptera are also situated in the rectum but are not used for jet propulsion.

FEEDING

Larvae appear to be stimulated by moving objects and they feed on a variety of animal matter: fish fry, tadpoles, water beetles, the larvae of mayflies and stoneflies and, also, the smaller larvae of other odonates; they will even consume almost moribund worms as they sink, still wriggling, to the bottom. Some are able to stalk their prey by walking among the submerged vegetation; others, which exist almost

totally buried in the substrate, must lie in wait until something edible passes within reach. In addition there are a few 'oddities' among odonate larvae: there are those that live in burrows, partially out of the water (e.g. some petalurids); those that live in rain water trapped in bromeliads and in tree holes (e.g. Pseudostigmatidae); and a tiny number that are totally terrestrial (e.g. *Megalagrion oahuense* and a few island species of Pseudagrioninae).

An exuvia of the southern African *Anax imperator mauricianus*, shows the unextended mask.

Final instar of an *Aeshna grandis* (Brown Hawker) consuming a stickleback.

Robert Thompson

Satisfying their voracious appetites is made simpler by a unique feature: on the underside of the head is a curious appendage known as a 'mask'. The mask is an extension of the lower 'lip' (labium) and is elongated, jointed and armed with a pair of pincers at the tip. It is called a mask because, in most species, when not extended it covers the lower part of the face. When something edible comes within reach, the larva shoots out this lip, grips its captive with the pincers and then retracts the mask to its original position, whence the meal can be transferred to the waiting jaws.

ENEMIES AND ESCAPE MECHANISMS

During the larval stage of an odonate's life, it is subject to predation by a number of creatures: fish and newts, frogs and toads, and larger larvae of their own order. The principal protective strategies used by larvae are immobility and concealment. Larvae are usually green or brown which allows them to blend with their backgrounds and some may be able to take on the predominant colour of their backgrounds when they moult. Many species of damselfly larvae have dark bands on their caudal lamellae (gills) which enhance their invisibility.

Some species feign death (reflex immobilisation) when disturbed and the larvae of *Megalagrion* species exhibit this to a marked degree. Other species will readily shed a leg or a gill grabbed by a predator, thus facilitating escape. These will be replaced over succeeding moults.

Finally, a dragonfly larva has a spectacular form of escape: it can expel water from the rectum, thus jet-propelling itself forward out of harm's way. Keith Wilson records that, 'the larvae of *Tetracanthagyna waterhousei*, although capable of jet propulsion, feigns death and makes

itself inconspicuous; it keeps perfectly still, with legs folded tightly against the body and strongly resembles a twig'. Larvae are at their most vulnerable during periods of moult. A female odonate may lay hundreds or thousands of eggs but the number of later larval instars is always vastly outnumbered by the earlier ones.

Although threats include predators, a more serious one is loss of habitat through water pollution, drainage and the filling in of ponds. From this kind of threat, larvae have no escape.

METAMORPHOSIS AND EMERGENCE

Although there are a number of interesting exceptions, the larval stage lasts from six months to five years, the actual time depending on species, the temperature of the water and the supply of food (specimens reared in an indoor aquarium and fed with live bloodworms, daphnia, etc. will develop much quicker than the same species in a garden pond). A species that spends a year in the larval stage in the tropics will be more likely to require two or three years in temperate zones. A number of species (*Pantala flavescens*, the Globe Skimmer, is a famous example, and Australia's *Hemicordulia tau* is another) have adapted to breed in temporary pools and these can complete development in as little as 40 days. At the other extreme, some of the primitive mountain species (e.g. the 'living fossil' *Epiophlebia superstes*) that develop in cold forest streams spend six or seven years as larvae.

By the time the aquatic larva reaches its final instar, it will have developed all the organs and other attributes needed to sustain life as a winged terrestrial insect; it will have undergone metamorphosis. It is generally possible to determine whether a dragonfly larva has reached its final instar: beneath the small separated eyes, large compound eyes can be seen; beneath the large labium (mask), a small adult-looking one is visible; and within the small wing buds, large contracted wings are evident.

The changes that take place during the final three instars can be compared to those that occur during the pupal stage of a lepidopteran. A day or two prior to emergence, feeding ceases and the larva will climb a suitable stem and, as Peter Miller writes, 'sit with the head and part of the thorax out of the water, as though contemplating the aerial world they are about to enter, but in reality exchanging gases through the first spiracle which is near the front of the thorax and can now be opened'. When the time for each particular species is right, aquatic respiration will come to an end and it will be time to leave the watery environment and commence a totally new, aerial existence. We have seen that times of moulting from one instar to another are times of high risk for larvae; emergence, and the period immediately following it, is an equally vulnerable time for adults. For this reason, in the warmer parts of the world, emergence will generally take place during the night; in temperate regions, however, emergence must be delayed until early morning when the air temperature has risen a little.

Although some species of Odonata (Clubtails, for example, and most damselflies) can emerge on a flat surface, the majority need a vertical one; the larva climbs up the stem of a reed or other plant, until it is well out of the water, and affixes itself to the plant by hooking the claws on its legs into the stem. There then follows a pause in visible activity, during which it is surmised that respiration changes from aquatic to terrestrial, then the larval skin breaks at the back of the head and, slowly and laboriously, the insect withdraws its head, thorax, legs and part of its abdomen. At this point there is a period of rest, during which the body dries out and the legs harden. Almost all dragonflies (gomphids are an exception) hang backwards with the head downwards (the 'hanging back' method) during this rest period (third picture in sequence), whilst damselflies and gomphids adopt an 'upright' rest position. Once the legs are adequately hardened, the emerging insect jerks itself upright and, using its now strengthened legs, takes a firm grip on the upper part of the larval skin. The remainder of the abdomen is then withdrawn and haemolymph (the insect's body fluid that takes the place of blood) is pumped strenuously round the body and into the network of veins running along the wings. This action expands the abdomen and also the wing-buds, transforming them into the beautiful wings of the adult insect. When the wings are fully expanded, the haemolymph is withdrawn leaving the veins to set hard as hollow tubes; the wings which were initially soft, pale and glistening with very pale pterostigmas, gradually harden and darken.

Although the majority of odonates choose rocks or plant material upon which to emerge,

At least five instar stages of the larva of the Hong Kong gomphid *Megalogomphus sommeri* which breeds in streams with a bottom of coarse granitic sand.

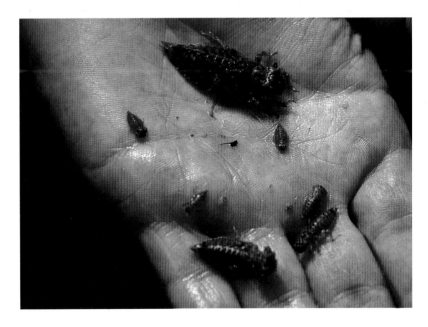

The emergence of the
Brachytron pratense
(Hairy Hawker)
photographed by
Robert Thompson.

there are exceptions. The larvae of *Gomphus vulgatissimus,* for example, can frequently be seen climbing the six or seven foot concrete wall beneath a viaduct on the River Thames (UK) and, if they fail to make it to the top in time, emergence will take place on the wall itself. This is not an ideal place as the wash from passing river boats can sweep them back into the river, a fate from which they will seldom recover. Another exception is the Australian *Hemicordulia tau* which is a very urban insect. Ian Endersby tells me they frequently emerge on the brick walls of his house on the outskirts of Melbourne.

DISPERSAL AND MATURATION

During its final, adult stage an insect is known as an imago. The necessary growth having been achieved during the larval stage, the imago can concentrate on ensuring the continued existence of its species — it is the stage of dispersal and procreation. Our odonate has made its remarkable transformation from a rather unattractive-looking aquatic larva, breathing through unique gills, into a spectacular aerial creature that inhales air, in the normal insect fashion, through spiracles on the thorax and abdomen. As in its larval stage, the adult is totally carnivorous and commences to catch prey within hours of emergence.

On its first flight, the teneral insect, still pale, soft and very vulnerable, instinctively flies away from the water. In the majority of species, this maiden flight takes place shortly before sunrise, thus avoiding predation by awakening birds.

For a period lasting a few days to two or more weeks, most immature odonates remain well away from water while their undeveloped gonads attain maturity; that is to say the males' testes are stimulated to produce spermatozoa and the females' ovaries to produce eggs. During this time the sexes mingle without showing any sign of sexual behaviour or of inter-male aggression; they feed actively and voraciously whenever the weather is suitable; and, should they encounter water, Philip Corbet tells us, they 'turn away and fly in another direction'.

Peter Miller presents an interesting exception to this. Referring to the immatures of two libellulids, *Tholymis tillarga* and *Zyxomma petiolatum* (see pages 180 and 181), he describes how they appear at their breeding sites just after sunset 'hovering and flying slowly about a metre above the water and remain there for several minutes after the departure of all sexually active individuals. Such behaviour may represent feeding and it may also assist immatures to learn about the location of potential egg-laying sites by observing the presence and activity of mature individuals.'

Males usually mature before females and make their way to suitable egg-laying sites where they hold territory until the females have developed batches of eggs that are ready to be fertilised.

Male *Ischnura aurora* with teneral female prior to mating.

Other changes take place during this period, particularly where males are concerned. During the first two weeks following emergence, the immature males of some species are, in colour, very similar to the females but as they mature many of them, particularly among the libellulids, undergo quite dramatic changes of colour (see Chapter 6).

The Australasian damselfly *Ischnura aurora* is an interesting exception. Males emerge first, females following about two weeks later. Mating occurs almost as soon as the females emerge; as Richard Rowe puts it, 'females are typically intercepted and seized by males during their maiden flight and then they mate'. After copulation the females rise high into the air and may get carried considerable distances on air currents. After four or five days the eggs will have developed and, since fertilisation has already been accomplished, egg-laying can take place immediately — sometimes hundreds of miles from where mating took place. The species also occurs in India and the Far East where, again according to Richard Rowe, they behave in a different fashion in that both sexes, on their maiden flights, are carried over considerable distances by the wind, as is the case for many migratory odonates.

Finally, it is well known that oceanic islands far from any mainland have, over the centuries, been colonised by birds and insects. Nick Donnelly finds it interesting to speculate whether the dispersal is via 'normal' low-velocity trade winds or whether it 'mainly takes place during infrequent, violent hurricanes'. Several observations, taking into account the direction of the trade winds (southeast to northwest) and the dominant storm track for hurricanes (northwest to southeast), favour hurricane dispersal.

Orthetrum cancellatum (Black-tailed Skimmer). Immature male (top); sub-adult male beginning to become pruinosed (middle); fully mature male (bottom).

MIGRATION

Migration is defined as 'the seasonal movement of complete populations of animals to a more favourable environment'. While this definition can be understood when applied to birds or to such creatures as the African wildebeest (gnu), it is not so clear when applied to Odonata. Odonates can seldom be said to make regular seasonal movements and the causes of odonate 'migration' are by no means fully understood.

It should be remembered that, from the earliest times, odonates have dispersed after emergence. From time to time long distance dispersal was necessary in order to find more favourable environments following major catastrophic events on the planet, but such movements could not be termed 'seasonal'. Long distance journeys are still taken, for reasons that are not understood, but neither can they be called seasonal. Smaller scale 'migration' also occurs but this is really no more than seeking new egg-laying sites and such movements are generally fairly local as can be seen when a newly excavated pond becomes colonised, particularly should there be similar pieces of water in the neighbourhood.

However, we do talk about migration and perhaps it will help if we split 'migration' into two groups: 'big-time' and 'small-time'!

Of the first group, *Pantala flavescens* is undoubtedly the species that springs to mind. It appears to be a compulsive migrant and is well named 'Globe Skimmer' in the Old World and 'Wandering Glider' in the New. It is thought to have originated in Africa although, as Michael Parr points out, there appear to be no facts to support the theory. The species breeds on either side of both the Atlantic and the Indian Oceans and there are frequent records,

A female *Pantala flavescens*. (The male is illustrated on page 5.)

Hemianax ephippiger
**(Vagrant Emperor) is a
compulsive migrant.**

from various parts of the world, of swarms of
the insects moving in off the sea. Over the
oceans they must be on the wing for several
days and nights at a stretch and there have been
many reports of sightings by the crews of ves-
sels sailing hundreds of miles from land. It is
said to be the most highly evolved dragonfly.
Its broad-based wings allow it to glide and drift
on the thermals and it is perfectly adapted for
feeding on the aerial plankton that is present in
the upper atmosphere. Perhaps this species
comes nearest to the 'seasonal movement'
definition because, according to J. Reichholf
(1973), in North America adults apparently fly
north to breed and the resulting generation
travels south in the autumn.

The same type of seasonal movement is said
to occur in *Anax junius*. Robert Cannings and
Kathleen Stuart tell us that fully mature adults
arrive in Canada from the USA in the spring
and early summer and that the females

immediately begin to oviposit. At the end of
August a new generation emerges which, since
no mature specimens are ever seen at this time
of year, 'probably migrates south in late
summer'. The authors continue: 'Since larval
development takes about a year, it appears that
adults of *junius* emerging in southern Canada
in late summer are the progeny of the previous
year's migrants from the south'.

Another example of a long distance traveller
is *Hemianax ephippiger* (Vagrant Emperor).
This species occurs throughout Africa, breeding
in any suitable water from the Cape to the
Mediterranean coast; its movements appear to
be complexly related to weather systems and
seasons. It quite regularly crosses the
Mediterranean into Europe and Asia and, as
frequently pointed out, it is the only odonate to
have been recorded from Iceland. Perhaps the
most surprising example of all is the tiny damselfly *Ischnura aurora*, illustrated on page 25

and whose migratory behaviour is described on page 26.

In all these cases (and a number of similar ones), it appears the insects are immature (even teneral and on their maiden flights) when they set out and there would seem to be, therefore, an innate migratory instinct.

In contrast, 'small-time' migration is generally undertaken by mature insects, searching for new egg-laying sites. Although most 'small-time' movements are confined to short distances, there are quite frequent examples of arrivals from further afield, some of which may even have originated across considerable expanses of water. In Britain, 1995 was noted for an invasion of Darters from the Continent. On August 1st, nine *Sympetrum flaveolum* (Yellow-winged Darter) were reported in Great Yarmouth Cemetery; on the following morning there were 100 or so and, by the morning of August 3rd, the count had risen to several hundred. There were Darters everywhere (five species of them), perched on gravestones, on railings, on plant tips and on the branches of trees. After resting, they spread further afield and, by the end of September, there were few parts of England and Wales from which there were no records. Smaller landings clearly occurred along the coastline north and south of Yarmouth and there were other points of entry along the south coast from Kent to Cornwall and even Wales.

Needless to say, the questions on everyone's lips were, 'Why?', and 'From where?'. It is suggested by Bob Gibbon (and others) that such migrations depend on a combination of a high level of synchronised emergence, a shortage of food, and winds in a suitable direction. In 1995, on the Continent, high temperatures and constant sunshine in July were preceded by very high spring rainfall: a combination that ensured maximum emergences of Darters. Following waterways, young adults (some of which had

The Palaearctic *Aeshna mixta* (Migrant Hawker) once an uncommon migrant to Britain, has been steadily extending its range and is now a common breeding resident.

Male *Sympetrum flaveolum* (Yellow-winged Darter) in Surrey, England.

been marked) travelled, and were traced, from southern Scandinavia, via Schleswig-Holstein, to Amsterdam. On July 31st hundreds were observed leaving the shores of Holland and it was on August 1st that the first arrivals were recorded from Great Yarmouth, which lies north-west across the North Sea. High pressure and the south-easterly winds which were prevalent during the last week of July and the first week of August undoubtedly facilitated passage and the exceptionally hot weather experienced during the same period would have encouraged the visitors to fly inland in an attempt to find suitable sites in which they could breed. In other words, all they were really doing was seeking new egg-laying sites.

There are a few other examples of mass odonate movement that do not fit into either of the above groups. For example an unusual form of migration has been recorded by Yutaka Arai in the Saitama Prefecture, Japan. The eggs of *Stylogomphus suzukii* are laid in the upper reaches of mountain streams and, on hatching, the larvae commence a long journey downstream, a journey, taken in stages, that lasts throughout their larval life. After emergence, the adults reverse the movement and migrate back to the breeding areas upstream prior to commencing reproduction. According to Kiyoshi Inoue, another species to make this downstream migration as larvae and upstream as adults is *Sinogomphus flavolimbatus*.

There are also instances where odonates must make regular yearly migrations because of particular seasonal climatic changes: Philip Corbet terms such individuals 'obligate migrants' and Inoue refers to such movements as 'round trip migration'. This obligate or round-trip migration could be said to be more nearly related to the definition given in the first paragraph: it is indeed a seasonal movement to a more favourable environment.

4
The perfect hunting machine

Dragonflies and damselflies can hunt and feed on the wing and the voracious appetite displayed during the larval stage is equalled during adulthood. In many respects they are the 'perfect hunting machine'. This is a good description of an odonate and four features of its anatomy help make it what it is.

The compound eyes are well adapted to detect movement and the thousands of facets enable the insect to see forwards, to the left and to the right, below and above. With at most a slight turn of its head, it can effectively see what is happening behind it as well.

The thorax shows evidence of its antiquity, odonates having specialised to feed while in flight from an early stage in their evolution. The first segment (the prothorax) is small but otherwise 'normal'; the second and third segments (which are fused together) are large, set at an oblique angle and concertinaed towards the front.

The shape of the thorax means that the legs are thrust forward in a fashion unlike that of any other insect. The legs are armed with stout bristles which interlock to make a 'basket' into which the insect scoops its prey and, from the basket, the meal is easily transferred to the mouth.

Aeshna mixta (Migrant Hawker). **The large compound eyes of odonates are well adapted to detecting movement.**

Macromia bifasciata (Natal Macromia). **The unique shape of the odonate thorax results in their legs being thrust forward.**

Male *Trithemis stictica.* Because their fore- and hindwings are not connected, odonates have exceptional manoeuvrability.

The wings are structurally very strong and, unlike those of almost all other insects, the fore- and hindwings are not connected with each other and thus can beat out of phase. This give the insects exceptional manoeuvrability. They can take to the air vertically and they can hover almost motionless for long periods at a time. They can fly forwards and backwards and make the most incredible twists and turns within very limited space.

Having discarded the wings of their prey, odonates will feed on flies, beetles, butterflies and moths, and will even devour caterpillars if they are swinging on threads from the branches of a tree. Damselflies will often use their legs to snatch small insects resting on the stems of plants. The South American *Megaloprepus caerulatus* (wingspan 20 cm) feeds on spiders plucked from the centre of their webs. Feeding activity is high in immatures and increases to a peak as they approach reproductive maturity. Once fully mature the activity becomes less urgent.

Generally speaking, two hunting methods are used — one by 'fliers' and the other by 'perchers'. There are seven families of 'fliers': Aeshnidae, Neopetaliidae, Cordulegastridae, Chlorogomphidae, and the three Emerald families, Macromiidae, Synthemistidae and Corduliidae, plus a few of the Libellulidae. 'Perchers' consist of Gomphidae, Petaluridae, most Libellulidae and almost all damselflies. Basically, fliers catch and consume their prey while flying, and perchers take off from an observation post, catch their prey and return, often to the same perch, to consume it. According to Michael Parr, damselflies have been reported trying to remove small galls from leaves.

It is sometimes possible to witness swarms of aeshnids congregating where food is abundant, for example where there has been an emergence of flying ants. Considerable numbers have also been known to gather on the leeward side of trees and bushes in windy weather, waiting to catch insects as they are blown off the vegetation. Species that congregate in swarms are generally those with large wings and light bodies such as *Rhyothemis*, *Tramea*, *Tholymis*, *Zyxomma* and the two *Pantala* species. Swarms of *Pantala* have been reported following people, large animals or even slow vehicles in anticipation of the prey they stir up.

There are some fascinating variations on this 'accompanying behaviour' as a means of acquiring prey. Philip Corbet and Peter Miller have observed both sexes of the *Brachythemis*

Ceratogomphus pictus (Common African Clubtail). Odonates usually discard the wings of their prey, here a ladybird.

leucosticta (4-square Groundling) fly close to the legs of large vertebrates (including humans) as they move through open grassland and it is presumed that such following behaviour enables the dragonflies to feed on insects put up by the moving vertebrates. I too have experienced this in Africa with the 4-square Groundling and, also, beside the Amazon in Peru with the similarly marked *Erythrodiplax attenuata* (Smoky-winged Dragonlet). They are sometimes so numerous that it might seem impossible to avoid treading on them. Such fears are unnecessary: they are very alert!

Dragonflies usually need warmth in order to fly and will take shelter when dusk approaches or should the sky become overcast. Most people will have noticed how the hordes of small insects seem to multiply towards dusk and how mosquitoes appear after the sun has set. A small number of dragonfly species take advantage of this. In Europe, the best example is *Boyeria irene* (Crepuscular Hawker) which flies long after nightfall. It is attracted to lights and can easily satisfy its hunger by consuming the hundreds of smaller insects that are likewise attracted. In the streets of a small town in central France I have seen them flying just a foot or so above the tarmac and, next morning, the battered corpses of some of them have lain beside the road as a result of being run over by passing cars. Interestingly, in northern Queensland, I have witnessed (long after dusk) numbers of the closely related *Telephlebia tillyardi* flying about 23 cm above the ground along a dirt track in the forest. In this case there was no electric, nor any other, lighting to attract possible prey.

In a forest clearing in Japan, a couple of hours after dusk, I have seen dozens of male and female *Aeschnophlebia anisoptera* ('Ao yamma') and *Anaciaeschna martini* ('Martin yamma') flying over a large boggy pool; the fol-

lowing morning, just before sunrise (and in the pouring rain!), they were there again feverishly feeding on thousands of small insects before disappearing into the trees for their daytime slumbers. A little later, at about 6 a.m., *Anax parthenope julius* ('Gin yamma') appeared on the scene and, a little later still, *Polycanthagyna melanictera* ('Yabu-yamma').

There are other tropical species active when it is raining. For example, in Queensland, *Austroaeschna pulchra* is noted for flying high among the treetops in daytime while rain is falling and disappearing as soon as the sun comes

Male *Brachythemis leucosticta* (4-square Groundling) at Duiwelskloof, South Africa.

Telephlebia tillyardi is one of Australia's crepuscular species.

out; and in Borneo, according to Allen Davies, many of the night-flying anisopterans, including the giant *Tetracanthagyna* species, will make welcome appearances on drizzly afternoons.

TEMPERATURE REGULATION

Insects are cold-blooded creatures and thus odonates can only fly when they are warm. In the tropics this seldom presents a serious problem but, in temperate regions and particularly in cold mountainous areas, the problem can be acute. In Japan, anisozygopteran *Epiophlebia superstes* emerges in mid-April when the temperature can be very low indeed. Each morning, in order to raise its body temperature sufficiently to enable it to fly, the insect engages in a session of strenuous wing-whirring which can last well over an hour. This vibrating of the wings can also be witnessed in newly emerged dragonflies: emergence generally takes place early in the morning and it is important that the young adult raises its body temperature as quickly as possible.

A very wet and cold *Anax imperator mauricianus* below Cathedral Peak, South Africa.

In 1964 and 1968, Philip Corbet studied various aspects of dragonfly migration in Canada. He noticed that roosting *Anax junius* had the ability to change from the west to the east side of a piece of vegetation, 'thus mitigating the effects of cool autumn nights when migrating.' Having settled the previous evening on the still sunny west side, some 30 minutes or so before sunrise, they commenced to vibrate their wings. A few minutes later they took off and darted round to the other side, resettling low down on grasses facing east and the rising sun. As a result, their body temperature was sufficiently high to allow them to be active shortly after sunrise.

In July 1998, Michael May reported on an investigation into the ability of *Sympetrum vicinum* to cope with cool conditions: 'Because of its late flight season, this species is faced regularly with cooler environmental temperatures than most dragonflies investigated heretofore. By virtue of postural adjustments and perch selection, individuals are able to maintain both thoracic and head temperatures within a relatively narrow range even at ambient temperature as low as 10°C.' The species appears to be adapted to cool conditions by the possession of a low minimum temperature requirement for effective flight and a relatively rapid digestive function at low temperature, both of which enhance the ability to cope with cool conditions.

On a cold, wet and miserable morning in February 1990, I and two companions arrived at a resting place on the side of Cathedral Peak in the Natal Drakensbergs. Sheltering from the rain were two *Anax imperator mauricianus* almost totally hidden under the bank of a small pond. I picked one up and placed its cold, rigid body on a piece of plant material where it remained motionless, except for a reflex action which caused it to take a firm grip on the stem with its legs. We went on our way and, three hours later, returned to the same place. The Emperor appeared not to have moved although he was clearly beginning to warm up. The sun had almost emerged from behind the clouds and the rain had stopped; he was wiping his face with his forelegs but had not yet attempted to dry out his wings.

Ian Endersby describes how *Austrolestes annulosus* is one of those species which shows a temperature-dependent variation in colour: 'When cold they are darker in colour as a black body absorbs radiation faster than a reflective one, thus enabling them to reach their flight temperature sooner than a species that has not developed this adaptation. Conversely, a black body also radiates heat more rapidly than a reflective one and so there is a further advantage for *A. annulosus* to become reflective (bright blue with small black markings) when at operating temperature.'

An added advantage possessed by *A. annulosus* and others like it, is that by heating up more quickly, they will gain earlier access to food and to the best territorial spots.

Dragonflies like to bask in the sun but overheating is sometimes a problem. In such cases, some insects (*Crocothemis* and *Trithemis* species are examples) assume the 'obelisk' position, raising the abdomen up in the air so that it presents the least possible body area to the rays of the sun. Abdomens are angled so that the tips point directly at the sun and, as the day progresses, the insects rotate so that they track the sun's movement.

There are other ways of keeping cool. Some libellulids, especially in the tropics, may be seen 'water-dipping'; and many zygopterans retire into the shade. One is more likely to find *Ceriagrion* and *Pseudagrion* species under trees and in deep shade during the heat of the day than by sunny, watery sites. Finally, the wings of some libellulids are almost totally dark

Male *Crocothemis erythraea* in Italy, in the 'obelisk' position to prevent overheating.

coloured while others have red, brown or black basal regions and it is thought that, as well as providing visual identification to the opposite sex, they may act as sunshades, preventing the thorax from overheating.

In corroboration of this idea, Marcel Wasscher witnessed an interesting piece of behaviour: 'In Surinam, I saw a *Diastatops* species use its wings as a 'sunshade umbrella' at noon and in the afternoon. It turned one wing up at an angle of 45 degrees towards the sky in the direction of the sun so that it provided direct shade on its thorax; the other wing was held at an angle of 45 degrees in a downward direction'. This beautiful libellulid has completely black wings, with two patches of red in the hindwings.

A variation of this method was witnessed by David Pryce on a very hot day of 43°C near Death Valley in California: he described how a male of the brilliant red *Libellula saturata* carefully and minutely moved position in order to keep his body in the shade provided by the stem on which he perched.

Perhaps the dark colouring at the base of the wings on this *Libellula luctuosa*, in Upper New York State, USA, acts as a sunshade.

Libellula saturata shelters from the sun in Death Valley, California, USA.

David Pryce

SIZE

In Palaeozoic times, giant 'dragonflies' with wingspans of over 60 cm flew above the prehistoric fern forests. They must have been a formidable sight as they moved, rather clumsily, through the air but, since they had no competition, their somewhat inefficient flying abilities were not likely to have been a serious handicap. Around 100 million years would pass before pterodactyls appeared and 150 million years before birds as we know them. *Meganeura monyi* with a wingspan of 68.5 cm which has been found in carboniferous deposits in Commentry, France and the Permian *Meganeuropsis permiana* with a wingspan of 72 cm are among the largest fossil dragonflies yet discovered. Philip Corbet, in his *Dragonflies*, deduced that a full-grown larva of the first species must have been about 30 cm long, but fossil larvae from these eras have yet to be found.

Even in those distant times, not all dragonflies were giants; a number of fossils from the Carboniferous and Permian deposits are not particularly large. And the same, on a much smaller scale, is true today. The largest dragonfly I have seen is Australia's *Petalura ingentissima* whose female has a wingspan of 158–162 mm and a body length of 125 mm. Although some species of *Anax* (e.g. *A. tristis*) are as long in body length; some of China's *Tetracanthagyna* have longer wings (168 mm); and *Chlorogomphus papilio* has the greatest wing area, no species yet discovered surpasses *P. ingentissima* in all respects. One of the smallest is the libellulid

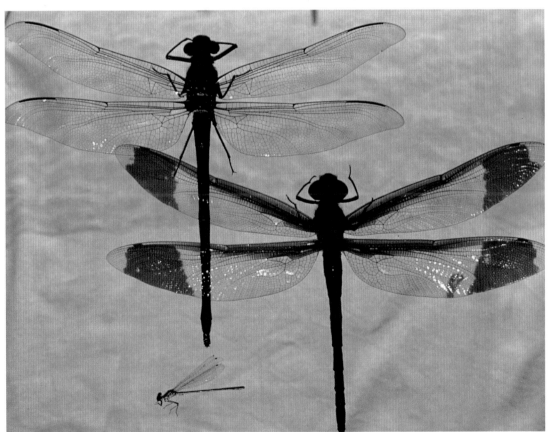

Collection of Allen Davies

Two giants: *Petalura ingentissima* (left) and *Tetracanthagyna plagiata* (right), with *Enallagma cyathigerum* beneath.

This male *Notogomphus praetorius,* in north-eastern Transvaal, South Africa, is unlikely to survive long due to the damage to its wings during emergence.

Nannophya pygmaea with a wingspan of 26 mm and length of 17 mm but the smallest known anisopteran of all is another libellulid, *Nannophyopsis clara* (see page 162).

There is an equal diversity in the size of damselflies: some of the tropical rainforest species are huge, with the males often being larger than the females. The South American *Mecistogaster lucretia* (see page 123) is the longest known zygopteran with a body length of 150 mm; the wingspan of this particular species is 125 mm but those of others in the genus reach around 200 mm. At the other end of the scale, the tiny Far Eastern *Agriocnemis femina* is just 20 mm.

Even within a particular species there can be quite a big difference in size. Europe's *Anax imperator* has an average wingspan of 100 mm but the subspecies found in South Africa

(*A. imperator mauricianus*) is considerably larger, with a span of around 105–110 mm.

LIFE EXPECTANCY

The average life expectancy of an adult odonate depends on the part of the world in which it lives. In 1960 R. M. Gambles observed that in temperate zones, the largest portion of an odonate's lifetime, which may amount to several years, is spent in the larval stage, while the adult phase is reduced to one or two months. In species common to the tropics and subtropics, however, larval development is often reduced to a few months and the adult stage may last a full year. In temperate zones, adult odonates that survive the extremely vulnerable period between commencement of emergence and successful maiden flight, have an average life expectancy of 4–6 weeks (dragonflies) or 1–2 weeks (damselflies). One or two examples of damselflies' life span are: *Enallagma civile* (temperate), two days; *Palaemnema* spp. (neotropical), 3–10 days; *Ischnura gemina* (temperate), 6–23 days; *Megaloprepus caerulatus* (neotropical), a maximum of 165 days.

An interesting exception is found in the temperate subfamily Sympecmatinae, some of whose members emerge in late summer and, while still sexually immature, overwinter in fallen leaves or at the base of tall grasses, recommencing an active procreative life in the following spring.

In those years in which northern Europe enjoys an 'Indian Summer', some late-season species will survive into October or even November. The longest survivor I have seen in Britain was an *Aeshna cyanea* (Southern Hawker) which, on 16 December 1989, was settled on the inside wall of a covered area outside our back door; the following day, it had fallen to the ground and was dead — is an attempted hibernation possible?

There have been one or two recorded instances of suspended animation. In July 1994, what appeared to be a dead Emperor Dragonfly, in a perfect state of preservation, stretched out on a lily-pad in a small pond, was spotted by a friend. It was such a beautiful specimen that he lifted it off and carried it (quite stiff) back to the car. On arrival home, it was placed on the top of the kitchen boiler so that people could admire it. Some two hours later, my friend's eye was caught by movement: the head was moving and then the wings began to move too. A few minutes later, when it was obvious the insect was very much alive, he picked it up, released it outside and watched as it flew strongly up the garden.

ENEMIES AND ESCAPE MECHANISMS

It is always fascinating to watch the food chain in operation. A warm sunny day will find hundreds of small insects dancing just a few inches above the water; these will be chased and caught by voracious dragonflies which, in their turn, may be trapped in the jaws of jumping fish. (Tillyard mentions the finding of as many as 35 undigested heads of dragonflies in the stomach of a single trout!) Completing the chain, a kingfisher, perched on an overhanging branch, will make frequent dives and, more often than not, emerge with a fish in its bill.

Adult odonates are at their most vulnerable during emergence and during the 'drying out' period that follows. Fortunately newly emerged specimens are generally less brilliantly coloured than they are when mature and are thus less

A *Calopteryx splendens* (Banded Demoiselle) caught in a spider's web.

A Rainbow Bee-eater consuming *Hemianax papuensis* in Queensland, Australia.

This *Calopteryx splendens* (Banded Demoiselle) laying its eggs on the River Dordogne, France, would be difficult to spot by a swooping swallow.

likely to be spotted by predators. Most species emerge during darkness: nature's way of protecting them against predating birds, frogs, rodents and small mammals. Darkness does not, however, protect smaller species from capture in spiders' webs and such a fate commonly awaits damselflies.

There have been a number of reports of quite large dragonflies being attacked by small bees and wasps. After numbing a dragonfly with its sting, the hymenopteran will remove the head, suck up the internal juices and fly off, leaving behind what appears to be an almost intact odonate.

Birds probably present the most serious threat to adult dragonflies. Falcons catch them and so do swallows, bee-eaters and rollers. As has been seen, dragonflies are adept at twisting and turning in the air and it is fascinating to watch the aerobatics they perform when being chased by swooping swallows and martins. It is reminiscent of dogfights between warring fighter planes and one feels like cheering each time a dragonfly succeeds in eluding its enemy — which it frequently does. Lizards are another enemy and Fraser mentions that they not infrequently attack those species which are given to alighting on the ground.

Although superb manoeuvrability is their principal method of escape, camouflage is also a great help. *Tachopteryx thoreyi* (Grey Petaltail) 'disappears' as soon as it lands on the bark of a tree (see page 53), and *Bradinopyga geminata* (Indian Wall Dragonfly) rests with its wings pressed so close against a wall that it makes no shadow at all. *Aeshna grandis* (Brown Hawker) almost invariably chooses something brown on which to settle (dead ferns, copper-coloured leaves, etc.) and females of many other species are extremely hard to spot as they lay their eggs into thick water weeds.

Bradinopyga germinata makes no shadow as he vanishes into the bricks of a wall in southern India.

Another method is 'playing possum'. I have witnessed this being used very successfully beside a small ornamental pond at Skukuza in South Africa's Kruger National Park. *Philonomon luminans* (Barbet) is a very shy and alert species which, when threatened, will collapse and lie sideways on the ground, looking dead. When the danger has passed, the 'corpse' will right itself and fly away.

Dragonflies are often enemies to smaller species of their own order. Such predation is generally by dragonflies on damselflies or smaller species of dragonfly but Sidney Dunkle tells us *Hagenius brevistylus* (Dragonhunter) eats species up to 73 mm long such as *Nasiaeschna pentacanthus*. There are also cases of true cannibalism when an individual is devoured by a member of its own species.

Finally, smaller dragonflies and many damselflies get trapped or entangled in such insect-eating plants as sundew or, as reported by Michael Samways of Natal University, on the hundreds of minute hooked trichomes (hairs) on the seed heads of *Desmodium repandum* and *Bidens pilosa*.

The shy *Philonomon luminans* feigns death when threatened.

Female *Orthetrum icteromelas* (Cannibal Skimmer), in Botswana, eating a *Diplacodes*.

Enallagma cyathigerum (Common Blue Damselfly) trapped by a sundew plant.

5
Lords of the air

GEORG RÜPPELL

Dragonflies move their shimmering wings too fast for human eyes to see, but their own visual perception is so quick that they can detect, and immediately analyse, the movements of other flying insects, correctly identifying prey, enemy and potential partner. In order to compensate for this inequality, I use 'slow-motion' film of up to 500 frames per second. The film is shot so fast through the camera that, when projected at normal speed, all movements are slowed down 20 times and we get the effect of slow motion. When watching these films we are, in effect, looking through the eyes of the dragonfly!

No other order of insects is able to exhibit the fantastic flight manoeuvres displayed by Odonata. They can hover for a minute at a time and then dart away forwards or backwards or on a breathtaking zigzag course through the reeds. Some species can fly immense distances and a male is often capable of towing his much heavier mate for 20 kilometres or more. Generally speaking, odonates have managed to adapt to a changing environment because of these superb flying abilities. Some of the larger species can reach speeds of up to 70 km per hour; some travel to places thousands of miles

away and no gust of wind will disturb their flight direction. High up amongst the treetops they can chase and catch their prey and they are able to avoid most birds without difficulty — bee-eaters and hobbies being exceptions. Without rest, the so-called 'fliers', such as Emperors (e.g. *Hemianax papuensis*) or Hawkers can remain on the wing for several hours at a time. Damselflies, on the other hand,

Hemianax papuensis in flight, photographed in Queensland, Australia.

which need to rest more frequently, are weak fliers. Their flight is slow, only around 10 km per hour, but they are very manoeuvrable. Low over the surface of the water or in the dense jungle of waterside plants they can circle, twist and hover. How do our odonates do it?

Speed and power

Damselflies

Most zygopterans move their two pairs of wings alternately: one pair, on its way downwards, meets the other pair going upwards. Thrust is generated with each downward beat and, because one pair of wings after the other is pro-

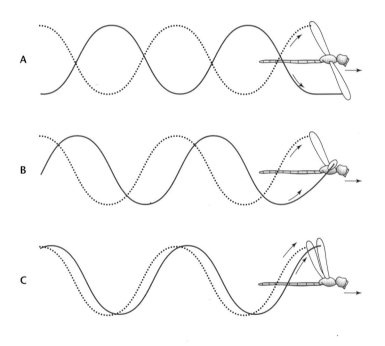

Different phase relationships between forewings (solid lines) and hindwings (broken lines). A, Counterstroke movement: fore- and hindwings beat alternately (always used by zygopterans (other than calopterygids) and by anisopterans when hovering); B, Phased movement: hindwings lead the movement (used in normal forward flight of anisopterans); C, Synchronised movement: all wings beat in same direction at the same time (used by calopterygids, except in courting flight, and by anisopterans in short bursts).

ducing it, the thrust is continuous. This type of wing movement is called 'counterstroking' and it is an economical way of flying as it results in steady flight (unsteady driving costs us humans a lot of fuel too). For damselflies such economy is important because they must conserve energy. Their very light bodies (0.02–0.05 g) have only little inertia and, because of the relatively large surface of body and wings, they are all too easily slowed down by air friction. The relative surface is much higher in small animals than in larger ones and this may be a reason for the heavy wing action that damselflies exhibit. They beat with all the power their small flight muscles (relation to total body weight 1:5) allow, and they move them in a wide angle of about 120 degrees, with a high frequency of about 35 beats per second (35 Hz). Despite this, their actual wing movement is not very fast, the wingtips only reaching velocities of between 2 and 2.5 m/s. Wings with a length of 12–22 mm (as in almost all common damselflies except Broad Wings) are too short to produce the lift and thrust needed for faster flight. Passage through the air depends on the frequency and the actual speed of the wingbeats; the latter is obviously highest at the tips of the wings. If we divide a damselfly's wing into two halves, the outer one covers more area than the inner because the latter ends in a thin stalk, and this is ideal for wide movements.

Dragonflies

In contrast to the wings of damselflies, those of dragonflies are broad at the base, particularly in the hindwings. Why? Well, they act as aerofoils and these are used in gliding and soaring. Indeed the members of Libellulidae, which forms one of the most advanced groups of dragonflies, are called in German 'Segellibellen' (soaring dragonflies). Damselflies are not able to soar nor even to glide (although I did once see *Megaloprepus coerulatus* (Forest Giant Damselfly) soaring over a short distance, but this amazing Central American species possesses a wingspan of up to 18 cm!). Dragonflies are better equipped for fast flight than are damselflies. Their high mass (0.1–1 g) has a lot of inertia; their huge flight muscles (relation to body weight 1:3 or 1:2.5) are able to beat the 25–55 mm long wings with a frequency of 30–50 Hz and, at an angle of 70–90 degrees (during normal forward flight), which gives a velocity of 4 m/s at the wingtip. Should faster flight be required, the dragonfly is able to increase its power output: the frequency by 40% and the flight angle by 50%, which means the maximum wingtip speed can reach 7 m/s.

The wings must be stable enough to bear this velocity — and they are. The folded structure and the highly sophisticated architecture of the wing veins have been modified over more than 100 million years of evolution to guarantee a maximum of stability at a minimum of material weight.

In forward flight the hindwings lead the movement and the forewings follow one-quarter out of phase. When the wings beat like this, in the same direction, the dragonfly attains more speed than when the counterstroke is used. The counterstroke (used, as we have seen, at all times by most damselflies) is used by dragonflies only when hovering. It is possible that the use of the counterstroking flight technique is in some way a question of body size: the very small *Perithemis tenera*, an American libellulid, nearly always uses this beat.

On the other hand, the larger calopterygids mostly use 'synchronous' wingbeats, in which all four wings are beaten in the same direction at the same time. Dragonflies have more 'gears' than damselflies and they have this excessive fuel-using movement in their repertoire too! They use the synchronous wingbeat in fast

upward and upward-backward flight, but only for short spells because it uses too much energy. This type of flight is used during, for example, escape from a predator or to confront a rival male appearing with the intention of whisking a female away. On such occasions, the angles of attack — which are the angles between the incoming air and the wings' surface — are very large, so that stalling is very possible; the wings are now used as shovels (rather as in rowing) and it means flying with drag (not as elegant as with lift). All fliers, even aircraft, do this on occasions.

MANOEUVRABILITY

The wingbeat direction shown in slow motion films of anisopterans flying with drag, corresponds very well to the precise morphological findings of K. H. Pfau. He judged that dragonflies, owing to their wing joints, are only able to beat their wings downwards. Damselfly wings, on the other hand, are freer and can beat in different directions, varying between vertical and horizontal. This is one important reason for their high manoeuvrability. Largely as a consequence of their different flight abilities, dragonflies and damselflies usually occupy different space: the former more in the open and the latter among vegetation or near the water surface. Of course they do meet, frequently with fatal consequences for the damselflies. Indeed damselflies occupy a choice position on the menu of their larger cousins although a high degree of aerial dexterity allows many of them to escape.

This leads us from symmetrical flight manoeuvres, where the wings on both sides of the body exhibit the same movement, to asymmetric ones, where the wings on one side of the body are moved differently from those on the other. The ability to do this shows, even better than high-speed flight, the highly evolved flight capabilities of odonates.

Generally speaking, a slowing down or acceleration on one side of the body causes a turn: the greater the difference, the sharper the turn. But they have other ways of executing a turn: during fast forward flight, a sudden banking, as in aircraft, will lead the insect round and this is a method frequently used by dragonflies. It is, aerodynamically, the most economical way of turning but it has a large radius and sharp changes of direction cannot be executed in this manner.

Damselflies need only one wing beat to turn 180 degrees and just one and a half beats can be sufficient for a *Calopteryx* to swing round 360 degrees. I surmise that such sharp turns are made possible by using high angles of attack: both wings on the outer side of the curve beat backwards at high angles and those on the inner side beat forward at high angles. The action takes about 0.05 s and, in accomplishing it, the practically weightless damselfly does not lose any measurable height; to obtain more thrust on one side of the body, the angle of the wingbeat on that side must be increased. In addition, they

Wing movement during the execution of turns: top, *Anax imperator*; right, *Calopteryx splendens*; centre left, *Lestes viridis*; centre, *Megaloprepus coerulatus*; left bottom, *Aeshna cyanea*. Small black arrows show the stroke direction of the wings, large shaded arrows indicate the direction of the turn.

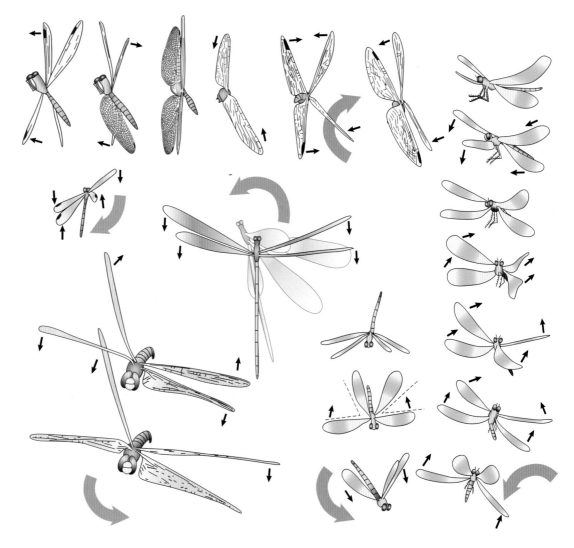

A male *Anax imperator* (Emperor Dragonfly) attempted to catch a pair of *Orthetrum cancellatum* (Skimmers) flying in tandem. Coming in, he banked sharply but missed his target; immediately he swung back to a horizontal flight position and then banked to the other side. Banking was achieved by setting the wings on one side of the body in a negative angle of attack which meant that the incoming airstream hit the upper surface of those wings which were pushed downwards. He again missed the target and, having lost height by these manoeuvres, he beat all four wings synchronously in the same direction at high angles of attack, so that his flight path rose again. He then gave up the chase and normal forward flight, with its slightly phased movements, was recommenced. The Emperor was unsuccessful and this is often the case: large insects often fail to catch smaller ones, particularly if the smaller ones are damselflies.

Parallel stroking during the flight is indicated in the drawings by grey wings. The time courses of the upstrokes (rising lines) and downstrokes (falling lines) are shown. In the shaded areas, the wings beat in the same direction. A, flight of *Anax* from its beginning until shortly after the steep curve; B and C, the same flight from the heavy black arrow until the end. In B, both forewings (continuous line) are held still for some time and then, for one cycle, only one is moved. A hindwing (dashed line) is also held still for one cycle in C.

are able to vary the wingbeat speed of port and starboard and also to beat their wings in different directions: almost anything is possible! All these kinematic patterns are used for turns at low flight velocity and, at these particular feats, damselflies are the champions.

The high variability of an odonate's flight is not only shown in twisting and turning, it is also used in braking and accelerating. By varying the angles of the wingbeats, or the frequency of the wingbeats, or the angles of attack, odonates are capable of almost immediate changes of speed. And should an individual be flying too fast when he needs to make an emergency stop, he can still achieve it, even if it means a crash landing into the undergrowth: his body structure is robust enough to withstand it.

FLIGHT AS A MEANS OF COMMUNICATION

Flight is not only used to cover distance, in odonates it is a language too. Calopterygids, some of the Giant Damselflies of the New World, and some of the coloured-winged libellulids use their wings in territorial display. Calopterygids display their wings whenever possible: flashing their wings, males threaten each other and chase intruders from their territories. When two males meet frontally, the normal wingbeat pattern is changed and the wings beat from a thrust-forward position, thus showing the signalling area of their wings. When they meet laterally, they show their side view and try to enlarge the optical effect in another way: wings beat synchronously in threatening flight and, at the end of the upstroke, they are held still for a short time. Non-beating wings are not conducive to good flight and each time such an action occurs, the male will lose height and must act in a way necessary to regain it. This is not disadvantageous as it results in a waving flightpath which increases the conspicuousness of the threatening flight. The male who does best in threatening and flying at the same time will win. On one occasion, a slow motion film showed particularly interesting behaviour: a territorial male flew frontally against an intruder, obviously using a frontal threatening display; the intruder passed by, threatening laterally. To increase the effect he flew using only his hindwings, holding the forewings totally still for two wingbeat periods. He began to lose height and so brought one of his forewings into action but still signalled with the one facing his opponent. It was not enough and he ended up in the water!

When all their skills are added together, it can be seen why odonates are considered the lords of the air.

6

Colour and polymorphism

PETER MILLER

The colours of odonates can be as striking and beautiful as those of any other insects. However, their colours usually fade after death which may explain why they are more attractive to photographers than to collectors. It is typically the mature males that are the most brightly coloured, females and young adults of both sexes tending to be duller, with browns, greens and yellows predominating. As they mature and return to their breeding sites, males take on the strong blues, reds, yellows and greens that make them such prominent features of the waterside when they display to each other and defend their territories.

In a number of families, however, there is not much difference between male and female colouring: in petalurids both sexes are dull brown; in most gomphids, both sexes are black or brown with yellow markings; and male and female corduliids share the same metallic blue-green on thorax and abdomen; such species tend not to be so territorial and conflicts between males may be less common.

Odonate coloration is due either to the possession of pigments lying below the cuticle in the epidermal cells, or to very thin cuticular

Robert Thompson

layers which reflect specific wavelengths of light according to their spacing. Maturing males of some species develop a waxy bloom or pruinescence on the upper side of the abdomen and thorax which gives them a white, blue or, in a

The striking facial colours of *Aeshna juncea* would frighten any intruder.

few cases, a red appearance, obscuring other colours below . Those dragonfly colours which depend on cuticular layers or on pruinescence may be preserved after death.

An odonate's head is dominated by its eyes and the eyes are often strikingly coloured. Below a brown 'eyeshade' the facets may be blue, green, red or yellow. The thorax also in many species bears a bright patterning of colours: in damselflies, clubtails and hawkers it is typically striped with alternate dark and pale areas, whereas in libellulids it is more usually a single colour. Likewise, the upper surface of the mature male libellulid abdomen tends to be a single strong colour, commonly blue or red, whereas it is banded in many cordulegasterids, gomphids and coenagrionids, and often tessellated with an intricate patchwork of several colours in aeshnids.

The wings of some species are also strongly marked with red, brown, black or purple patches, particularly in males. In several species (*Chlorolestes* and *Tholymis* for example) these patches only develop with maturity. The shimmering purple-black wings of many calopterygids (the name means 'beautiful-winged') make for spectacular displays near streams and rivers around the world. Some African calopterygids (*Umma* and *Phaon*) appear to have transparent wings but, when they fly, their wings glitter, reflecting rainbow-like patterns of light and making them highly visible as they flit about in the shady parts of forests.

Erythemis simplicicollis (Eastern Pondhawk). Female (top). A male that has started to pruinose (middle). A fully mature male (bottom). Immature males have the same colouring as females. Photographed in Bays Mountain Park, Tennessee, USA.

Chlorolestes fasciatus (Mountain Sylph), on Cathedral Peak in the Natal Drakensberg, South Africa.
In the immature male (top) patches are just beginning to form on his wings. A mature male (below).

Although the bright colours of odonates serve mainly behavioural functions, they have other functions as well: for example in connection with temperature regulation or with cuticular hardening. The tarsal claws and the tips of the ovipositor may be black in many species in order to be hard rather than because they need to be dark.

Sexual behaviour

Colour plays a major role in sexual behaviour. The spectacular colours of mature males enable them to be readily visible to females as well as to rival males when they are at the breeding sites. Males may compete for territories at the water side, displaying coloured parts of their body in aggressive interactions with rivals. Libellulids may raise the abdomen to show its colourful upper surface; *Platycypha* displays its colourful legs and calopterygids fly in a way which allows their strongly marked wings to be visible.

Rival males often confront each other head on and perhaps this is why the face and front of the thorax are so strikingly patterned in some species. *Pyrrhosoma nymphula* (Large Red

Damselfly) presents a threatening grin when facing rivals and the face of *Aeshna juncea* (Common Hawker) is, one would imagine, very alarming (see page 49).

Some libellulids (*Trithemis* and *Palpopleura* for example) possess a reflective metallic disc in the middle of the face, the colour of which may be distinctive for the species. In addition, the beating wings of many species form a halo, patterned by the pterostigmas and other wing marks. The pterostigma has a major aerodynamic function but it may also act as a visual marker, particularly in species where its colour contrasts with that of wing patches, as in some *Brachythemis, Palpopleura* and *Calopteryx*.

Courtship

Colour is also important in many species during courtship. Many calopterygids reveal the brightly coloured lower surface of the last few abdominal segments to females settled nearby; male *Palpopleura* display their strongly marked wings and *Platycypha* shake their red and white legs at perched females (see page 59). Although humans cannot see ultraviolet light, odonates are well able to perceive it and are thus able to detect distinctive patterns of UV-reflectance or absorption on the wings or the body of other species, perhaps using it in the detection and courting of potential mates.

Colour forms

Mature females of some species (*Ceriagrion, Enallagma* and *Ischnura,* for example) occur in more than one colour form. One of the forms always resembles the male — which would appear to be disadvantageous since it might prevent mating. However, such male-like females do mate and they probably receive less harassment from males, which could be an advantage during egg-laying at high population densities. Colour forms are known to be geneti-

The pterostigmas contrast strongly with the black wing marking on this *Palpopleura lucia portia*.

A tandem pair of *Ceriagrion tenellum* (Small Red Damselfly). In this species there are three female forms. One resembles a male, being all red; another is black; and a third ('normal') form, shown here, is partly red and partly black.

cally inherited and there is still much to be discovered about this fascinating topic. Maybe those female darters, skimmers and chasers which become increasingly male-like in colour with age, gain a similar advantage.

Camouflage

Alternatively, colour can contribute to making dragonflies inconspicuous. The soft browns, greens and yellows of immature forms and of females help to conceal them from predatory birds, lizards and frogs as well as from praying mantids and larger dragonflies. Both sexes of the tropical *Bradinopyga* are coloured to resemble the rocks on which they commonly perch (see Enemies and escape mechanisms). North America's *Tachopteryx thoreyi* merge into the barks of the trees on which they settle, while the yellows of immature *Orthetrum* match the dry grasses among which they are often found. Such camouflage may also enable dragonflies to avoid sexual harassment from males of their own species.

Mimicry

In a few cases, colour patterns may enable dragonflies to resemble creatures which possess powerful defensive mechanisms. The female *Libellula depressa* resembles a hornet. So if a bird has previously encountered a hornet, it

Carlo Utzeri

Tachopteryx thoreyi is perfectly camouflaged on the bark of this tree in Tennessee, USA.

The female *Libellula depressa* (Broad-bodied Chaser) mimics a hornet.

may avoid this dragonfly. Similarly some small black tropical dragonflies resemble black wasps, while the gomphid species which rear up their expanded posterior abdominal segments when grabbed may deter further attack by reminding predators of scorpions or even of snakes. However mimicry does not seem to be a common feature of dragonflies.

Temperature regulation

Colour in dragonflies is also of importance in temperature regulation. Black, brown and red species absorb radiation and they are able to heat up more rapidly in the sun, whereas paler species may reflect radiation and thus be better equipped to remain cool in hot environments. Species such as *Sympetrum danae* (Black Darter) and *Libellula quadrimaculata* (4-spotted Chaser), with a northern temperate distribution, are dark in colour, but there are also plenty of dark species in the tropics (e.g. some *Brachythemis*, *Diplacodes* and *Erythrodiplax*) and the microclimate they nor-

mally experience may be as important as the latitude at which they occur for understanding their thermoregulatory requirements. In some species, forms occurring in temperate climes have a dark coloration while desert forms are almost white. *Selysiothemis nigra* is a good example (see page 182).

Temperature changes

In addition to the slow changes which occur as they mature, some species can change colour rapidly when they are cooled or warmed. The bright blue areas on the abdomens of some *Enallagma*, *Coenagrion*, *Platycypha* and a few hawkers change to a sombre grey when they are cooled, the change taking about 30 minutes. On return to higher temperatures, the bright blue reappears. The greying is due to the distal movement of small black granules in the epidermal cells which can obscure other granules responsible for the normal blue colour. Red species of *Sympetrum* and *Chlorocypha* may also change colour on cooling, turning a dingy brown. The darker colours of cool, inactive dragonflies help protect them from predators and may also increase their rate of warming up in the sun. Brighter colours, in contrast, enhance visibility as well as reflecting excess radiation.

Nick Donnelly reminds us that in Fiji, where there is a marked difference of climate between one side of the islands and the other, there are dramatic examples of variation in coloration, manifested in the extent of pale and dark abdominal colour. For example in populations of *Nesobasis selysi* from the 'wet' (cold) side of the island Viti Levu, adults are almost completely dark whereas on the 'dry' (hot) side their bodies are embellished with large areas of pale blue. He remarks: 'I know of no mainland Zygoptera which are so variable within such a restricted area.'

7
Territory and reproduction

A territory is defined as a fixed area that an animal defends against intrusion from others of its species. In the case of odonates, a male's territory will generally contain egg-laying sites suitable for his species and its size will vary considerably according to species and also according to the number of conspecific males present. The density of males generally increases as the day progresses so that competition for good territories will increase and their size decrease.

In the case of, particularly, libellulids a 'good' territory serves as a rendezvous and a male that is able to hold one will be rewarded by the arrival of satisfactory numbers of females since they will be seeking suitable egg-laying sites such as he is defending.

In some species males are highly selective in their choice of egg-laying sites and members of the genus *Perithemis* (Amberwings) are known to be among them. The genus has been much studied, for example we learn from Hansruedi Wildermuth that the South American species, *Perithemis mooma,* will fly slowly along the bank of a pond, 'examining emergent root-felts of water plants, logs, stones and other matter as possible oviposition sites by repeated short

dips, touching the substrate quickly with the hind leg tarsi'. Having found the ideal site, he will perch on a low stem or leaf and aggressively see off intruders. Wildermuth found that neighbouring males tolerated each other provided their egg-laying sites were not closer than 3 m apart. Other Amberwings elsewhere in the Americas show similar behaviour.

Matt Holder tells us that, while defending a territory in a small area of a beaver pond in

The male *Plathemis lydia* (Common Whitetail) uses his white abdomen to ward off intruders.

A confrontation between *Crocothemis erythraea* (left) and *Nesciothemis farinosa* (right), in South Africa's Kruger National Park.

Ontario's Algonquin Provincial Park, a male *Plathemis lydia* (Common Whitetail) will hold his abdomen in the air, showing off the white colour as a threat and will repeatedly chase other males away.

Some ultra-territorial males will take exception to males of other genera entering their terri-tories. *Libellula quadrimaculata* will aggressively chase off *Anax imperator* males and also those of *Cordulia aenea*. It is not uncommon to observe confrontation between two unrelated males as if they were daring each other to move another inch into the other's territory.

Among non-libellulids, *Anax imperator* is one that shows strongly territorial behaviour. Aeshnid territory holders need a greater expen-diture of energy: there is no perching on promi-nent plant tips, rather the male will have a beat, up and down which he will fly for lengthy peri-ods that will be punctuated by only short rests. On any warm sunny summer's day in Europe or Africa, a male Emperor will be seen quartering a portion of a large lake or the whole of a smaller one. Visiting females will be swooped upon and as many as four or five may be spotted busily laying their eggs into floating aquatic plants within the area of a single male's territory.

Male corduliids will attempt to hold, not a corner of a piece of water, but a stretch of its

Pseudagrion hageni makes use of its bright red face to defend its territory. Photographed in South Africa.

bank and will patrol the stretch vigorously. Territories of macromiids are perhaps the biggest of all: a male *Macromia bifasciata* (Natal Macromia), for example, will arrive at a stretch of well-wooded river and, keeping to the middle of it, rush past the observer to disappear round a bend, return again a few minutes later and disappear once more, in the other direction.

Among zygopterans, territoriality has been declared by many researchers to be absent in Platycnemididae, most Lestidae and many Coenagrionidae, but several members of the superfamily Calopterygoidea exhibit it strongly. Generally speaking, the species whose males are brightly coloured are the ones that exhibit territorial behaviour. Such males advertise their occupancy as they perch on the tips of prominent pieces of vegetation. A male with brightly coloured legs (e.g. *Platycypha*) or vividly marked wings (e.g. *Disparoneura*) will flash them aggressively to signal approaching males that he is holding territory. Ivan Meskin, who has studied territoriality in *Pseudagrion,* reckons that in many of these species it is those with brightly coloured faces that are the territorial ones: *P. hageni*'s is red; *P. citricola*'s bright yellow, but *P. salisburyense*'s, a nondescript blueish-grey. The first two are territorial and the third is not. Species of the primitive and diverse South American genus *Heteragrion* are endowed with bright yellow 'lamps' (iridescent spots) on the top part of the face which they use as a signalling device by flashing at one another.

The males of most *Calopteryx* species will hold a territory of about 3 m along a stretch of stream or river bank that contains suitable floating vegetation. They may hold territory for several consecutive days and even, according to Sidney Dunkle when discussing *C. maculata*, hold a single perch for more than one week.

The reason for some species being territorial while others are not is not yet understood.

Brightly coloured portions of the body may help territorial males but cannot constitute a reason for territorial behaviour. An interesting explanation is given by Jurg De Marmels when referring to some Polythoridae species. Male *Euthore fasciata*, which perch on sunny twigs in forested seepages in Venezuela, show no signs of territoriality probably, as De Marmels suggests, because they are constantly moving to keep up with the changing sunspots. On the other hand, species of *Cora* which also occur in forests, perch almost exclusively in the shade and, since there is no need for them to be constantly on the move, males are extremely territorial and have been observed (by A. M. Fraser and T. B. Herman) holding a particular territory (often around pieces of rotting wood) for over 15 days at a time. Nick Donnelly tells me of a remarkable reversal of territorial roles in many Fijian *Nesobasis* species: the females guard territories and the males lurk in the bushes! Donnelly has no explanation for this behaviour.

RECOGNITION AND COURTSHIP

Many of the ploys used by males to warn off conspecific intruders are similarly used for recognition purposes. They will display the brightly coloured regions of their bodies: the colour of eyes and legs, and the characteristic pattern made by whirring wings. In addition, the ventral surface of male abdomens in most species of *Calopteryx* are distinctively coloured on segments VIII, IX and X, the so-called 'taillights'. These are brilliant white in Japan's *Calopteryx cornelia*; and, among European species, off-white in *C. splendens*, rose-coloured in *C. virgo*, and carmine in *C. haemorrhoidalis*. A male will turn his back on a female and raise his abdomen to display his identity.

When a female enters a male's territory it is

Kiyoshi Inoue

A male *Calopteryx cornelia* displays the colour of his 'tail-lights'.

an indication that she is carrying eggs which are ready for fertilisation and the male will commence appropriate action. Courtship is defined as behaviour in animals that plays a part in the initial attraction of a mate or as a prelude to copulation. As well as ensuring that the prospective mate is of the same species, the male's courtship performance may allow females to choose between males according to some quality or qualities unknown to us. Georg Rüppell tells us that the male of at least one species demonstrates the suitability of his particular territory in a very practical manner. Landing on the surface of the water, a male *C. haemorrhoidalis* will float and allow himself to be carried downstream. This behaviour lets a prospective mate gauge the strength of the current and from this she will be able to weigh the survival chances of her future offspring.

Generally speaking it is zygopterans that perform courtship displays although members of the libellulid genus *Perithemis* also exhibit conspicuous courtship behaviour. This varies a little according to species, but *P. tenera* (Eastern Amberwing), which has been well studied, is a good example. As a female approaches his terri-tory, the male will fly out to intercept her, lead her to his chosen egg-laying site and hover over it with wings whirring and abdomen raised.

Another libellulid to court a female is the African species *Brachythemis lacustris* (Scarlet Groundling) which, according to Peter Miller, hovers at the water surface beside an emergent plant, 'as though indicating a good place for egg-laying and, after copulation, the female may then glue her eggs to it'. In both these cases, females are given an opportunity of accepting or refusing copulation.

Apart from such exceptions, in the majority of anisopterans there is no recognisable courtship behaviour. When a female approaches a suitable piece of water, she will immediately be grabbed by a watchful male and the pair will mate. It is by no means uncommon for more than one male to make the attempt and, in such cases, fierce skirmishes will take place.

Courtship among damselflies takes many forms but it is always aimed at displaying, to its best advantage, the male's most conspicuous feature. Just as a courting bower bird displays his glorious plumage, so a damselfly will display his face, his legs, his abdomen or the pattern of his wings.

Female *Calopteryx*, on entering a male's terri-tory, will perch at the edge of the water, where-upon the holder will fly towards her and hover, with a mixture of slow and rapid wing move-ments, directly in front of her. If the female approves (is 'receptive') she will remain perched, thus inviting the male to grasp her; if not she will immediately depart to another territory where an alternative male may be more successful.

Chlorocyphids, like calopterygids, are renowned for their courtship displays. *Platycypha* use their legs: two or three males may hover just in front of a female, displaying the dazzling white side of their legs as they thrust them forward in front of their faces.

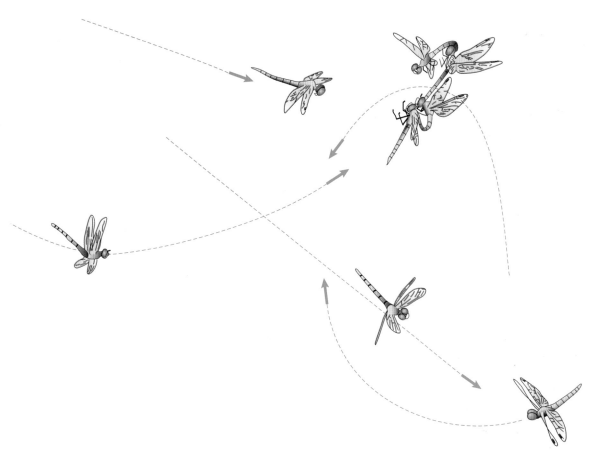

Seven male *Leucorrhinia rubicunda* compete for a female who is already caught by three of them. Only dragonflies are strong and agile enough to perform such manoeuvres. Drawing after Georg Rüppell.

The male *Platycypha fitzsimmonsi* uses his legs to attract a female and also in aggression when another male enters his territory.

Rhinocypha males dance up and down before the females displaying their wings and colourful bodies. I have watched some half dozen males at a time, bobbing over the fast flowing water running between large boulders and have frequently wondered what it is that determines the female to make a choice.

Another family in which some males exhibit courtship behaviour is the Protoneuridae. Although the majority of these species have hyaline wings, a few have wings that are heavily marked and it is these that carry out courtship displays by actively displaying the wing pattern to visiting females. Yet another example comes from Rosser Garrison who tells me the male *Chalcopteryx rutilans* hovers almost motionless in front of the female, displaying his outstretched hindwings to show their brilliant colours.

MATING

Females wishing to reject mating attempts will make various signals, the most common being the downward curving of the abdomen. Once a female has indicated acceptance, either as a result of the male's courtship display or of having investigated and approved the proposed egg-laying site, the male will, typically, grab her by the thorax with his legs and then curve his abdomen so that he can place his apical claspers over the prothorax (in the case of a damselfly) or on to the back of the eyes (in the case of a dragonfly), thus freeing his legs. The method of mating practised by Odonata is very nearly unique in the animal kingdom (some spiders use a similar one). As in all insects, the genital opening for sperm is situated on the underside of the ninth

The accessory organ of a male *Somatochlora metallica* (Brilliant Emerald) is very prominent.

A male *Aeshna palmata*, in the Canadian Rockies, showing his anal appendages with which he will grasp a female behind the head.

abdominal segment but, in odonates, there is a secondary, 'accessory', organ on the underside of segments II and III. Before mating, the male must transfer his sperm to this secondary organ. In dragonflies the act is usually carried out before the pair take up the tandem position; in damselflies immediately afterwards.

An anisopteran male's anal appendages (claspers) consist of a single inferior appendage (epiproct) and a pair of superior ones. Working together, they form an adjustable clamp and, using this, the male clasps the female tightly at the back of her head, behind the eyes: at this point, the pair is said to be 'in tandem'.

In the case of male zygopterans, a pair of inferior appendages (paraproct) takes the place of the single one possessed by anisopterans. Using all four, he grips the female round her pronotum (plate covering the prothorax). In order to ensure conspecific mating, a male damselfly's appendages will only fit the pronotum of a female of his own species — they fit together rather like two pieces of a jigsaw.

With his sperm safely translocated, the male bends his abdomen in a downward arc while his mate curves hers upwards so that her genital opening is pressed against his. The mating pair thus form an uneven heart shape which is referred to as the 'wheel position' and they are said to be in copula ('in cop').

It is not known at what point in Odonata's long history this unique method of mating evolved or why it should have become necessary for males to possess two sets of reproductory organs. However, they have been acting like this for many millions of years so it obviously works! Allen Davies has a theory that it originates way back when most living creatures were hermaphroditic, that is each individual possessed both male and female reproductive organs: an earthworm is an example of such a creature that survives to this day.

Prior to ejecting sperm, the males of many species will attempt to ensure that it will be their own sperm which fertilise the eggs. This is achieved by two principal methods: a male will

A male *Coenagrion puella* (Azure Damselfly). Note the short appendages at the tip of his abdomen.

Before mating, the male *Chlorolestes tessalatus* (Mosaic Sylph) transfers his sperm (far left) while the pair is already in tandem. With the sperm safely transferred, the mating pair go into the 'wheel position'. Mating is not a common sight in members of this family.

A mating pair of
Sympetrum striolatum
(Common Darters).

The pruinosity on the sides of this male *Libellula fulva* (Scarce Chaser) has been rubbed off as a consequence of several matings.

either use his tufted, spoon-shaped penis to scoop out the sperm deposited by previous suitors, or else to ram them into the depths of the female organ making them virtually inaccessible. This action is known as 'sperm displacement'.

The length of time taken to complete copulation varies considerably according to species. In general, pairs fly off to a secluded spot in a tree or into thickly growing reeds and rushes where they may remain for as short a time as a few seconds (*Tetrathemis polleni* takes between 15 and 20 s) or for as long as well over an hour. Some species (*Libellula fulva* is one) mate briefly in mid-air, others (*Orthetrum cancellatum* for instance) may be seen bumbling along 'in cop', sometimes alighting on a reed or, at other times, crashing to the ground to complete the operation there. Damselflies, when disturbed, will not be deterred but will float off gently and alight together on a neighbouring piece of foliage.

While in tandem, the male dragonfly's abdomen curves downwards so that the inferior appendage presses against the back of his mate's eyes, often leading to considerable damage and resulting in noticeable scars. In a few species, notably among gomphids, similar wounds can be inflicted by spines on the male's superior appendages. (Damage of this kind is not made by male zygopterans because females are grasped by the prothorax, not behind the eyes.) Signs of previous mating can often be observed by examining the rear of a female's head and they may also be found on some species of male dragonfly, particularly on those whose bodies pruinose: the pruinosity will often be rubbed off by the legs of their female partners.

MATE GUARDING BEHAVIOUR

Vicky McMillan

In some odonates, the members of a mated pair part company soon after copulation and the female lays her eggs alone. In many other species, however, the male remains with his mate after copulation and guards her from other males while she lays eggs.

Mate guarding behaviour takes two major forms. In 'contact guarding', the male stays physically attached to the female in the tandem position. Such behaviour is common in the damselfly families Lestidae and Coenagrionidae for example, as well as among libellulid dragonflies and a few aeshnids. Some tandem pairs (*Sympetrum* for example) fly about actively while the female releases eggs into water or over wet ground; others (many damselflies) move more slowly while the female inserts her eggs into the tissues of aquatic plants. In some cases, contact guarders hang on even when their mates submerge to lay eggs in underwater vegetation, or they may separate temporarily and grasp them again when they resurface.

In the second type of guarding, 'non-contact guarding', the male separates from the female but hovers or perches nearby, chasing away intrusive males. Non-contact guarding is common in many territorial libellulids, as well as in *Calopteryx* damselflies and it has been suggested that this behaviour allows a male to keep up territorial defence even as he monitors the female.

Mate-guarding reduces interference with egg-laying and lessens the chance that the female will be seized and re-mated by a different male before she has laid all her eggs. From the guarder's perspective, preventing takeover (re-mating) of his mate protects his sperm investment, since studies of many odonates have shown that the female's most recent partner tends to fertilise most of her eggs. Jonathan Waage was the first to demonstrate the striking tactic in damselflies (he used *Calopteryx maculata*) where the male uses his penis to remove most of his rivals' sperm before inseminating the female himself. Waage's discovery, 'last male advantage', was of major importance in helping to understand odonate reproductive strategies.

Compared to non-contact guarding, egg-laying in tandem offers a male greater security against rival takeover. Clearly, other males cannot easily grasp a female while she is still in the clutch of her mate. Females of non-contact guarders are more vulnerable, especially at high

A male *Chlorolestes tessalatus*, in the Natal Drakensbergs, 'non-contact guarding' his egg-laying mate.

A pair of *Celithemis fasciata,* in Bays Mountain Park in Tennessee, USA, provides an example of pre-copulatory guarding.

Guarding patterns vary markedly among odonates. In some species, a particular guarding type seems characteristic (for example, non-contact guarding in *Libellula pulchella*; contact guarding in *Sympetrum vicinum*) but, in many odonates, both types may be seen. In *Sympetrum parvulum*, territorial males perform contact-guarding, as do 'wandering' males at high male densities (high takeover risks) but otherwise the wanderers may switch to non-contact guarding. In many species, males guard at the outset but may show weaker guarding before the last eggs are laid, and may even leave their mates to finish alone.

A number of factors seem to be related to guarding variability in odonates. Among these are the probability of female takeover, the length of the egg-laying period, and the availability (to the guarder) of other potential mates. Georg Rüppell suggests that, generally speaking, it is non-territorial species whose males remain in tandem during egg-laying whereas, in most cases, territorial males will practise non-contact guarding. It has also been suggested that guarding may be moulded by predation risks and physiological factors, such as the temperatures most conducive for tandem flight.

Finally, in a few species pre-copulatory guarding has been observed. For instance, in *Sympetrum depressiusculum*, males hold females in tandem for as long as three hours prior to the pair eventually copulating.

male densities. On the other hand, contact guarders are unable, themselves, to make other matings while still clasping their females. This option is at least potentially available to non-contact guarders. *Plathemis lydia* males sometimes interrupt guarding to mate with a second female; then the male stands guard over both at the same time. Occasionally, males have been seen to seize a third female while still protecting a second. *Calopteryx atrata* has been seen guarding four females at once and *Cora semiopaca* as many as five!

8
Habitats and refugia

With only a handful of exceptions, odonate larvae develop in water and, in order to protect them, it is necessary to study the exact habitat requirements of each individual species and then to protect, conserve and, where possible, increase the number of suitable habitats. The requirements of some species are narrow and these are obviously the ones that are most at risk. Other species are catholic in their needs and will survive in almost any kind of water, acidic or alkaline or, in a few cases, water that is brackish, even saline. The majority fall between these extremes, some occurring in running water, some in still water and some in bogs and marshes. Generally speaking, the more uncommon odonates breed in running water: rivers and streams, canals and dykes. A large proportion of the remainder breed in still water: lakes and ponds, bogs and marshes. This leaves a relatively small number of species that inhabit a variety of unexpected breeding sites. A requisite for the habitats of almost all species is that the water be unpolluted.

Running water

Large, open, fast-flowing rivers only seldom provide good breeding sites for Odonata.

Larvae living in this kind of habitat must be endowed with features that will prevent them from being swept downstream: some will take refuge under stones and small rocks, some are able to cling to the surface of rocks and plants, others bury themselves in the substrate, only their feeding and respiratory parts obtruding. Wide, shallow and slow moving rivers, on the other hand, prove more hospitable.

Streams running through woodland and, particularly, rainforest are often hosts to lesser

The fast-flowing Wit River in South Africa's Cape Province has a series of shallow cascades and, at the sides, areas of almost still water. This caters for a good mix of species including *Zygonyx* (Cascaders).

Cindy Allen

The large Suwanee Canal in the Okefenokee Swamp, Georgia, USA, plays host to a large range of odonates — as well as the *Alligator mississippiensis*!

A river with margins of coarse granitic sand in Hong Kong, China, provides a home for the larvae of *Megalogomphus sommeri*.

known odonate species, in the latter case because few people are able to penetrate the difficult terrain in order to study them. A further factor to be taken into account is the make-up of the substrate. For example, Keith Wilson found that fast-flowing streams with margins of coarse granite sand in China were home to the larvae of *Megalogomphus sommeri* while others with muddy sand margins played host to *Asiagomphus hainanensis*.

Waterfalls provide habitats for a number of species: the larvae of some attach themselves by their flat limpet-like abdomens to the rockface behind the fall, others develop in the rock pools formed at the bottom. Adult members of the

genus *Zygonyx* (Cascaders) may be found skimming the tops of waterfalls and cascades. The monotypic *Thaumatoneura inopinata* breeds behind large waterfalls and is known as the Giant Waterfall Damselfly.

Ditches, dykes and canals will often provide something between moving and stagnant water. Some well-vegetated ditches can be very productive: in Britain, *Lestes dryas* (Scarce Emerald Damselfly) (see page 92) breeds in a few Essex ditches; *Anaciaeshna isosceles* (Norfolk Hawker) (see page 128) has recently recolonised many of the East Anglian dykes; and some of the better kept canals have good numbers of breeding odonates.

Stagnant water

Lakes and ponds can be large or small, natural or artificial, open or heavily overgrown. Species of *Zygoptera* and *Libellulidae* will probably be breeding in almost every one and even the smallest garden pond will soon be colonised.

Swamps, marshes and bogs on all continents provide excellent habitats but, sadly, too many of them are disappearing. Marshlands are being drained to provide space for housing estates or the grazing of livestock; raised peat bogs are ravaged by giant mechanical contraptions that eradicate valuable habitats: a loss equally as disastrous to the total earth environment as the destruction of rainforests.

Oases are as welcome to wildlife as they are to travellers in the desert. Some are large and lush, some only a damp patch surrounded by scrub but, however big or small, they will attract any odonates that may find themselves in the inhospitable neighbourhood. And it is surprising how often one does come across dragonflies in desert areas.

Magpie Geese share this Queensland, Australia, swampy marsh with zygopterans, libellulids and with aeshnids *Hemianax papuensis*, *Anax guttatus* and *Aeshna brevistyla*.

The cold, dark Lochs Finnert and Monaghan in Tayside, Scotland, have small breeding colonies of *Aeshna caerulea* (Azure Hawker) and *Somatochlora arctica* (Northern Emerald).

A Little Bittern in the Okavango Delta swamp in Botswana. Several species of gomphid breed here as well as many libellulids and corduliids.

Cindy Allen

The large lake within Bays Mountain Park in Tennessee, USA, supports a multitude of aeshnids, gomphids, corduliids and libellulids.

An oasis in the desert not far from Riyadh in Saudi Arabia. *Anax parthenope* was one of the species flying here.

Unusual breeding sites

A number of tropical and subtropical species live and develop in phytotelmata, which are small waterbodies found in plants: holes in tree trunks; the axils in bromeliads and other parasitic plants; in the hollow stems of bamboo. All of these require highly specialised egg-laying and larval development: examples are the Pseudostigmatidae of Central and South America, the coenagrionid genus *Leptagrion* from the same area, Borneo's *Lyriothemis cleis* and Australia's *Podopteryx selysi*. Several anisopteran species (e.g. *Anax grubaueri* and *Orthemis ferruginea*) are opportunistic tree hole breeders that will more usually use forest ponds.

Water held between the buttresses of a forest tree in Brunei was found to contain larvae of *Indaeschna grubaueri*, *Lyriothemis cleis*, *Pericnemis triangularis* and, once or twice, *Cratilla metallica*.

New Zealand's *Uropetala carovei* (Bush Petaltail), like most members of the genus, is a burrower. Its breeding sites are extremely hard to find but, after several years of study by a number of odonatologists, it became possible to recognise the kind of habitat likely to be productive: small swampy clearings in Southern Beech forest where the presence of Perching Lilies and sedges were a hopeful sign. In such places, a search for muddy hummocks

John Mason

A swampy clearing within a Southern Beech forest in North Island, New Zealand, provides a breeding site for the burrowing *Uropetala carovei* (Bush Petaltail).

emerging just above the water level often results in success.

In addition, there are a handful of fully terrestrial species. According to Nick Donnelly, the Hawaiian *Megalagrion oahuense* is one such with larvae living on steep hillsides in the tangled rhizome mats of the fern *Dicranopteris linearis*. Donnelly remarks: 'Ironically, because these ferns are highly successful colonisers of newly stripped hillsides, the conservation prospects of this terrestrial species might be enhanced by disturbance!'

Breeding sites of South Africa's *Chlorolestes* species are seldom found because they are almost invariably in such unexpected locations: in hidden, almost stagnant backwaters, well away from the places where they generally disport themselves. Mating and egg-laying of Australia's *Synlestes* are equally hard to witness and I suggest that a search for similar unlikely sites might prove rewarding.

Bert Orr

Finally, there are a number of tropical species (*Pantala flavescens*, the Globe Skimmer, is the best known example) that often breed in temporary pools. This kind of breeding place can hardly be called a 'habitat' and can be found in any location; they may be rain-filled puddles at the side of the road, water-filled tyre tracks sunk in mud, swimming pools and even bird-baths in gardens. It is difficult to imagine what the larvae find to feed upon but they obviously manage somehow and some of these species are adapted to complete the larval stage in as short a time as just five or six weeks.

Where and when to find Odonata

Despite the preference of several species for diffuse light or shade, odonates are essentially lovers of sunshine. Unlike the vegetarian insects (aphids, lepidopterans, etc.), our carnivorous odonates are not limited to any marked degree by flora but rather by the purity of water, the strength of its currents and to a great extent its temperature.

Odonates, being cold-blooded creatures, mostly only appear when the sun is shining. Warm sunny days will bring forth many species over almost any kind of water and there will be plenty to observe as they couple, mate and oviposit. Feeding aeshnids may also be seen in woodland clearings and along firebreaks, sometimes at considerable distances from water. When the sun goes behind a cloud they will fly off to find shelter only to appear again suddenly, as if from nowhere, when the cloud passes over.

Generally speaking odonates are late risers and early retirers but there are a number of crepuscular species, for example, all members of *Gynacantha* and their closest relatives fly well after dusk and again before the sun rises. Some species which take to the wing only after dark or at dusk, live entirely on mosquitoes: proving a real boon to those living in malarial areas.

In many tropical regions lack of sun does not necessarily mean lack of Odonata. Allen Davies tells us: 'The day in my life which turned up far more dragonflies, both Anisoptera and Zygoptera, than I could ever hope to see again, had pouring rain from dawn to dusk. This was in a subtropical island (New Caledonia).'

Similar experiences have been documented in many other such areas and one memorable one took place in Japan. Six of us roused ourselves at 4 a.m. in order to witness crepuscular aeshnids enjoying their early morning feeding flights. It was teeming with rain and we sloshed through deep, slimy mud but the rain did not affect the flight of *Aeschnophlebia anisoptera* and *Anaciaeschna martini* at all.

Refugia

In addition to recognising good habitats in whatever part of the world one finds oneself, it may be useful to learn about some of the centres of high endemism so that, if opportunities come along, they can be visited before it is too late. Often called 'refugia', there are a number of such places dotted around our planet.

Chlorolestes tessalatus breeds in the small artificial backwater on the bottom left of this picture.

Allen Davies

A small remnant of Madagascar's diminishing rainforest.

Madagascar is one and the island probably contains more endemic species than anywhere on earth but, due to serious deforestation, it may not be so for long.

Cameroon in West Africa is another region of high endemism, as is the extreme southern region of Africa (the southern Cape). Parts of Brazil and Amazonian Peru, which are suffering the same devastation as Madagascar, can still be rewarding as can Venezuela in Central America. Central and South-East Asia possess many centres of endemism. Thailand, Philippines, Malaysia, Indonesia, Hong Kong and mainland China are all well worth visiting, as is Melanesia which includes New Caledonia, Papua New Guinea and the 'Top End' of Australia.

It is interesting to speculate why there are these refugia. A refugium is defined as a geographical region that has remained unaltered by climatic or other fundamental changes affecting surrounding regions and that therefore forms a haven for relict fauna and flora. Millions of years ago, when the two super-continents, Laurasia and Gondwanaland, broke up these refugia were left behind and pockets of endemism they have remained to this day. The splitting of the super-continents also accounts for some of the very strange distributions of fauna and flora. Among many other examples, the split of Gondwanaland explains why marsupials are found in Australia and in South America, and it also explains how remnants of the zygopteran subfamily Rimanellinae are found in small pockets in West Africa's Cameroon mountains and in the highlands of Venezuelan Guyana. It is also considered possible that it was from these centres that, millions of years ago, odonates began to spread; it certainly appears true that, for example, the Gomphidae originated in what is now China and that North America was the original home of the cordulegastrids.

It cannot be stressed too strongly that, if deforestation continues at its present rate, the ancient refugia will not survive much longer.

Allen Davies

Birdwings and *Petaluras* inhabit this cloud forest in north Queensland.

9
Odonata around the world

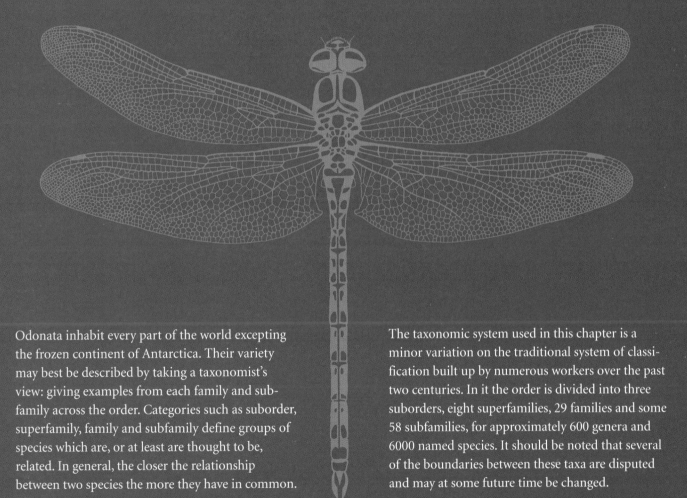

Odonata inhabit every part of the world excepting the frozen continent of Antarctica. Their variety may best be described by taking a taxonomist's view: giving examples from each family and sub-family across the order. Categories such as suborder, superfamily, family and subfamily define groups of species which are, or at least are thought to be, related. In general, the closer the relationship between two species the more they have in common.

The taxonomic system used in this chapter is a minor variation on the traditional system of classi-fication built up by numerous workers over the past two centuries. In it the order is divided into three suborders, eight superfamilies, 29 families and some 58 subfamilies, for approximately 600 genera and 6000 named species. It should be noted that several of the boundaries between these taxa are disputed and may at some future time be changed.

SUBORDER	SUPERFAMILY	FAMILY

Odonata

Zygoptera (Damselflies)

- **Calopterygoidea (Broad Wings)**
  - Amphipterygidae
  - Calopterygidae (Demoiselles)
  - Chlorocyphidae (Jewels)
  - Dicteriadidae (Barelegs)
  - Euphaeidae (Gossamerwings)
  - Polythoridae (Bannerwings)
- **Lestoidea (Open Wings)**
  - Synlestidae (Sylphs)
  - Lestidae (Reedlings)
  - Lestoideidae
  - Megapodagrionidae (Flatwings)
  - Perilestidae (Shortwings)
- **Hemiphlebioidea**
  - Hemiphlebiidae
- **Coenagrionoidea (Closed Wings)**
  - Coenagrionidae (Pond Damselflies)
  - Isostictidae (Narrow-wings)
  - Platycnemididae (Brook Damselflies)
  - Platystictidae (Forest Damselflies)
  - Protoneuridae (Pinflies)
  - Pseudostigmatidae (Forest Giants)

Anisozygoptera

- **Epiophlebioidea**
  - Epiophlebiidae

Anisoptera (Dragonflies)

- **Aeshnoidea (Angle Wings)**
  - Aeshnidae (Hawkers)
  - Gomphidae (Clubtails)
  - Neopetaliidae (Redspots)
  - Petaluridae (Petaltails)
- **Cordulegastroidea (Golden Rings)**
  - Cordulegastridae (Goldenrings)
- **Libelluloidea (Dippers)**
  - Chlorogomphidae (Tigerbodies)
  - Macromiidae (River Emeralds)
  - Synthemistidae (Southern Emeralds)
  - Corduliidae (Emeralds)
  - Libellulidae (Perchers)

SUBORDER ZYGOPTERA SUPERFAMILY CALOPTERYGOIDEA (BROAD WINGS)

The members of this superfamily usually have metallic colouring on the body. Their wings are generally tinted and are only slightly stalked. They possess at least five antenodals (generally many more), of which at least two are complete; postnodals are not usually in line with the crossveins below; the arculus is close to the base of the wing; quadrilaterals are rectangular and generally crossed. Larvae have triquetral (3-sided in cross section) or saccoid (sack-like) anal gills. Six families are generally recognised.

Robert Thompson

A typical calopterygoid larva, *Calopteryx virgo.*

Robert Thompson

A typical calopterygoid imago, *Calopteryx splendens.*

Family Amphipterygidae

This is an ancient family whose lineage goes back to the days prior to the split-up of Gondwanaland. There are two extant subfamilies: Amphipteryginae with species in tropical rainforests of Asia and North Africa, and Rimanellinae which consists of two genera, one in Venezuela and the other in Cameroon. As a family, it has suffered from constant reclassification and, since there are many inconsistencies, there may well be more.

Members of this family are medium sized and sturdy with long, narrow, petiolate (stalked) wings each bearing two primary antenodals and three or four incomplete secondary ones, that is to say these veins do not extend from the costa into the subcostal spaces; venation is not as close as in Calopterygidae. At rest, the wings are held away from the body. Larvae have saccoid gills which are embellished with tufts (as are those of the Lestoideidae genus *Diphlebia*). Graham Vick explains that, in amphipterygines, the bases of the gill tufts are cylindrical and there is a strap-like process ending in a sclerotised plate whereas, in the rimanellines, the bases of the gill tufts are elliptical in section and they issue from a nipple-shaped process.

Subfamily Amphipteryginae

Amphipteryginae contains two genera, one (*Amphipteryx*) is confined to Central America, and the other (*Devadatta*) to South-East Asia. Pterostigmas of *Amphipteryx* species are long and narrow, those of *Devadatta* less so. Secondary antenodals are only present in the costal space.

Amphipteryx agrioides was for many years the sole known member of the genus *Amphipteryx*. It was observed by Nick Donnelly in Guatemala where it inhabited leaf litter banked at the lip of small waterfalls. The

ZYGOPTERA

CALOPTERYGOIDEA

Amphipterygidae

recently discovered *Amphipteryx longicaudata* is apparently restricted to the Oaxaca area in Mexico where it breeds in fast flowing water, or in seepages, in remnants of tropical rain or cloud forest. Three further species (all as yet unnamed) have been discovered in the past few years, two in Mexico and one in Honduras.

Devadatta species are generally found by muddy, lowland streams, particularly in still water below waterfalls where they will take refuge among bent and broken plants. These damselflies hold their wings away from the body on first coming to rest but once they are fully settled, they close them on top of the abdomen.

The small rocky streams where all these species occur are within tropical rainforests, in places where, as Allen Davies has put it, 'an equable climate has existed longest, places where the oldest of all known land animals is still found: peripatus itself, the existing (not missing) link between worms and arthropods'.

Little is known of adult behaviour, their habitats not being conducive to investigation.

Devadatta argyoides at Yala in the extreme south of Thailand.

Amnuay Pinratana

Subfamily Rimanellinae

Graham S. Vick

This subfamily has an extraordinary distribution. It contains just three species, in two genera, which are among the most unusual in the entire order. All three damselflies have red

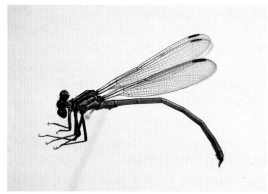

Graham Vick

Male *Rimanella arcana*.

abdomens with a black thorax marked with yellow or brown. There are distinct markings on the last three abdominal segments. They are fairly large and sturdily built, the African species being about the size of *Calopteryx splendens*, with hindwing about 37–41 mm. The South American species is smaller, with hindwing about 26–28 mm. The wings are long and narrow, with dense venation and they are slightly enfumed with yellow or brown. There are between four and six antenodal crossveins in the two African species but only three in the South American one (occasionally only two). They rest with their wings closed, frequently perching on vertical twigs with their bodies held just below the horizontal.

Rimanella arcana occurs on the cool submontane streams of the ancient Guyana Shield, having been found in both Guyana and southern Venezuela. It is characteristic of the 'pantepuyan' region which has a particularly interesting and endemic fauna. This consists partly of neo-endemics: species which, having evolved relatively recently in isolation in the cool regions of the tepuis, have their nearest relatives in other parts of South America, for example the Andean chain. There are also palaeoendemics, such as *Rimanella*, which are ancient survivors: relics of a once-widespread fauna which is almost extinct.

In Africa, two other close relatives occur which, although larger insects, bear a close resemblance to *Rimanella*. Both have been placed in the genus *Pentaphlebia* and they only occur in the montane regions of the borders between Cameroon and Nigeria, another region noted for its biodiversity and the presence of palaeoendemics.

Pentaphlebia stahli occurs on Mt Cameroon, Mt Kupe and on a few other mountains in the area, provided the original evergreen forest-cover has been preserved. The third species, *P. gamblesi*, was described as recently as 1977 by Michael Parr, who found it in 1973, at 1520 m, on the Obudu Plateau in Nigeria; it appears to favour the same habitat as *P. stahli* but it is isolated on mountains further to the north.

David Chelmick

Pentaphlebia stahli in Cameroon.

The larvae of the three species are among the most curious known. They are adapted to live on submerged rocks where they can be seen crawling on the surfaces, searching for prey. They have a strong preference for the darker (volcanic) rocks over the paler quartz rocks; presumably they will be less noticeable to predators on the darker substrates.

Larvae bear two large cerci which are prolonged as long tapering spines, with the bases expanded. They bear many long hairs which perhaps assist with adhesion in the strong currents. The median appendage covers a central gill tuft which projects from the last segment of the abdomen. This is a feature of all the true amphipterygids (shared by the genus *Diphlebia*) and is unique in the Odonata. The cerci of rimanellines look superficially like those of a perlid (stonefly) but they are quite different in structure. However, I mistook a *Rimanella* larva for a stonefly larva when examining it quickly with the naked eye but the presence of a labial 'mask' made the separation easy when looked at more carefully. The mask is, in fact, rather simple and gomphid-like, without setae.

David Chelmick

The very curious larva of *Pentaphlebia stahli*.

Family Calopterygidae (Demoiselles)

This family contains some of the loveliest of all zygopterans. They are characterised by broad, non-petiolate wings with numerous veins and at least five antenodals; those of most males are without pterostigmas while those of most females have white spots called pseudostigmas in their place. Bodies are generally metallic and abdomens slender. Not only are they lovely to look at but they are often gregarious and active; a cloud of male *Calopteryx* performing their aerial ballet over a stretch of river is a stunning sight.

The family has representatives in almost all parts of the world, in both tropical and temper-

ZYGOPTERA

CALOPTERYGOIDEA

Calopterygidae

ZYGOPTERA

CALOPTERYGOIDEA

Calopterygidae

ate zones. They are absent from Australia and New Zealand but plentiful as far south as Papua New Guinea.

Subfamily Caliphaeinae (Clearwings)

Until 20 years ago, this small subfamily was thought to consist of just two species, *Caliphaea confusa* and *C. consimilis*, recorded from India and China but, in 1976, S. Asahina described two new species from Thailand. One of these was *C. thailandica* and the other *Noguchiphaea yoshicoae*, the latter being a very elusive and particularly primitive species which seems to be on the wing only during the heaviest rainy season. Unlike the other Demoiselles, caliphaeines have clear (but iridescent), petio-late wings which are exceptionally long and narrow and which bear dark pterostigmas. They possess a strangely simple (reduced) venation, one which puzzled Selys so much that (in 1859) he named the type species 'C. confusa' to convey his confusion over where the insect should be placed in the classification. The discoidal cell, which is almost a true rectangle with a straight upper side, has just one cross vein; the anal vein runs straight and there is a distinct row of cells

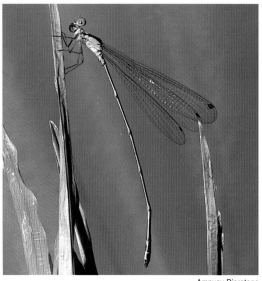

Caliphaea thailandica **in Chiang Mai in the extreme north of Thailand.**

Amnuay Pinratana

between it and the posterior border of the wing. They rest (frequently in the shade) on the tips of leaves overhanging the water, holding their wings spread wide in the manner of many Lestoidea species.

The fact that Clearwings differ in many major ways (in features and in habits) from the rest of the Calopterygidae would seem to make change a sensible solution. Unfortunately the species are elusive which makes much needed research extremely difficult.

Subfamily Calopteryginae (Demoiselles)

This very large subfamily contains 12 established genera and occurs in all parts of the world except Australia and New Zealand. The non-petiolate wings are broad, densely veined with numerous antenodals; the discoidal cell is long and narrow with several cross veins. They fly only short distances and rest with their wings closed above the abdomen.

Demoiselles generally breed in running water, some preferring a pebble base, some mud and some sand. In most species females lay their eggs alone, sometimes guarded by their mates; eggs are generally inserted into plant stems, sometimes well below the level of the water. Males are very territorial but their territories are small and, consequently, large numbers may be seen perched on the tips of pieces of long grass and there will be frequent skirmishes as one male intrudes into the territory of another. Prior to mating, as an aid to recognition by the female, the males of many species raise their abdomens above their heads to display the colour on the underside of the tip: in the case of *Calopteryx haemorrhoidalis* this area is blood red, while in *C. cornelia* it is gleaming white.

The genus *Calopteryx* boasts the largest number of species, all spread across the northern hemisphere. Most species have a blue or green metallic sheen on the abdomen

Male *Calopteryx haemorrhoidalis* (Mediterranean Demoiselle) in southern France.

David Pryce

A female *Phaon iridipennis,* posing unusually in a sunny spot in Cameroon.

(*C. haemorrhoidalis* is an exception) and the male's broad wings are tinted to a greater or lesser extent: *C. virgo* (Beautiful Demoiselle) is a good example. This lovely and aptly named damselfly has a wide distribution which stretches across Europe, through North Africa and the Near East, to northern Asia. The largest member of the genus is the shade-loving and very spectacular, copper-winged *C. cornelia* from Japan, and the smallest is north America's *C. dimidiata. C. hyalina* is endemic to Syria and Lebanon and is unusual in that both sexes have uncoloured wings.

It is strange that there is only one demoiselle, *Phaon iridipennis,* in southern Africa. This is a large, seemingly sombre insect and very secretive; it is seldom seen out of deep shade but, when it does move into sunlight, it is transformed into an iridescent beauty. West Africa, however, in addition to *Phaon,* boasts two more genera: the large, robust, enormously broad-winged *Sapho* with strikingly marked wings and the much smaller *Umma* with green abdomens and, generally, iridescent green wings; recently an interesting large species belonging to this last genus, *U. mesumbei,* was discovered on Mt Kupe in Cameroon, which is a well-known centre of endemism.

Iridictyon myersi and *I. trebbaui* are the sole representatives of the subfamily in South America. Both are very local and extremely hard to find, the former being a resident of Guyana and the latter of Venezuela.

The genera *Echo, Matrona, Mnais, Neurobasis* and *Vestalis* are confined to India and the Far East with the exception of three species of *Neurobasis* which extend as far south as Papua New Guinea. The genus *Echo* contains the Chinese (north Guangdong Province) species *Echo (Archineura) incarnata* which Keith Wilson describes as, 'the most impressive calopterygid I have ever seen: 80 mm total length and bright carmine bases to male wings'. The Japanese *Mnais nawai,* with its pale, metallic grey abdomen and red-gold wings, is also particularly lovely.

South-East Asia's *Neurobasis chinensis* is one of only a few green odonates.

ZYGOPTERA

CALOPTERYGOIDEA

Calopterygidae

Male *Vestalis amethystina* in Thailand.

Members of the very lovely genus *Vestalis* possess a number of unusual characteristics. Although female calopterygids almost invariably oviposit alone into the stems of aquatic plants, *Vestalis* species use other methods: for example, Allen Davies has witnessed female *V. beryllae* (a rarely seen Borneo endemic), while in tandem, dropping eggs into the rushing water of a forest stream; other members of the genus (*V. amethystina* is one) oviposit into plant stems overhanging streams, sometimes several feet above the water and, in these cases, the larvae, as soon as they hatch, drop into the water below. *V. beryllae* is unusual in other ways too: the male is about twice as long as any other in the sub-family, with a body length of around 75–80 mm, and they appear to be more solitary than other species. *V. anacolosa* (another Borneo endemic) is, according to Robert Kemp, unusual in that the male has only vestigial inferior appendages.

Subfamily Hetaerininae

Rosser W. Garrison

Members of this subfamily have an entirely New World distribution and can be separated from other calopterygids by the crossed basal space. The subfamily is divided into two large genera. *Hetaerina* species are commonly known as 'Rubyspots' because males usually have a ruby-red spot on the basal fourth of their wings. The intricate, reticulate venation within this red area is often brilliant white. Some species have red or brown wingtips and the bodies are usually metallic red or, less commonly, metallic green. Females have shorter abdomens than males and all lack the red basal wing spot. Rubyspots are very numerous and examples are found in almost any collection of Odonata: 37 species are currently recognised.

The second genus, *Mnesarete,* consists of about 20 brilliant metallic green or red species, mostly with hyaline wings. In one species, *M. pudica*, from south-eastern Brazil and northern Argentina, the male has broad

Female *Hetaerina americana* (American Rubyspot) in North Carolina. The male is illustrated on page 8.

Rosser Garrison

***Mnesarete devilei* in Peru.**

Rosser Garrison

Mnesarete cupraea in Brazil.

wings that are almost entirely wine-red while the female's are rose pink.

Separation of tropical American representatives of these two genera presents a real challenge to the collector. Many species resemble one another closely and identification is only assured by examining the secondary sexual characters.

All members of these genera are stream dwellers with up to four species occupying different reaches of the same stream. In southern Peru, I found *H. rosea* common along small open rivulets while its larger relative, *H. charca* was confined to shady areas of larger streams. Adults perch facing toward the stream on tips of snags or leaves at the water's edge. When disturbed, they will usually return to the same or a similar perch. Copulation has rarely been observed but, according to Clifford Johnson, is of short duration (about five to six minutes for *H. americana*).

The long, spider-like, sluggish larvae are found clinging to vegetation in streams.

Family Chlorocyphidae (Jewels)

Members of this colourful family are easy to separate from those of any other. They have short, stout bodies and long narrow wings; the clypeus (central portion of the face between the frons and the upper lip) protrudes, giving the face a strangely snout-like appearance.

Generally speaking chlorocyphids do not travel far from the streams in which they breed.

Chlorocyphidae is not divided into subfamilies but is, nevertheless, a large family with over 120 species in 17 genera, distributed over Asia, Africa and Australasia.

In some genera, the petiolate wings are partially or wholly iridescent (e.g. *Rhinocypha*), in others they are hyaline (e.g. *Chlorocypha, Platycypha*); venation is less dense than in other Broad Wings; primary antenodals are present and there are between five and 10 secondaries, none of which are proximal to the primaries. In most genera, males have pterostigmas in all wings (e.g. *Platycypha, Rhinocypha* and *Cyrano*), in some they are absent in the forewings (e.g. some species of *Libellago*). Larvae have spine-like gills which are often not developed in the earlier instars.

Jewels breed in running water and are generally shade-loving; both sexes roost on the tips of branches and, as dusk approaches, can quite often be seen perched on the top of tall shrubs or high up in trees. Females remain in such places until ready to lay their eggs. Mature males choose prominent rocks in fast-flowing water or the tips of overhanging branches on which to await approaching females. When males fly over the water, despite their bright colours, they can be very difficult to pick out against the ripples.

David Pryce

ZYGOPTERA

CALOPTERYGOIDEA

Chlorocyphidae

This male *Chlorocypha selysi* on Mt Kupe in Cameroon has a body length of 30 mm.

ZYGOPTERA

CALOPTERYGOIDEA

Chlorocyphidae

Male *Cyrano unicolor* at Mud Springs on the Philippine island of Luzon.

It is known that in several damselflies, body colour (particularly in blue species) changes when the temperature gets really low but, in 1992 and 1993, Peter Miller found that the bright red abdomen of *Chlorocypha straeleni* became dark grey when the temperature dropped a mere 5°C to around 25°C.

The genus *Cyrano* has two species, both of which are endemic to the Philippines. They are interesting in that, in both cases, males have two totally different colour forms: red and black, and totally black. The species can be seen beside fast-flowing forest streams, its flight resembling that of a dragonfly rather than the more usual fluttering flight of damselflies. I found *C. unicolor* flying beside a clear mountain stream which flowed just a few metres from a bubbling, unpleasant smelling, sulphuric mud spring into which the locals threw live chickens, etc. to placate the local goddess.

The Asian genus *Libellago* and the African genus *Platycypha* contain some of the world's most striking and photogenic damselflies; male *L. lineata* are black and bright golden-yellow with black patches at the tips of the forewings; male *P. caligata* and *P. fitzsimmonsi* are beautiful jewel-like creatures with bright blue and scarlet bodies, and legs with flattened and distended tibia which

are scarlet on the outer surface and white on the inner. These are flashed to ward off intruding males and also to attract females. The cream and ochreous-brown females are very uninteresting compared to the glamorous males.

Members of the genus *Rhinocypha* usually perch in the shade, with their wings alongside the abdomen, thus obscuring its colour and they can look very nondescript indeed. However, when they take to the air and if the sun is shining, some of them present a beautiful and entirely different picture. This genus is the only one that extends into the Australasian region.

Matjaz Bedjanic

Libellago greeni in Sri Lanka.

Male *Platycypha caligata* from the Kwa-Zulu Natal Drakensberg, South Africa, showing his bicoloured legs. Note the snout-like appearance of the face which is a feature of the family.

A female *Platycypha caligata* in the Kwa-Zulu Natal Drakensberg, South Africa.

Rhinocypha tincta semitincta, which ranges from the Moluccas to the Solomon Islands, has been recorded from Australia's Cape York but, according to Tony Watson, all known specimens date from the nineteenth century. However, it is present in New Guinea and, in 1993, Stephen Richards was delighted to find large numbers of them in a stream near the Fly River.

Family Dicteriadidae (Barelegs)

Sidney Dunkle

The most notable features of these medium-sized damselflies are their long, thin legs which lack the bristle-like spurs found on the legs of other odonates, and the large movable hooks on each side of the mouthparts. It is possible that they use their legs less for capturing prey than do other odonates, but use the labial hooks to assist in aerial prey capture. The femora (thighs) of the legs are curved so that the folded legs fit tightly against the thorax during flight, thus undoubtedly decreasing air resistance.

Only two species, both rare, are known in the family and they all live by the streams and rivers which flow through the tropical forests of amazonian South America. *Dicterias atrosanguinea* (Red Bareleg) is a species in which males have bright red abdomens while, in *Heliocharis*

amazona (Blue Bareleg), the males' abdomens are mostly blue; females of both species are olive green.

Larvae of *Dicterias* are unknown; those of *Heliocharis* show a marked resemblance to those of Calopterygidae and Megapod agrionidae (Demoiselle and Flatwing families). They possess long basal segments on the antennae and have long thin legs. The caudal gills are as long as the rest of the body and are triangular in cross section.

Nothing has been recorded about the habits of the Red Bareleg and only a very little is known about the Blue species. They perch with their wings spread horizontally, males choosing sunny spots on the leaves of overhanging branches. They are remarkably wary and shy of humans, seldom allowing an approach closer than several metres. Females, perching in both sunlight and

Sidney Dunkle

Sidney Dunkle

Heliocharis amazona, male (top) in Ecuador. Notice the long legs which are bare of spines. *Heliocharis amazona* female (bottom).

ZYGOPTERA

CALOPTERYGOIDEA

Dicteriadidae

shade, seem more secure in their camouflage of olive green and usually allow a closer approach. The reproductive behaviour of both species is unknown but, since the inferior appendages of males are vestigial, they must grasp their mates only with the forceps-like superior ones; and, because female ovipositors and the teeth on them are small, it is probable that eggs are laid in soft plant tissues such as decomposed wood.

Family Euphaeidae (Gossamerwings)

This family with some 60 species in 11 genera is restricted to the Old World and, with one exception, to India and the Far East. The exception is *Epallage fatime* which has extended its range to the Middle East and countries bordering the eastern Mediterranean and is also recorded from Bulgaria, Hungary and Romania.

Larvae, which are found under stones in fast flowing water, are unusual in that, as well as the three saccoid gills at the tip of the abdomen, there are seven pairs of supplementary gills running down the sides. The adults' scarcely petiolate, gossamer wings have very close venation, there are numerous antenodals, quadrilaterals are short and pterostigmas well developed. In

The whole body of a fully mature male *Epallage fatime* (European Gossamerwing) is pruinosed.

many species the wings are brilliantly coloured due to metallic reflections. Their bodies are short and sturdy. The wings of male *Anisopleura* are of interest in that the leading edge of the hindwing bulges out anteriorly, producing an extension to the costal area which underlaps the hind edge of the forewing. F. C. Fraser treats this as something unremarkable but it does appear to be unique in odonate wings.

Although all Gossamerwings breed in running water, some species breed in small forest streams (e.g. *Cyclophaea cyanifrons*), some in pools below waterfalls (e.g. *Euphaea refulgens*), some in irrigation channels running through tea plantations (e.g. *Anisopleura* spp. from India).

Their habits are equally varied. Some perch on twigs in heavy shade (e.g. *Cyclophaea*), some prefer prominent rocks in the sun (e.g. *Bayadera indica* from India) and some will settle on rocks in deep shade (e.g. *Euphaea refulgens*); some species rest with their wings open (e.g. *Indophaea fraseri, Epallage fatime*), others hold them closed above the abdomen (e.g. *Euphaea refulgens*). Females may be found in neighbouring jungle where they perch on prominent twigs, from which they launch themselves at passing prey.

Copulation and oviposition has seldom been witnessed but Fraser, referring to *Bayadera indica*, tells us that 'many pairs may be seen in copula, a very unusual circumstance in the larger Zygoptera, and these pairs take long flights down stream seemingly looking for a suitable spot to deposit their eggs, though oviposition is rarely seen.'

Generally speaking, the flight of all Gossamers is fluttery and of short duration. *Dysphaea dimidiata* is one of those widespread species whose wing markings differ dramatically according to the locality in which it occurs; in southern Thailand for example the basal half is black but, elsewhere, the black area may totally cover the wings or only be present at the base.

The wings of *Dysphaea dimidiata,* in Thailand, glisten in the sun with shades of deep purple.

Euphaea refulgens (Radiant Gossamerwing) from the Philippines.

ZYGOPTERA

CALOPTERYGOIDEA

Euphaeidae

Euphaea guerini in Bori Phut, Thailand.

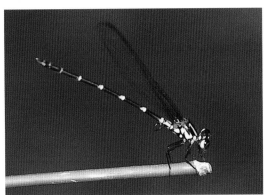

Strange ventral appendages can be seen on this male *Cyclophaea cyanifrons* on Palawan, Philippines.

Euphaea refulgens is endemic to a few of the Philippine islands. When settled in the shade on rocks in mid-stream, the insects hold their wings closed above the abdomen and, since the underside of the wings is dull blackish-brown, it is only when they take to the air that their incredible beauty is displayed. Members of the genus *Euphaea* can easily be mistaken for that of the calopterygid genus *Neurobasis*: both rest on rocks with their wings closed above their abdomens so that the uppersides are concealed and, in flight, both use their hindwings as planes and the forewings as propellers. However, closer investigation reveals that one (*Euphaea*) has pterostigmas and the other (*Neurobasis*) does not.

Structurally, one of the most interesting damselflies is another Philippines endemic, *Cyclophaea cyanifrons*, from the island of Palawan. The male is a lovely black, blue and yellow damselfly with unusual ventral appendages. On either side of the secondary genitalia, there is a long, black, incurving protuberance and it is interesting to speculate what the function of these might be. The most likely explanation is that they serve a similar purpose to the auricles on most anisopteran dragonflies. This species, incidently, also occurs in a red form.

ZYGOPTERA

CALOPTERYGOIDEA

Polythoridae

Family Polythoridae (Bannerwings)

Sidney Dunkle

This family of about 55 species is found deep in the tropical forests of Central and South America where the majority inhabit cool, shaded forest streams.

Bannerwings are robust damselflies, medium to large in size, with broad wings which they close together over the top of the abdomen when at rest. The wings bear large pterostigmas and those of most species are patterned with some combination of black, brown, white, yellow and orange; in sunlight, the black markings may be iridescent red or blue. In the genus *Chalcopteryx*, the iridescent hindwing of the male is both shorter and broader than the forewing, indicating that its signalling value is more important for species in this genus than aerodynamics.

In flight some Bannerwings (e.g. *Polythore manua*) mimic distasteful Clearwing Butterflies (Ithomiidae); the mimicry is quite good and one cannot tell until it perches whether the insect is a butterfly or a damselfly.

There are three subfamilies: Euthorinae with 10 species in the genus *Euthore*; Miocorinae with seven species in four genera; and Polythorinae with many more species placed in three genera. Since the subfamilies are largely separated by the number of crossveins in their discoidal cells (five or six in the first, three or four in the second and six to eight in the third), it is easier to discuss them as a family.

Bannerwings apparently identify the opposite sex of their own species by coloration and behaviour, because the genitalia within each genus are similar in structure. For example, in the genera *Polythore* and *Euthore* the bodies of all species are mostly black with similar colour

Male *Polythore mutata* in Peru.

Sidney Dunkle

patterns, but the wings are differently patterned. In the genus *Cora*, which has mostly unpatterned wings, the body of each species has a different colour pattern, in most cases bright blue and black. In Bannerwings with a wing pattern, the females often have a different pattern from that of the males. In some species of *Polythore*, females have two different wing patterns and in one species (*Polythore procera*) even three different patterns! In these cases one of the female forms mimics the male and it is thought that, although this form is mated less often than the others, it is harassed less by males when busy laying eggs. There are also age changes: in species with white wing markings, the white areas change to yellow or orange as the insect matures and, in *Cora obscura*, the blue sheen on the hyaline wings fades with age.

Depending on species, the short, stocky, brown Polythoridae larvae cling to rocks and other objects in flowing stretches of water that range from mere seepages to quite large rivers. The larvae are unusual in two respects: the presence of ventral abdominal gills and the unique shape of the caudal gills. The soft, finger-like abdominal gills are found in pairs on abdominal segments II–VII and apparently serve as supplementary sources of oxygen. The only other odonates with such gills are the closely related Old World Euphaeidae, in which ventral gills occur on segments II–VIII. The three caudal gills of Bannerwing larvae are uniquely shaped in that they are swollen, each with three to six finger-like projections; they are probably not efficient in absorbing oxygen but they possibly make the larvae more difficult to attack from the rear. Gordon Pritchard, in 1996, suggested that the abdominal gills allow the cuticle of the body to become thicker, since the caudal gills and body surface are not needed for oxygen absorption; the thicker skin then allows the larvae to survive the buffeting of wet-season flash floods. Other interesting features of larvae belonging to this family include a covering of scaly hairs, and a row of dorsal hooks on the abdomen. Such hooks or spines are common in dragonfly larvae but are seldom found in the larvae of damselflies.

Since Polythoridae inhabit very out of the way, hard to reach areas, their behaviour has been somewhat sketchily documented. However, observations have been made on a few species.

Cora marina (Aquamarine Bannerwing) was studied by E. Gonzalez Soriano and M. Verdugo Garza in 1984. Between 9.30 and 10 a.m., a bright blue male would find a piece of water-logged wood in a stream, perch above it on a bare twig and then defend it against other males. Should there be no bare twig nearby, he kept watch from a twig high in a tree and might maintain a suitable territory for periods of up to six weeks. When a female appeared on the scene, which usually happened towards the middle of the day, the waiting male flew out to meet her, hovered briefly before her and then slowly led the way to his chosen oviposition site. On arrival, he would turn to face the female, with his

ZYGOPTERA

CALOPTERYGOIDEA

Polythoridae

Cora marina in Mexico.

Sidney Dunkle

abdomen raised to show its blue coloration, and hover briefly over it for about three seconds. Should the female not be attracted to either the site or the male, she would make a quick decision and leave. If his advances were accepted, however, the pair settled down to mate for about four minutes. Copulation complete, the female flew to a new perch while the male made a final brief inspection of the piece of wood before returning to his observation post. After spending some five minutes cleaning her ovipositor, the female flew down and proceeded to lay her eggs in the selected piece of sodden wood. Oviposition might take an hour, during which time the male guarded his mate, as best he could, from the attentions of other interested males.

In 1993 A. M. Fraser and T. B. Herman published the results of a study they had conducted in Costa Rica in 1989 and 1990. They examined the behaviour patterns of three members of the genus *Cora*: *C. semiopaca*, *C. notoxantha* and *C. obscura* and a number of interesting facts emerged. Unlike most forest species, these three

Male *Chalcopteryx rutilans* in Brazil.

Rosser Garrison

perched almost exclusively in the shade and did not keep on the move chasing sunspots: perhaps as a result of this, they are extremely territorial and males were commonly found holding a particular territory (around pieces of rotting wood in the creek bed) for over 15 days at a time; ovipositing females were closely guarded by their mates and *C. semiopaca* males were observed guarding as many as five females at a time. At the time it appeared there was considerable interspecific mating but it now seems likely that the three 'species' are, in fact, just polymorphs of a single species and it is felt that further studies will reveal similar cases in other Bannerwings.

Another species, *Euthore fasciata* (Banded Bannerwing), was studied by J. De Marmels in 1982. The species is found in the Coastal Andes Mountains of Venezuela and breeds in forested seepages on steep canyon walls. Males, which have black and white wing bands, perch on sunny twigs and leaves, close to the ground. They are not territorial, probably because they must keep moving with the changing sunspots. When a female arrives, the male lands on her wingtips, without any courtship, and then runs down her wings to take her in tandem. They mate for about a minute, with the male fanning his wings every few seconds. The female then lays her eggs in soil or among wet roots, intermittently clapping her wings as she does so.

The genus *Chalcopteryx* is endemic to Brazil and Rosser Garrison reckons *C. rutilans* provides one of the most spectacular odonatological sights in the world: males perch on tips of twigs in shaded areas but make brief sorties into sunlight, often chasing off another nearby male and, as they fly, the brilliant metallic orange flash of the hindwings is enough to make any observer gasp. The more sombre coloured females oviposit into damp logs and, still according to Garrison, each male will guard one or two females.

SUBORDER ZYGOPTERA SUPERFAMILY LESTOIDEA (OPEN WINGS)

The members of this superfamily can be separated from other damselflies by their resting stance, with their abdomens hanging down and wings held, at varying angles, away from the body (there are one or two exceptions). Wings are petiolate (stalked) and usually have two antenodals; postnodals are in line with the crossveins below them; the arc is at, or distal to, the level of the second antenodal. Larvae are large, long and slender, with long caudal lamellae and very wide heads. Five families are generally recognised.

Robert Thompson

A typical lestoid larva, *Lestes sponsa.*

A typical lestoid imago, *Lestes virgatus.*

Family Synlestidae (Sylphs)

This very ancient family of damselflies has for long been known as Synlestidae in Australia but as Chlorolestidae in Africa. The former name is now generally accepted. The family is of considerable genetic interest and includes one of the most primitive odonates known, *Chorismagrion risi.* Most experts consider synlestids are Gondwanan relicts and, as Michael Samways puts it, 'have probably remained unchanged for millions of years'.

However, the distribution is a puzzling one since, in addition to Australia and southern Africa, representatives are also found in China (10 species in the genus *Megalestes* and three in *Sinolestes*) and on the West Indian island of Hispaniola (one species, *Phylolestes ethelae*).

Members of this family breed in running water, or in stagnant offshoots beside it. They are somewhat ethereal looking and have strongly petiolate wings. A close look at these will show the unique, strongly pronounced forward arching of the cubital vein as it leaves the distal end of the quadrilateral (discoidal cell). Most species hold their wings wide apart when at rest. The wings of many of the males belonging to the South African genus *Chlorolestes* are spectacularly adorned with black and white patches.

Subfamily Synlestinae

The Australian genus *Synlestes* are large (up to 60 mm long), metallic green or black damselflies which live in clear, cold streams on the eastern side of Australia. Adults of both sexes can be seen suspended (with abdomens hanging straight down and wings spread) from reeds and grasses, or else from the tips of twigs but, during daylight hours, always overhanging the water. According to John Trueman, the borders of mountain streams can be thick with *Synlestes weyersii* and yet *Synlestes* have apparently never been recorded

ZYGOPTERA

LESTOIDEA

Synlestidae

ZYGOPTERA

LESTOIDEA

Synlestidae

mating or ovipositing. He suspects, from the size and strength of the female ovipositor, that eggs are laid into something fairly tough.

Episynlestes, which are found beside streams in untouched forest on the eastern slope of the Dividing Range and nearly down to the sea, are even longer and slimmer than *Synlestes*; they are jet black with brilliant white markings and the anal appendages of both sexes are exceptionally long and always white. In *E. cristatus*, the underside of the thorax is also totally white.

The genus *Chlorolestes* occurs in South Africa and, on warm sunny days, individuals are generally to be found beside clear, fast-running streams. They all have localised distributions, specific altitudes and individual habitat preferences. The genus contains some fairy-like species: in most, as they mature, the hyaline wings of the males each becomes patterned with a patch of white and another of smoky grey and, in the majority of species, the pterostigmas are bicoloured: one half black and the other white, cream, yellow or orange, depending on maturity.

The body of *Chlorolestes fasciatus* (Mountain Sylph) is a bright metallic green,

The rare *Chlorolestes draconicus* in a wilderness area of the Natal Drakensberg, South Africa.

Synlestes weyersi at Foster, Victoria, Australia.

which turns coppery with age and, in males, a pale pruinosity generally forms to cover the apical segments. (see page 51). In *Chlorolestes umbratus* (Cape Sylph) a pale pruinosity also covers the top of the thorax. The much more robust Cape species, *C. conspicuus* (Conspicuous Sylph), is very handsome with bright yellow bands across the dark green abdomen. In the last two species mentioned, the pterostigmas are not bicoloured.

Breeding sites for *Chlorolestes* have seldom been found and mating and egg-laying have very infrequently been recorded. In 1990, I watched *C. fasciatus* (Mountain Sylph) larvae in a small hydrology research tank near the top of Cathedral Peak in the Natal Drakensburg; they were swimming just under the surface of the water and were attractive little things with striped bodies and long leaf-like lamellae marked with black and white (somewhat similar to the adult's wing markings). Adults of both sexes abounded in all stages of maturity on the nearby trees and shrubs but no sexual behaviour was exhibited.

In 1993, quite by accident, I witnessed shade-loving *C. tessalatus* (Mosaic Sylph) mating and egg-laying in what would seem a highly unlikely habitat and I later found several exuviae, as well as emerging imagos. It was a very small,

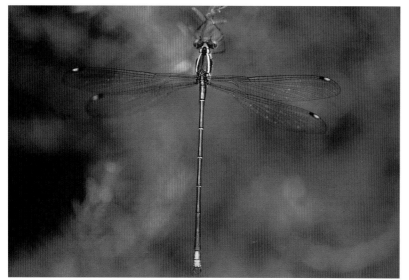

Michael Samways

Male *Ecchlorolestes nylephtha*, a rare shade-loving species, deep in the Tsitsikama Forest, Cape Province, South Africa.

scummy, artificial backwater beside a small fast-flowing forest river in Kwa-Zulu Natal.

In 1996, I found *Chlorolestes umbratus* (Cape Sylph) abundant on the vegetation beside the Storms River in the Eastern Cape river. Both sexes were present but showed no signs of being sexually aware of each other. Searching for small, almost stagnant backwaters, I found the expected 'hidden spot' almost under the wide stone road bridge and well away from the main part of the river. As usual there was a small, stout-stemmed shrub growing to one side of the somewhat insalubrious piece of water and on it there were two pairs of Cape Sylphs mating, two females ovipositing and one male guarding.

The other South African genus, *Ecchlorolestes*, has two species both of which are rare. I was pleased to find two or three good colonies of *E. nylephtha* in a deep forest locality beside a tiny stream that wound its way through tree ferns and enormous, ancient, indigenous yellowwood trees. A bright blue patch covering the top of the prothorax helps one to pick them out from the dark background. The female of this species is very rarely seen as she inhabits the deeper reaches of the forest and only visits the water briefly to mate and oviposit. The

extremely localised *E. peringueyi* is mottled, brownish grey, enabling it to blend into the lichen-covered boulders on which it rests.

Keith Wilson discovered some of the beautiful *Sinolestes* species while on trips to the Chinese mainland and tells me how similar they are to the South African *Chlorolestes*. Some have almost completely black wings with white patches near the tips. The island of Hispaniola is host to *Phylolestes ethelae*. Rosser Garrison tells me he found a number of adults perched along cold mountain streams in the Dominican Republic, 'they perched on overhanging ferns or snags at margins of rushing water'. He watched an adult that had just emerged from a large clear pool, leaving its exuviae on a small twig just a few inches above the water's surface. The species is unusual for synlestids in that they perch with their wings held closed on top of the abdomen.

ZYGOPTERA

LESTOIDEA

Synlestidae

Male *Phylolestes ethelae* in the Dominican Republic.

Rosser Garrison

Subfamily Chorismagrioninae

This subfamily contains only one species: the north-eastern Australian endemic *Chorismagrion risi*. This dull reddish-brown coloured damselfly, with yellowish markings, is

The wings of *Chorismagrion risi* show the unclosed discoidal cell on the forewing and the typical synlestid forward curving cubital vein.

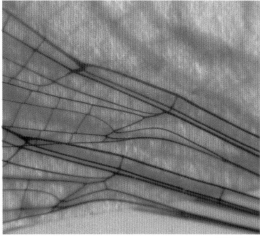
Allen Davies

Chorismagrion risi (Badger Damselfly) in Paluma, Queensland, Australia.

smaller and more compact with a much shorter abdomen than those of the Synlestinae. It perches horizontally on the upper side of leaves and twigs bordering the tropical rainforest streams where it lives, not letting the body hang downwards. It almost always holds its wings out away from the body. Finally, and most famously, the crossvein which forms the lower sector of the arculus in all other Odonata except *Hemiphlebia* is missing in the forewings which means that the discoidal cell is not closed at the base. However,

Stephen Richards

as John Trueman points out, 'the rest of the wing is so obviously synlestid-like that this can only be by secondary loss of the vein'.

The larvae are of typical synlestid shape though somewhat shorter, and have two very distinct, deep black badger-stripes, one on each side, which run down the whole length of the abdomen. For this reason, Trueman has named *Chorismagrion risi*, the Badger Damselfly.

Subfamily Megalestinae

There is just one genus (*Megalestes*) known from China, Vietnam, Thailand, north-east India and adjacent countries. Generally speaking, they are species of higher altitudes, from around 900–2500 m where the larvae must often undergo freezing conditions. Males can be recognised by the unusually long, slender abdomens, which are considerably longer than the narrow wings and, at close quarters, by the acutely pointed discoidal cells. In colour their bodies are bright, metallic, emerald green, marked with yellow.

F. C. Fraser records finding the larva of *Megalestes major* at 2500 m in a sandy and gravelly stream at Ghum, near Darjeeling. It was in the month of May and the water was icy cold but 'the larva, nevertheless, full grown.' Lower down the hill slopes, at about 1850 m, in a scrub jungle and hillside marsh, he 'found tenerals emerging from small brooklets which formed a network throughout the marsh.'

In 1996, 10 years after a visit there by Matti Hämäläinen, Rosser Garrison visited the Siriphum waterfall in Thailand (c. 1200 m) where he found good numbers of *Megalestes kurahashii* at the edge of bamboo thickets below the waterfall. He tells me they perch almost perpendicular to the ground with their wings fully extended and that they seem to prefer shady areas.

Amnuay Pinratana

Megalestes kurahashii at Chiang Mai, Thailand.

Family Lestidae (Reedlings)

Michael Samways

Some say these alert, mostly dark, metallic bronze to green damselflies derive their name from the French *leste*, meaning 'nimble'; others claim lestes comes from the Greek for robber or pirate and that it refers to the predatory nature of the species, especially of the larvae which are agile hunters.

There are two subfamilies, 14 genera and some 160 described species. The group has a worldwide distribution, from Siberia through the tropics to the southern tips of Africa and New Zealand. They breed in still water, some in small pools, including those trampled by buffaloes. Others, at an elevation of 3000 m in the Natal Drakensberg, can be on the wing even when snow is on the ground. Europe's *Lestes viridis* is exceptional in that it will breed in slow-flowing rivers as well as ponds, lakes and canals.

If not quite as spectacularly beautiful as the Sylphs, Reedlings are very lovely and even ethereal in appearance. Wing venation is different from that of other damselflies: many cells are not quadrangular, but five-sided, like a 'wonky' honeycomb. There are also conspicuous and long pterostigmas, often of two colours. Discoidal cells have an acute distal angle.

Subfamily Lestinae (Emerald Damselflies or Spreadwings)

These can best be distinguished by the position of the wings when the damselflies are perched: they are held out from the body at an angle of about 45 degrees. Their mostly greenish or brown colouring provides good camouflage. Males often have small, pale blue pruinosed areas on the thorax and at the base and tip of the abdomen.

Most species are short-distance fliers, flitting from one prominent perch to another. But they clearly have the ability to disperse far afield, probably with regular rests, because some species such as *Lestes plagiatus* appear at newly flooded, grassy pools within a few days. Males and females commonly occur at the water together, generally perched conspicuously on grasses or on bushes overhanging or beside the water.

The Holarctic species *Lestes dryas* (Scarce Emerald Damselfly) is less easy to spot as both sexes remain low down in the thick vegetation growing in ditches or at the sides of small ponds. They are one of a few species whose larvae will tolerate brackish water. Mating pairs remain in the same area and eggs are mostly

ZYGOPTERA

LESTOIDEA

Lestidae

Male *Lestes plagiatus* (Common African Spreadwing) in the Natal Drakensberg, South Africa.

ZYGOPTERA

LESTOIDEA

Lestidae

Male *Lestes dryas* in Essex, England.

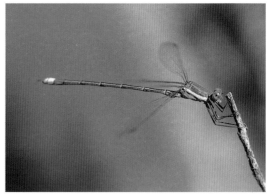

Rosser Garrison

Male *Archilestes grandis* in Arizona, USA.

laid in the stems of floating plants, tandem pairs often becoming totally submerged.

Lestinae larvae are large, long and slender, with long caudal lamellae and wide heads. They develop rapidly (eight weeks in temperate climes, less in warmer ones) and generally emerge on plant stems, leaving conspicuous exuviae. Sometimes, as in the African *L. virgatus* (Virginal Spreadwing) there can be a mass emergence with the pondside alive with fluttering tenerals.

The closely related genus *Archilestes* occurs in Central and South America, and the southern USA.

The genus *Orolestes* occurs in South-East Asia and contains some striking species whose long, slender abdomens are longer than the span of the wings: *O. octomaculatus* is a splendid example with its large size and heavily marked wings. *O. selysi* is interesting in that the male comes in two wing forms: hyaline or heavily marked black with white patches near the tip.

Subfamily Sympecmatinae

The unusual feature of these Reedlings is that they rest with their wings closed at the side, or on top, of the abdomen. The discoidal cell in the forewing is shorter than in the hindwing. They are seldom metallic and many are coloured in shades of dull brown; members of the Australasian genus *Austrolestes* are exceptions, often being coloured bright blue and black, and New Zealand's *A. colensonis* is black (male) or greenish with non-metallic brown (female). Richard Rowe tells us the last species is the largest damselfly (length 40–47 mm) in New Zealand and that it is also unusual among the New Zealand fauna in perching with the body held almost perpendicular away from the stem, the two characteristics making identification simple.

Male *Orolestes octomaculatus,* wingspan 78 mm, in Thailand.

Rosser Garrison

Robert Kemp

Sympecma fusca (**Common Winter Damselfly**) **in Crete, Greece.**

In Reedlings, the egg is generally the over-wintering stage but *Sympecma* species, and a few other species belonging to the same sub-family (Japan's *Indolestes peregrinus* and Australia's *Austrolestes leda*) overwinter as adults. Having emerged in late summer, they move to woodland shelter, generally with a carpet of long grasses, and there hibernate until the following spring although they may be stimulated to activity by warm spells in the middle of winter. The adult stage in such species is thus very long and can last for nine months or even more.

Habitats are varied. Although generally associated with grasses, sedges, reeds and bushes, some species have a close association with rocks. *Indolestes obiri*, for instance, inhabits shallow caves and overhangs along the Australian Arnhem Land escarpment. Europe's *Sympecma fusca* is less choosy in the selection of habitat than most other species and is known to tolerate slightly brackish water, and other similarly catholic examples are *Austrolestes leda* and *A. annulosus*. Most members of this genus breed in a wide range of still and sluggish waters including, in some species, temporary ponds and swamps.

Family Lestoideidae

This is one of the more confusing zygopteran families. Before 1995 it consisted of just two species in the single genus *Lestoidea* and many odonatists still consider this is as it should be. In 1995 (Novelo-Gutierrez, followed by nomenclature changes by van Tol), it took its present form of three genera in two subfamilies, the new classification being primarily based on small differences in wing venation. However it is still difficult to describe the family's adult features: habits, build (and wing venation) of the two subfamilies are totally dissimilar and, in addition, many individual features are shared with amphipterygines; for example, *Philoganga* has many incomplete antenodals and *Diphlebia* larvae possess gill tufts. It seems inevitable that a further reclassification must take place before long.

The genera at present in Amphipterygidae and the genera in Lestoideidae would appear to possess a mix of Calopterygoidea and Lestoidea characteristics. However, Lestoideidae, as it stands, consists of three genera split between two subfamilies and, however they are classified today or reclassified tomorrow, the genera themselves contain some of the most interesting and beautiful of living damselflies.

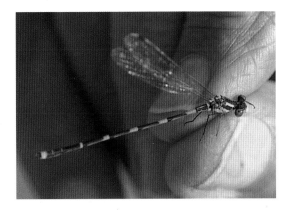

Austrolestes leda **in Queensland, Australia.**

ZYGOPTERA

LESTOIDEA

Lestoideidae

Subfamily Philoganginae

Of the two genera *Diphlebia* and *Philoganga*, the former has proved particularly difficult to place. For a time it enjoyed family status, then it was placed (where it had actually started) in Amphipterygidae, as a subfamily. Now, following Novelo-Gutierrez, it has been demoted again and the genus, together with *Philoganga*, has been placed in Philoganginae. Certainly these two genera are similar in build and habit: they are medium large forms with sturdy bodies, they hold their wings away from their bodies at an angle of 180 degrees and, from a distance without a look at the shape of the wings, their build and posture resemble anisopterans.

There are five known species of *Diphlebia*, and all but one (which extends into Papua New Guinea) are confined to eastern Australia. They breed in streams and rivers, often in dense rainforest, and the larvae of at least one species, *D. euphaeoides*, is capable of surviving in seasonally dried up river beds. The larvae of *Diphlebia* have gill tufts.

Males are black and bright, non-metallic, blue with narrow, petiolate wings that are gen-

Male *Diphlebia euphaeoides* basking on a rock in Birthday Creek, Queensland, Australia. This is surely one of the most striking damselflies in the world.

Female *Diphlebia euphaeoides*. Note the characteristic long narrow wings.

erally adorned with black, brownish yellow or white markings. The females' thorax and abdomen are either dark olive green or brownish yellow with black bands and their wings, except for *Diphlebia nymphoides*, are unmarked. The wings are densely reticulated; there are two complete primary antenodals and four or five incomplete secondary ones distal to the primaries; postnodals do not coincide with the crossveins beneath them. According to Stephen Richards, *Diphleba euphaeoides* is the favourite food of large water spiders.

The genus, *Philoganga*, containing four species, is recorded from Myanmar, northern India and China. They are exceptionally large for zygopterans and the long, narrow wings (with a span of some 110 mm) are unusually petiolate, bear short, wide pterostigma and the secondary antenodals extend into the subcostal spaces. Both males and females have very long anal appendages. They are found in primeval forests and males often fly over rocky streams at treetop level.

Philoganga vetusta is, according to Keith Wilson, quite common in Hong Kong during the months of May and June and will continue on the wing until late summer: 'It does not stray far from its mountain stream breeding sites

Keith Wilson

The striking *Philoganga vetusta,* in the New Territories, Hong Kong, China.

and, in its deep shade roosting sites, it hangs down in the style of an aeshnid with body vertical and wings outspread.' The Assam and Bengal *P. montana*, on the other hand, has been reported resting horizontally, in the manner of a gomphid, on the top of bushes bordering the montane streams. Larvae, before emerging, have been known to climb several metres up vertical rock faces from the streams below.

Subfamily Lestoideinae

This interesting Australian endemic subfamily is restricted to the north-eastern parts of Queensland. It is represented by just one genus containing two species. One of these, *Lestoidea conjuncta*, was discovered by R. J. Tillyard in 1913 and the other, *L. barbarae*, by J. A. L. Watson in 1967. Specimens of *L. conjuncta* are in various museums around the world but they are all a dingy black, having lost whatever colour they had had when living. The larvae have tufts on their caudal gills.

Whether or not *Lestoidea* belongs in superfamily Lestoidea is arguable. *Lestoidea* shows features of four clearly distinguished family-level taxa. According to John Trueman: 'the overall appearance of the adult is of a small lestid damselfly with a bright yellow to dull orange thorax

and a coppery-brown abdomen which glints deep metallic green when the sun shines upon it. The wing venation is like that of Australian Lestidae (subfamily Sympecmatinae) except for three features. One of these, the presence of intercalated veins, would place the wing with Megapodagrionidae. The second, a rectangular discoidal cell, suggests either Megapodagrionidae or Coenagrionoidea, but certainly not Lestidae. At rest the wings are held together as in the Sympecmatinae and Coenagrionoidea, not straight out sideways as in Megapodagrionidae. The third peculiarity of the venation is that the cubital is very short, running to the wing margin just 1–2 cells beyond the discoidal cell, while the anal vein is so completely reduced as only to form a little triangle around the site of the anal crossing. The larva, on the other hand, is short-bodied, with a wide head and the abdomen terminates in three-pointed, saccoid gills: nothing could be less like a lestid, megapodagrionid or coenagrionoid larva than this.'

Lestoidea are species of the rainforest, breeding in shady forest streams and seldom moving out of the shade or far away from the water. According to Allen Davies, they frequently

Lestoidea conjuncta (wingspan 46 mm) in northern Queensland, Australia.

Rosser Garrison

ZYGOPTERA

LESTOIDEA

Megapodagrionidae

perch on the upper side of leaves, right at the top of the trees. One would imagine this would make them impossible to see but, fortunately, since tracks cut across the deep ravines at different levels, it is sometimes possible to look down on to the treetops and observe the resting damselflies from above. This is not always necessary, however, since the insects do also alight on the upper sides of vegetation down low near the stream bank.

At the water, they fly very close to the surface and males, according to F. C. Fraser, will keep a watching brief from overhanging vines and creepers.

Family Megapodagrionidae (Flatwings)

This is a large and heterogeneous family of well over 200 species confined to small tropical rainforest streams around the world. Strangely, only four species occur in continental Africa, although many live on the nearby island of Madagascar. It is a primitive family, having existed for more than 100 million years.

The 'average' Flatwing is a dull-coloured, medium-sized damselfly that perches on vertical stems beside small rainforest streams, with the wings spread flat, or nearly so. But there are many exceptions which will be discussed within their subfamilies. Sidney Dunkle has provided much useful information for two of these: Argiolestinae and Thaumatoneurinae.

Subfamily Argiolestinae

This is the largest of the subfamilies, having no fewer than 28 genera which are spread around both New and Old Worlds. The scientific names of some members of this group are annoyingly similar to species in the family Lestidae — it is only too easy to confuse *Austroargiolestes* and *Argiolestes* (both Argiolestinae) with *Austrolestes* which is a lestid.

This male *Austroargiolestes icteromelas* was roosting on the fronds of a tree-fern in Victoria, Australia.

The number of antenodals in Australian species is fixed generally at two but John Trueman tells us that *Austroargiolestes icteromelas* varies a bit, especially in the high country of the northern tablelands of New South Wales. There, *A. icteromelas* often has a third or even a fourth incomplete antenodal in each wing (sometimes the number differs between the two sides or between fore- and hindwings). Although most Flatwings within this subfamily perch with their wings spread open, a few like the Colombian *Mesagrion leucorhinum* hold their wings together above the abdomen; some species perch on the ground or on rocks, others on large flat leaves or the thinner leaves of tree ferns. Species belonging to this subfamily do not have exceptionally long legs.

Most are of medium size although there are variations. Among Australian species, for example, is the large, spectacular tree hole dweller *Podopteryx selysi* (abdomen over 42 mm, wingspan 94 mm) which is black with pink markings, and there is also the small metallic *Argiolestes pusillisimus* (abdomen 21 mm, wingspan 34 mm). In colour the group covers almost all the colours of the spectrum. The lovely New Caledonian species *Argiolestes ochraceus* is one of a few species to be tri-

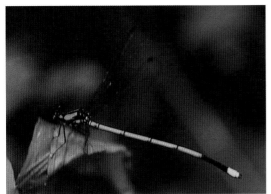

Neville Yates

Male *Argiolestes ochraceus* (wingspan 65 mm), lit by a sunbeam in a New Caledonian forest.

coloured, the thorax and most of the abdomen being brilliant orange, segments VII, VIII and X black and segment IX iridescent sky blue.

Another endemic from the same Odonata-rich island is *Trineuragrion percostale* which is deep metallic green. Most argiolestines have clear wings but a few have dark wingtips or bands and fewer still have white wing patches (certain *Nesolestes* of Madagascar and *Paraphlebia zoe* of Central America). Some species go through pronounced colour changes, for instance the thoracic stripes of the male *Austroargiolestes chrysoides* of Australia change from white to yellow to orange to red in six days. *Austroargiolestes alpinus*, a species of high altitude bogs, changes from blue to purple-brown at low temperatures, the darker colour probably helping it to absorb heat from sunlight. John Trueman points out that, in some eastern Australian species, particularly of the *Austroargiolestes calcaris* group, older adults develop a strong pruinescence on the thorax which makes them appear bluish-white and completely hides the thoracic pattern. A few female argiolestines have two colour forms, for example *Argiolestes ornatus* of New Guinea has one form like the male, with pale markings and black legs and a second which is dark brown with reddish legs.

Male damselflies rarely have two colour forms but such is the case in two genera of Central American Flatwings. In the genus, *Paraphlebia*, one form of male is large with black wing tips while the other mimics the female in both its smaller body size and its clear wings. The first male form is territorial, the second avoids territorial conflicts and attempts to mate with females surreptitiously. The other genus, *Thaumatoneura*, belongs in the subfamily Thaumatoneurinae and is described on page 101.

Genera in other parts of the world include: *Protolestes*, all of whose species are endemic to Madagascar; the beautiful monotypic *Trineuragrion* which is a New Caledonian endemic; and *Rhinagrion*, which is confined to South-East Asia. A fourth, represented by a single species, *Agriomorpha fusca*, is confined to China, including Hong Kong, where they occur

Allen Davies

Male *Trineuragrion percostale* in New Caledonia.

***Rhinagrion mima*, in Thailand, is a tricoloured species that rarely emerges from deep shade.**

ZYGOPTERA

LESTOIDEA

Megapodagrionidae

ZYGOPTERA

LESTOIDEA

Megapodagrionidae

Keith Wilson

Agriomorpha fusca in
Hong Kong, China.

quite widely. Another monotype, *Neurolestes trinervis*, an endemic of Cameroon, was named by Selys in 1885. It was recorded on Mt Kupe in 1996, where it is just one of the ancient relics that have survived in an area renowned for endemic invertebrates.

Most members of the subfamily breed in small forest streams but a number prefer other types of habitat, particularly in seepages where the larvae stay wet but are not actually submerged. A few species, such as *Podopteryx selysi*, will breed in water-filled tree holes. Malaysia's *Podolestes* will also breed in tree holes but, according to Lieftinck (1954), more generally choose lowland swamps, information that is corroborated by Matti Hämäläinen.

Larvae are remarkable for variability in the form of their caudal gills. In the Oriental genus *Rhinagrion*, the gills are flat and held vertically as

Stephen Richards

Podopteryx selysi in a
Queensland rainforest,
Australia.

in most damselfly larvae; in the Australian *Austroargiolestes* and *Argiolestes*, the gills are flat but held horizontally. In the latter type of larva, the gills can form a suction cup for holding on to rocks in swift currents but strangely *Podolestes*, a tree hole breeder, also has this type of gill. All other known Flatwing larvae have inflated sausage-shaped gills, each gill having a trailing tail. This type of gill may be unadorned, covered with hairs or it may have rows of hooked spines.

In 1982 T. E. Shelley, when comparing the feeding strategy of adult damselflies in a Panamanian forest, made some interesting observations on female *Heteragrion erythrogastrum* (Scarlet Flatwing). Males of this species have bright red abdomens but females look like brown twigs with wings. The males of some species of *Heteragrion* use a fluorescent yellow 'lamp' on the frons as a signalling device and they are known to flash at one another. Shelley found that females perched on twig tips in the shade and flew out to catch prey about once every three minutes and that they retained the same perch for considerable lengths of time. He concluded that the Flatwings' foraging strategy made them less conspicuous to predators than other species in the same observation area. In the late 1980s, John Trueman watched a pair of female *Austroargiolestes icteromelas* on the Gara River in northern NSW behave in exactly the same way: perching on twigs, rising up to catch chironomids every half-minute or so and returning to the same spot. Trueman reckons they must have taken at least 50 each but, as they were doing it before he got there, he could not tell how many they might consume at one 'sitting'.

Also in 1982, E. Gonzalez Soriano and M. Verdugo Garza studied the reproductive behaviour of *Heteragrion alienum* (Golden Flatwing) in Mexico. The males are primarily bright yellow, including a glowing yellow face, while the females are mostly brown. The damselflies roosted overnight several meters back from a stream in forest undergrowth, then made for the stream in the morning, reaching a peak of reproductive activity between 3 and 5 p.m. Males perched facing the bank as they waited for females and vigorously defended their perch from other males. An average of two hours per day was spent on the perch with some males returning daily for two weeks or more. Males in territorial conflict hovered facing each other with their abdomens slanted downwards and with the flexible tips angled so as to display the yellow coloration. They would then repeatedly fly towards and away from each other while, at the same time, rising 1 or 2 m in the air; each

Male *Heteragrion albifrons* in Veracruz, Mexico.

The very beautiful male *Heteragrion aurantiacum* in Brazil.

Sidney Dunkle

Male *Heteragrion alienum* (Golden Flatwing) in Belize.

would then fly backwards and downwards to repeat these dance-like manoeuvres. From these actions they would somehow decide who got which perch. When a female appeared she was seized, without courtship, and the pair would perch to mate for about eight minutes. Still in tandem, they then oviposited for about an hour, in leaves floating in the stream, with the male balancing erect on the female. Up to nine pairs might lay eggs in the same leaf simultaneously.

Subfamily Coryphagrioninae

This East African subfamily is represented by just one species: the very large *Coryphagrion grandis*. It is the largest damselfly recorded in Africa, with abdomens of 96–99 mm (male) and 79–91 mm (female). The face, sides of the thorax, thoracic stripes and the base of the abdomen are yellowish green; the rest of the body, plus the wing venation and pterostigmas are black.

Restricted to the thick forest of the coastal belt of Tanzania and Kenya, it may be seen flying in sunlit spots or glades, often settling on lianas (woody climbing plants) or dead twigs, usually high up but occasionally close to the ground. E. C. G. Pinhey noted that, when disturbed, it can show surprising bursts of speed and that, despite its shape, it is a graceful flyer. *Coryphagrion* is an interesting case of parallel

ZYGOPTERA

LESTOIDEA

Megapodagrionidae

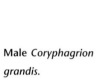

Male *Coryphagrion grandis.*

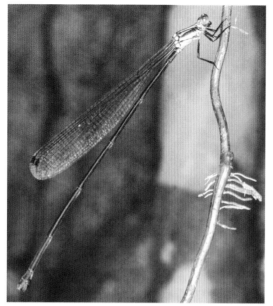

Viola Clausnitzer

Sidney Dunkle

Sidney Dunkle

Hypolestes trinitatis **in the Dominican Republic. Male (above) and female (below).**

evolution with the Pseudostigmatidae (Forest Giants) of Central and South America and, like them, it breeds in water-filled tree holes.

Subfamily Hypolestinae

This subfamily consists of just two species in the single genus *Hypolestes* and is known only from the West Indies, with variants on Cuba, Jamaica and Hispaniola. It is uncertain whether these populations should be regarded as species or subspecies. Females and immature males are black, marked with yellow but, as they mature, males become totally black and partially covered with grey pruinosity.

Males perch, with outspread wings, in the shade over small streams or, sometimes, on rocks in the stream. Like many other island animals, they are unwary and can be easily caught with the fingers. Pairs mate on stream-side vegetation and then the female lays her eggs, while still in tandem, into leafy debris at the water surface. Larvae are very similar to those of the argiolestine *Oxystigma petiolatum*, and like them possess sausage-shaped gills.

Subfamily Megapodagrioninae

This subfamily has a wide, but very local distribution. One genus is spread over Central and South America, one is found in New Guinea, one in Tibet and Thailand, and the fourth is confined to Madagascar. They can be identified by their exceptionally long legs. Sadly the nine red-bodied *Tatocnemis* species endemic to Madagascar are in danger from loss of habitat (as are so many relicts from other families that were once plentiful on that island). On the other hand, the two Tibetan *Mesopodagrion* species seem safe in their vast forest areas; *M. tibetanum* is, according to Davies, quite common in the eastern foothills of the Himalayas. It is a large black damselfly with bright yellow markings.

Gerhard Jurzitza

The exceptionally long legs of a Megapodagrion species (possibly *M. macropus*) in Argentina.

Collection of Allen Davies

Philosina buchi.

ZYGOPTERA

LESTOIDEA

Megapodagrionidae

Of the *Megapodagrion* species Gerhard Jurzitza observed in Argentina, he wrote: 'They flew along cool mountain streams, about 2000 m above sea level and generally perched on vegetation with their wings horizontally extended. Oviposition took place in tandem, apparently into mosses covering large stones. They are hardly visible and, therefore, overlooked despite the fact that they occurred in good numbers.'

Subfamily Philosininae

This subfamily is represented by a single species, *Philosina buchi,* named by F. Ris in 1917. Found (but rarely observed) in China, it is a large heavy-looking damsel with a wingspan of 88 mm, and considered to be a primitive species.

Subfamily Thaumatoneurinae

This is another subfamily represented by a single species, *Thaumatoneura inopinata* which has forms in Panama and in Costa Rica.

The Giant Waterfall Damsel was studied by P. P. Calvert in 1914 and 1915. The species flies in the spray of waterfalls and, when it perches, usually holds its wings closed over the abdomen as water drips off them. However males do hold their wings open for the 10 minutes required for mating. Females lay their eggs unattended in

Collection of Allen Davies

Thaumatoneura inopinata (Giant Waterfall Damsel) from Panama.

moss and root masses at the sides of the waterfall. Larvae cling to wet rocks but do not actually enter the rushing water. Calvert also watched an adult emerge from its larval casing; the 'blood' in the expanding wings was green, so that the soft emerging adult resembled a trembling green leaf.

The nodus is unusually close to the base of the wing (almost at the arculus) and there are many extra crossveins. It is one of the few Flatwings to perch with their wings held together over the abdomen and one of two in which the males have two forms: one form has clear wings and the other has a wide black band across each wing. Females have brown wing tips, unlike either of the male forms.

Subfamily Rhipidolestinae

This subfamily was recently demoted from family status and is here treated as a subfamily. Wings carry no accessory antenodals, and postnodals are aligned with the crossveins below them. Kiyoshi Inoue, and others, consider the genus *Rhipidolestes* to be a group in Coenagrionidae linking the two superfamilies Coenagrionoidea and Calopterygoidea.

Rhipidolestines are tropical rainforest species, closely related to similar dwellers in South America. The genus *Rhipidolestes* is characterised by a small, unexplained dorsal spine on the male's ninth abdominal segment. They inhabit jungle forest where they dwell among the low vegetation and females oviposit into mosses beside the mountain streams. Imagos often perch on dead twigs in shade, with half-opened wings and they fly slowly, as though wafted on the breeze, among the forest undergrowth. Larvae are often found in moss or between moss and rocks moistened by drip water. Representatives are found in China, Hainan, Taiwan, Myanmar, and Japan.

As is the case with most Flatwings, they are

primitive and have undoubtedly survived due to their continuous occupation of a very specialised niche. The four Japanese *Rhipidolestes* species breed in steep, fast-flowing streams with mossy banks and deep jungle forest cover. *R. hiraoi*, with their dark bodies, red faces and pinkish legs, were not easy to spot as they perched on shady twigs. When the branches were shaken, however, it was possible to put up resting individuals and, once our eyes became accustomed to the dimness, it was easier to pick out their shadowy, floating movement. Females oviposit, alone and unguarded, into moss on the sides of the steep banks. Keith Wilson, who recently (1996) discovered a new species, *R. janatae*, in Hong Kong, says of it: 'it occurs in a natural monsoon forest at 500–600 m on one mountain, where the breeding locality is the gravelly bottom of seepages in amongst boulders of montane head streams'. Due to their extremely secretive habits and often inaccessible habitats, it is likely there are new *Rhipidolestes* species waiting to be discovered.

Pseudolestes mirabilis, which is endemic to Hainan, is unusual in that the hindwing is shorter than the forewing; it (the hindwing) is decorated with a metallic sheen of browns, greens and gold.

Family Perilestidae (Shortwings)

Perilestidae is a small family of about 20 species that inhabit the tropical forests of Central and South America. The only exception is *Nubiolestes diotima* of Cameroon and Nigeria, whose ancestors must have survived in Africa when, millions of years ago, the landmass now known as South America split off leaving a huge area that became filled by the Atlantic Ocean. Sidney Dunkle provided most of the information on the Neotropical species and Graham Vick that on *N. diotima*.

Shortwings have very long bodies and short wings. Their bodies are camouflaged with stripes

Male *Rhipidolestes hiraoi* beside a rainforest stream at Dogamori on the Japanese island of Shikozu.

and bands of different shades of brown and black which render them virtually invisible in the gloom of the forest understorey where they live, particularly as they often perch under overhanging leafy branches. Even the legs and antennae are banded in some species. Seen at very close range, the dull body colours are relieved by the metallic green face, green eyes and, in some species, pale blue thoracic stripes or red pterostigmas near the wing tips. The arculus is distal to the second antenodal, the basal portion of the radius is thickened and the discoidal cell extends to the posterior border of the wing.

Shortwings hang vertically under twigs, generally with their clear wings partly spread. Sometimes males (*Perissolestes castor*, for example) curl the tip of the abdomen slightly upward to display the pale underside of the last few segments. The abdomen is very long, twice as long as a wing in males, proportionately a little shorter in females. Despite a somewhat ungainly appearance, their flight is swift and sure as they move a few metres from one perch to another.

The female's ovipositor is unusual, with two large teeth at its tip instead of the series of small teeth found in most other damselflies. The egg-laying habits of Shortwings are unknown but the powerful ovipositor indicates that females oviposit in firm material, perhaps the bark of twigs. The male's inferior appendages are vestigial, so he grasps the thorax of the female with his forceps-like superior appendages.

Larvae live among dead leaves in small forest streams. The antennae are twice as long as the head; the caudal gills of all described species are flat and blunt. In *Perissolestes magdalenae* the body is spiny, with lateral spines on the sides of all 10 abdominal segments and a row of dorsal spines on segments IV–X.

The reproductive behaviour of Shortwings is virtually unknown. Males have been seen hovering face to face in what may be a territorial display and one male was seen to perch on the tip of the abdomen of a hanging female, then climb up to her head before grasping her thorax with his appendages.

Until recently, little was known of the West African member of the family, *Nubiolestes diotima*. The 1995 Cameroon Dragonfly Project expedition to Mt Kupe in the South-West Province of Cameroon, led by Graham Vick, found an exuvia and newly emerged adult on a boulder adjacent to a gently flowing section of a well-shaded forest stream and noted that adult *N. diotima* occurred fairly commonly by similar stretches. Vick reckons that the Mt Kupe habitats were undoubtedly similar to those described by Williamson and Williamson (1924) in Colombia and, in 1974, by Gonzalez Soriano and Del Pilar Villeda when discussing the neotropical perilestids. The larvae exhibit characters which agree with those of the relatively few described neotropical species and this strengthens the placement of *N. diotima* in this family.

Sidney Dunkle

Male *Perissolestes castor* in Peru. Note the way he is curving the tip of his very long abdomen upwards.

ZYGOPTERA

HEMIPHLEBIOIDEA

Hemiphlebiidae

SUBORDER ZYGOPTERA
SUPERFAMILY HEMIPHLEBIOIDEA

Family Hemiphlebiidae

The family, indeed the superfamily, is represented by a single species, *Hemiphlebia mirabilis*, which has no near relative among known living odonates. The species is very small and has an exceptionally weak and fluttering flight. The most eye-catching feature is a pair of long, white, feathery anal appendages which are waved around in the air as the insect hides among the long antipodean grasses.

The wing venation is unique: there are two antenodals and the arc is distal to the second; postnodals are not in line with the crossveins below them; and the quadrilateral of the forewing is open at its base.

The first known record of this unique little damselfly is presumed to have come from M. Weyers who sent specimens to E. de Selys Longchamps in 1877. Selys, noticing several singular features, gave it the specific name 'mirabilis', meaning 'wonderful' and 'amazing'. In 1920, C. H. Kennedy, having received newly

collected specimens from R. J. Tillyard, stated: 'It certainly has no near relatives among known Odonata'. Taxonomically the species enjoys a totally isolated position and, in 1940, Tillyard elevated it to superfamily status; it is considered by many to be the oldest relic among living odonates.

Although the location of Weyer's original sighting has been much debated, the tiny inconspicuous little damselfly was spasmodically recorded from one or two sites in Victoria. By 1980 however there was no known population in existence. Then, in 1985, a strong colony was discovered by Allen Davies in Wilson's Promontory National Park, the southernmost point of mainland Australia. Since then a number of small colonies have been found in Victoria and, in 1992, G. A. Howe discovered them in a National Park in the north-east corner of Tasmania. Victoria and Tasmania are separated by the Bass Strait and between these two pieces of rocky land lies a submarine link known as the Bassian Rise, parts of which rise above the surface of the water to form a group of islands, the largest of which is Flinders Island. It appeared possible, if not probable, that a search among the swampy areas on Flinders Island would result in the discovery of further colonies of *Hemiphlebia* and, in January 1993, the premise was proved correct when no less than three such sites were found bearing strong colonies of this exceedingly rare and unusual little insect. It was suggested by Davies that *Hemiphlebia* could survive in damp, marshy areas that were protected from predators by dense rushes. He also suggested the possibility that it could survive the seasonal drying out of its habitat: it is, after all, a survivor through geological time and must have come through many droughts over the eons; (in 1988, G. J. Sant and T. R. New deduced that the drought-resisting stage is the egg). However, as

A male *Hemiphlebia mirabilis* in Victoria, Australia, showing his white anal appendages.

Davies says: 'what *Hemiphlebia* cannot survive is the intensive drainage and wind-pumping that are used to allow for today's ever-extending cattle ranching.'

Hemiphlebia is a very small (length 24 mm) metallic green, blue-green or bronze damselfly. Having about the same colour and diameter as the reeds in which they shelter, they are extraordinarily difficult to spot until ones eyes get accustomed to their inconspicuous movements. The top of the head is green and there are no post-ocular spots. The dorsal surface of the thorax is metallic green and the sides are grey, neither surface being decorated with stripes. Wings are not petiolate but broadish at the base. Features of the wing venation are likened by R. J. Tillyard to a Triassic fossil, *Permagrion falklandicum*. In primitive species the arc was only present in its upper portion, thus leaving the quadrilateral of such species open at the base; only two modern species are known for certain to possess this feature, and *Hemiphlebia* is one of them.

Little has been written about the behaviour of this unobtrusive little damselfly. When disturbed they are as likely to walk backwards down the reed stem on which they are perched as they are to fly: they appear to fly as little as possible and spend most of their time hidden in rushes at the edge of shallow marshy water. Mating has rarely been observed and ovipositing has not yet been described. Tillyard in 1913, Davies in 1985 and Howe in 1992 were, in turn, fascinated by males flicking their abdomens up and down, exposing their white appendages, and deduced an intention of attracting the attention of females. Davies noted that females respond to male signalling by revealing their own snow-white appendages. John Trueman, however, records that each time they land they wave their abdomens and reckons it might be a warning to others of both sexes that 'this reed

stem is occupied' or, alternately, it might be a way of straightening and settling the wings. He has noticed that both sexes bring the abdomen up against the outside of the folded wings on each side of the body and rub it along the wing membrane. 'Sometimes they open the wings slightly and do the same to the inside (upper) surfaces. Perhaps males do use their long, white claspers for sexual signalling as they sometimes open and close them in a conspicuous manner but this is not part of the end-flight procedure.'

The phylogenetic position of *Hemiphlebia* is uncertain. As Trueman says: 'The question for morphologists is whether the peculiar features of *H. mirabilis* result from specialisation and reduced size or are retained from a remote ancestor of all odonates. It is possible that future studies of molecular sequence data will help to answer this question.'

ZYGOPTERA

HEMIPHLEBIOIDEA

Hemiphlebiidae

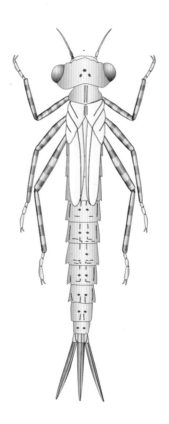

Full grown larva of
***Hemiphlebia mirabilis*,**
10 × life size.

ZYGOPTERA

COENAGRIONOIDEA

Coenagrionidae

SUBORDER ZYGOPTERA
SUPERFAMILY COENAGRIONOIDEA (CLOSED WINGS)

This superfamily forms an enormous group that includes species of all colours and all sizes: amongst them are both the smallest and the largest known damselflies. Their petiolate wings are generally uncoloured. There are two antenodals and the arc is approximately in line with the second; postnodals are usually aligned with the crossveins below them; the quadrilateral is uncrossed; the anal vein is fused with the wing border at the base of the wing and, in some cases, does not separate. The superfamily is divided into six families.

Robert Thompson

A typical coenagrionoid larva, *Enallagma cyathigerum*.

A typical coenagrionoid imago, *Coenagrion lunulatum*.

Family Coenagrionidae (Pond Damselflies)

This is a large, successful, dominant family with a worldwide distribution. Pond Damselflies are usually small and slender and, typically, rest horizontally with their wings pressed together just above the abdomen. They have short legs and the wings, which are generally uncoloured, are petiolate, the length of the stems varying according to subfamily. Most of the cells are rectangular, particularly those in the centre of the wings; the discoidal cells are trapezoid; and the distal angle is sharply acute. Although known as Pond Damselflies, a few species of *Argia, Cercion, Coenagrion, Ischnura, Pyrrhosoma, Pseudagrion*, etc. will occasionally, or even habitually, breed in running water.

Subfamily Agriocnemidinae (Midgets)

Several members of this subfamily are candidates for the smallest living zygopteran. They occur throughout the tropical zones of the Old World, including Australia. The stems of the wings are short; wing venation is scanty; the arc is widely distal to the second antenodal; and pterostigmas are often different on fore- and hindwings.

Agriocnemis pygmaea and *A. femina* (16–18 mm long), are tiny damselflies with wide distributions throughout the Oriental region and, in the case of the former, in Australasia as well. In *A. pygmaea*, the only noticeable colour on the otherwise dull ochreous males is on their anal appendages which are brick red. Both sexes are usually found low down among thick reeds and long grasses. *A. femina* is, if anything, the smaller. Males, as they mature, become pruinosed white on the thorax. They seem to float low down over shallow, often scummy water and most of their body disappears into the background,

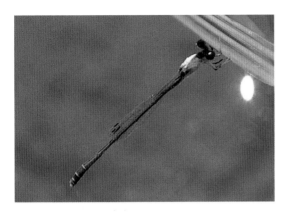

Male *Agriocnemis femina* with white pruinescence covering his thorax.

only tiny pinheads of white being visible as they 'dance' slowly among the water plants.

In *Agriocnemis falcifera* from Africa, the male is characterised by the brilliant scarlet on the terminal segments of his abdomen; they are slow moving and very secretive, generally skulking among thick reeds and rushes beside stagnant pools or slow moving streams where they can be very numerous. According to E. C. G. Pinhey, the female when egg-laying, rests almost on the surface of the water and curves her abdomen down until it is just submerged.

Another very small species, *Mortonagrion hirosei*, was first described from Japan in 1972, but has now been found by Keith Wilson in three Hong Kong sites, all of which are

Phragmites australis reedbeds. They are not easy to spot and may well be overlooked. In 1974, K. Mizuta recorded that, in Japan, *M. selenion* was known to commence reproductive behaviour very early in the day, with mating and ovipositing both starting before 6 a.m. This is exceptionally early for such activity in odonates.

Subfamily Argiinae (Dancers)

This subfamily is based on the huge New World genus *Argia*, with at least 110 valid species and another 20–30 awaiting description; the second largest, *Palaiargia* containing 20 species, is confined to New Guinea and its neighbouring islands, and there are four other genera containing one to three species each that occur in either New Guinea or South-East Asia. The wings are very briefly petiolate; postnodals converge posteriorly; females lack a vulvar spine.

Rosser Garrison has made an extensive study of the genus *Argia*. He writes: '*Argia* reaches its greatest development in the tropics. Adults are small (*A. bicellulata*) to large (*A. funcki*) coenagrionids which have tibial spurs longer than the interval separating them. In addition, the wings are stalked at the level of the first antenodal crossvein and males have a unique pair of soft pads located at the posterior

ZYGOPTERA

COENAGRIONOIDEA

Coenagrionidae

Keith Wilson

Mortonagrion hirosei in Hong Kong, China.

Rosser Garrison

A tandem pair of *Argia cuprea* in Mexico.

ZYGOPTERA

COENAGRIONOIDEA

Coenagrionidae

Rosser Garrison

Male *Argia oenea* in Mexico.

Onychargia atrocyana in Hong Kong, China.

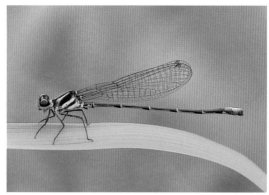

Keith Wilson

Argia fumipennis violacea in Tennessee, USA. The species generally has dark enfumed wings but they are not so in this subspecies.

end of abdominal segment X above the cerci; the purpose of these is not known. Males are most often blue, with a complement of dark thoracic stripes, and the abdomen is usually serially marked with dark bands. Others are violaceous. One group has red eyes and a largely coppery metallic mesothorax. Wings are often hyaline but some are light amber and a few, smoky to entirely black. Females can be marked like males but some are sexually dimorphic. Although easily recognized to genus, its members are probably the most difficult odonates to identify specifically. Any collection of these damselflies from the Neotropical region will probably yield undescribed species. Identification relies on the shape of the terminal appendages of the male and the hind lobe of the leaf-like structures at the front of the female's synthorax (the mesostigmal plate).'

Still according to Garrison: 'Almost all *Argia* species are stream dwellers and adults will often be found sitting on rocks, sandbars, dirt trails, or understorey in altered ecosystems but some are found in vacant lots in urban areas in the tropics. Adult behaviour is distinctive: after landing on a rock or the ground (rarely on vegetation), they open their wings to about a 30-degree angle and shut them again. This 'wing-clapping' appears to be unique in Coenagrionidae. Following copulation, the female proceeds to oviposit while still in tandem with the male. Larvae occur in rivulets or runnels frequented by the adults; some may be found in areas with little water so that they are exposed to the air.'

The South-East Asian genus *Onychargia* contains three species, the most widespread being *O. atrocyana*. This species occurs in wet, submontane areas of Myanmar, India, Sri Lanka and Taiwan. Although rarely plentiful, occasional large colonies are found and Keith Wilson tells us such colonies occur in Hong Kong, where they are found on marshy ground or abandoned paddy fields, often with no open water nearby. Their inclusion in Argiinae has been questioned by Yeh Wen-Chi, largely on the grounds of very different larval features.

ZYGOPTERA

COENAGRIONOIDEA

Coenagrionidae

Subfamily Coenagrioninae

This subfamily consists of a cosmopolitan collection of damselflies set into 10 genera that occurs in temperate and tropical parts of the world. Wings are the least petiolate of all coenagrionids; the discoidal cell is short; and the anal vein separates from the wing border well proximal to the arculus. Females (apart from some *Nehalennia* species) have no vulvar spines.

Of the larger genera, *Nehalennia* is confined to the Americas with the exception of *N. speciosa* which occurs throughout the Palaearctic; *Austroagrion* is Australasian; *Cercion* and *Erythromma* are abundant throughout Europe and Asia; and *Coenagrion* itself, upon which the group is based, has representatives in all parts of the world.

Cercion and *Coenagrion* both consist of small blue and black damsels, each individual species differing only slightly from the others and separation one from another is by no means easy. In the United Kingdom alone, where there is a total of only 41 resident species

of Odonata, there are no fewer than six different small blue and black damselflies and, at many still water sites, it is probable that at least two of them will be present. The shape of the black mark on the second abdominal segment helps identification but it is not infallible as it can vary a little from individual to individual. As with *Argia* (pages 107 and 108), sure separation of species depends on the shapes of the male's anal appendages and the female's mesostigmal plate. *Coenagrion lunulatum* (on page 106) occurs in continental Europe and in Ireland but has, for some reason, never been found in mainland Britain. *C. mercuriale* is a rare European species that just makes it into the south of England and Wales.

Coenagrion puella has been studied at a pond in the Liverpool area by David Thompson. According to him, mean length of mature adult life for both sexes is 5.5 days. The most successful male took 10 days to reach maturity, lived a further 26 days and obtained 18 matings; he struggled to the pond on just two and a half wings towards the end of his life. The most

A male *Coenagrion mercuriale* Hampshire, England.

Female *Coenagrion puella* in a Surrey garden.
The male is illustrated on page 61.

successful female lived for 30 days as a mature adult and produced 15 clutches of eggs (estimated 4 200 eggs!).

The genus *Erythromma* consists of three species, two of them common in Europe and Asia, the third confined to Siberia. They can be identified by the colour of their eyes which, in males, is deep red and, in females, rusty-brown.

Amongst all these very similar species, Europe's *Pyrrhosoma nymphula* is welcome. It is a robust damselfly whose body is red with coppery markings and is one of the earliest odonates on the wing each year. The only other member of the genus, *P. tinctipennis* occurs in China.

Nehalennia species are very small and very retiring: *N. speciosa* is one of the two smallest damselflies in Europe. Almost nothing is known of their reproductive behaviour. They spend their time low down in the grasses and reeds at the edge of ponds and other kinds of still water and can easily be overlooked. Many species have blue near the tip of the abdomen but others (Florida's *N. pallidula* for example) bear no such splash of colour and blend with the shadows and the surrounding vegetation.

Pyrrhosoma nymphula (Large Red Damselfly) on Thursley Common, south-eastern England.

Subfamily Ischnurinae (Blue-tailed Damselflies)

This subfamily contains the largest number of genera (29) and, like the previous one, it is cosmopolitan. The wings of Blue-tailed Damselflies (called Forktails in North America) are petiolate to a level proximal to the anal crossing and the arc is at the level of the distal antenodal. In males, the pterostigmas in fore- and hindwings are of different shape and, often, colour. In many species there is either a coloured band or a pair of spots on the top of the occiput between the eyes. Females usually possess vulvar scales.

Ischnurinae is noted for female dimorphism and polymorphism. One form takes on the same colouring as males (andromorphs) but, generally, larger numbers of females are heteromorphs. For example, in *Ischnura elegans*, females occur in five forms: the lovely *violacea* is a young form which matures to either an andromorph or to the dull brown *infuscans*; and *rufescens* is another young form which matures to an even duller brown *infuscans-obsoleta*.

Much study has been undertaken in attempts to determine the reproductive advantages and disadvantages of the different forms and much still remains to be discovered. Generally speaking it has been found that andromorphs, being more colourful and conspicuous, are more often attacked by birds and other predators, particularly during oviposition; on the plus side, however, it is probable that, resembling the other sex as they do, they receive less harassment from males as they oviposit, particularly at high population densities.

The genus *Ischnura* is represented in most parts of the world, perhaps its most widespread species being *I. senegalensis*. This very adaptable insect occurs commonly throughout Africa and Asia, tolerating most types of water, including

Immature female *Ischnura elegans* f. *violacea* in Surrey, England.

Mature female *Ischnura elegans* f. *infuscans* in County Down, Ireland.

that which is slightly brackish or in highly saline saltpans and even hot sulphurous springs. Europe's *I. elegans* and *I. graellsii* are also very tolerant species and North Africa's *I. fontainei* can breed in temporary pools in desert regions.

Another large genus is *Enallagma* which also has representatives in most parts of the world. In North America (where they are known as Bluets) there are 34 species and they could be said to take the place of *Coenagrion*. Probably the most widespread member of this genus is *E. cyathigerum* which occurs throughout the Palaearctic region. *Enallagma boreale* is a New World species whose range extends from Alaska in the north-west and Hudson Bay and Newfoundland in the north-east right down to California; it tolerates a wide variety of habitats: acid, alkaline and even (according to Robert Cannings) temporary saline waters.

Among other genera, the tiny Indian *Rhodischnura nursei* is a very brightly coloured insect and quite unmistakable, the abdomen of the male being almost equally divided into sections of crimson, pale yellow and black.

Two genera, both from South America, are very similar apart from colour: in the tiny *Acanthagrion* (wingspan *c.* 16 mm), the species are blue, while their close relatives *Oxyagrion* are red. The Neotropical genus *Cyanallagma*, on the other hand, contains species that are very typically ischnurine.

Enallagma boreale by Beaver Pond near Kananaskis, Canada.

Rosser Garrison

Male *Cyanallagma interruptum* in Chile.

An interesting genus, endemic to New Guinea, is *Oreagrion* with five species. They appear to be restricted to altitudes of over 3000 m and, presumably to protect them from the cold, their bodies are covered in hairs. The feature is also present in the two *Protallagma* species resident in the Andes.

Copulation generally takes a long time and many a female will only mate once in her lifetime, sufficient sperm being implanted during a single copulation to fertilise all the batches of eggs she is likely to produce. The extremely unusual reproductory behaviour in the Oriental and Australasian species *Ischnura aurora* is described and illustrated on pages 25 and 26. Females of this tiny odonate possess an extraordinary propensity for dispersal.

Subfamily Leptobasinae (Shadows)

Sidney Dunkle

This is a somewhat heterogenous group of neotropical damselflies held together by similarities in wing venation: the arc is almost level with the distal antenodal; the sectors of the arc arise separately; the costal side of the discoidal cell is shorter than the posterior side. Altogether 37 species in eight genera have been described but more species are already known and, no doubt, more are 'out there' waiting to be discovered. Although the ecology and behaviour of none of the species are well known, some interesting facts can be given here.

The two species of *Diceratobasis* are elongate, mostly metallic, black damselflies whose larvae live in the water of tank bromeliads in the West Indies. *D. macrogaster* lives in Jamaica, while *D. melanogaster* lives on the island of Hispaniola. Males of the latter species perch on bromeliads and it would be interesting to know if they defend a territory containing one or more of these plants. The larvae of *D. macrogaster* have many setae on each labial palp, forming a fine strainer, probably capable of capturing the smallest prey in their habitat, even protozoa.

In the three known species of *Inpabasis*, found in the Amazonian basin, the top of the male's segment X is notched and prolonged downwards between the terminal abdominal appendages to form part of the mechanism that grasps the female during mating. The monotypic *Leucobasis candicans* of Venezuela, is one of the world's few white damselflies.

The genus *Metaleptobasis* includes many elongate, furtive species that skulk in the dense undergrowth of seepages and swamps. Most species

Sidney Dunkle

A male *Diceratobasis melanogaster* on Hispaniola, West Indies.

have 'horns', usually larger in males, on the front of the thorax near the junction of the prothorax. The function of these is unknown but, in females, they might allow recognition by the male of the same species, while in males they would 'repel boarders' of the same or other species.

Finally, males of some Shadows are notable for having the lower terminal abdominal appendages much longer than the upper ones (e.g. *Diceratobasis*, *Mesoleptobasis* and *Metaleptobasis*), while some females (e.g. *Chrysobasis*, *Leptobasis*) are notable for their very long ovipositors which extend well beyond the tip of the abdomen.

Subfamily Pseudagrioninae (Sprites)

This is a large, ubiquitous subfamily and one that has attracted a considerable amount of interest and research. Wings do not have particularly long stems, legs have claw hooks and females have no vulvar spine. The anterior and posterior edges of the quadrilateral are parallel; the arculus is situated midway between base and nodus; and the pterostigma is very small, subtending one cell or less.

In the Afrotropical region the subfamily is dominated by *Pseudagrion*, the largest modern African genus of Odonata. I am grateful to Ivan Meskin for information on African species. He writes: 'There are well over 40 species in Africa, 26 of which occur in South Africa and there is much variation between the species as to habitat requirements, physical appearance and behaviour. Much of the fascination of the genus lies in the possibility of grading the variations in appearance and correlating it with behaviour. For example, at one end of the scale, in *P. hageni*, the males are brightly coloured and exhibit a high level of aggressive territorial behaviour, occupying the same territories for long periods of time (in one case, for at least 39 consecutive days). Territories are spaced out and always found on sluggish quiet pools. At the other extreme, the males of *P. salisburyense* are a drab darkish blue and do not exhibit any territorial behaviour at all, many males crowding together at suitable habitats. Between the two extremes, male *P. citricola* have bright yellow faces and exhibit a moderate level of territorial behaviour, establishing new territories each day; this species is found on streams with moderate currents. All African *Pseudagrion* are to be found along the margins of pools, streams or rivers, either in damp shaded localities in woodlands or among rushes or grasses. *P. massaicum* can be seen on sunny pools or even broad rivers, flying low and strongly over the water while *P. gamblesi* prefers fast flowing streams. Some species are widely distributed and common, while others are very local and there are a number of Cape endemics. The larvae of all known South African species are fully aquatic.'

Sprites also occur commonly throughout Asia and in Australasia. They are prone to speciation and many are endemic to quite small areas: for example *Pseudagrion siamensis* to Thailand, *P. pterauratum* to Madagascar, *P. rufocinctum* to Cameroon, *P. samoense* to Samoa.

ZYGOPTERA

COENAGRIONOIDEA

Coenagrionidae

Male *Pseudagrion pilidorsum* on the Philippine island of Luzon.

ZYGOPTERA

COENAGRIONOIDEA

Coenagrionidae

Another large genus with representatives throughout the Old World is *Ceriagrion*. The males of this genus are generally easy to recognise as the colour of their bodies is very uniform. Their abdomens range towards the red end of the spectrum, being yellow, orange or red; in some species the thorax is much the same colour as the abdomen, in others it contrasts dramatically. The abdomens of Europe's *C. tenellum* (see page 53) and Australia's *C. aeruginosum* are red, Far East Asia's *C. auranticum* and Africa's *C. glabrum* are orange and India's *C. coromandelianum* is yellow. Most species enjoy long flying seasons and they are mostly very common although *C. tenellum*, being dependent on acid heaths and bogs, is an exception. Females are less uniform in colour and, in many species, are polymorphic.

A number of Sprites are known to have semi or even fully terrestrial larvae — for example, some *Pseudagrion* species confined to small, isolated islands and also the extremely interesting Hawaiian *Megalagrion* species. Yet other members of the subfamily (the genus *Leptagrion* for example) are known to breed in tree holes.

Ceriagrion glabrum is found all over central and southern Africa.

Bert Orr

Female *Pericnemis triangularis* in Brunei.

A. G. Orr records from Borneo that the large *Pericnemis triangularis* 'apparently breeds exclusively in treeholes'. He relates that: '*Pericnemis* males tend to perch on the tips of leaves 10 to 20 ft [3–6 m] above the forest floor. Females oviposit alone and insert their eggs into moss or leaf litter just above the water surface. A female I watched ovipositing in a large hole worked around the rim of the hole, always remaining on the tree trunk. When the tip of her abdomen touched the water surface she withdrew it very rapidly. I think this may be a mechanism to avoid predation by larvae of *Lyriothemis* or *Indaeschna* which frequently occur at very high density in the surface water of treeholes.'

There are, in fact, a number of coenagrionids that breed in phytotelmata of one sort or another. Members of the South American genus *Leptagrion* specialise in this type of habitat and *Diceratobasis macrogaster* (see page 112) breeds in bromeliads. In all cases, the larvae of such coenagrionids are unusual in that they are similar to the larvae of pseudostigmatids (page 123).

Teinobasis is a genus of mainly bright red males, with a very wide distribution covering the Far East and Australia, including most of the islands in between. Only one species, *T. rufithorax,* actually occurs in Australia. This is an extremely slender orange-red damselfly, apparently inhabiting both still and flowing water, always in deep shade.

Xanthocnemis is a genus endemic to New Zealand where the species are named Redcoats. It is a difficult genus to place and Richard Rowe reminds us that, in 1913, R. J. Tillyard placed it on the boundary of Coenagrioninae and Pseudagrioninae.

Family Isostictidae (Narrow-wings)

The members of this Australasian family are very slim, very fragile and have exceptionally narrow wings. Because they are so slender and dull-coloured, it is scarcely possible to discern any difference in colour and, in many cases, one isostictid looks very much like another.

In 1984 there were seven accepted genera in the family, all of them natives of Australasia. In the late 1980s and early 1990s, J. A. L. Watson considered the generic classification of the Australian isostictids 'chaotic' and he carried out a complete reclassification. There are still seven genera but two of the original ones have disappeared, two new ones have been erected and species have been moved around within the genera. It has, undoubtedly, made classification more orderly.

Watson once described the genus *Isosticta* as 'wraiths on wings: if they were any thinner, the back of the abdomen would fall off'. John Trueman (to whom this was addressed) agrees: 'This is indeed true: *I. simplex* (since renamed *Rhadinosticta simplex*) is small, grey and flies close to the water in the deep shad-ows of overhanging bushes. I caught some one Christmas morning by swimming under the bank in deep river pools, with a net in one hand. It's like hunting for shadows in the shadows and, when you do catch them, it seems you are holding the head and thorax of a small damselfly with, some way after it, an ovipositor all by itself.'

In 1942, M. A. Lieftinck said he thought they laid their eggs in overhanging trees but Allen Davies has seen them laying their eggs on the bare rocks of waterfalls 'up to the eyebrows in water!'. Davies also tells us he has watched adults emerge from their larval casings, sheltering under boulders while the rain poured down.

Another genus is *Eurysticta* which has three named species, all of which were described by Watson and another unnamed one discovered by Davies in early 1991. In addition to being exceptionally fragile, they are shy and secretive. On the same visit Davies found a curious slow-flying damselfly that was totally colourless; it proved to be an isostictid, this time in the genus *Austrosticta*, but it was not either of the two known species. The genus *Oristicta*, which once held three species, has been reduced to just one, *O. filicicola* which occurs in north-east Queensland.

Male *Oristicta filicicola.*

ZYGOPTERA

COENAGRIONOIDEA

Isostictidae

Allen Davies

ZYGOPTERA

COENAGRIONOIDEA

Platycnemididae

Family Platycnemididae (Brook Damselflies)

Members of this Old World family can be identified by the dilation of the tibiae. This feature is, to a greater or lesser extent, always present in males and, in a few cases, in the females as well; the degree of dilation varies according to species. They may be found among the long grasses bordering brooks and streams. The two subfamilies are divided, somewhat nebulously, by the degree of acuteness in the distal angle of the pterostigma and the extent of dilation in the tibia.

Subfamily Calicnemidinae

The subfamily contains 23 genera which are distributed over Africa, Asia, New Guinea and some of the islands in between. Most genera in this subfamily have parts of the body that are strikingly coloured. The lower distal corner of the discoidal cell is acute; the tibia in males is said not to be dilated although the blue legs of *Allocnemis leucosticta* males are slightly enlarged as they are in several other species.

The widespread African *Allocnemis leucosticta*, with its blue legs, dark-veined wings with

Allocnemis leucosticta (Firetail), in the Natal Drakensberg, South Africa.

Keith Wilson

Calicnemia sinensis in Hong Kong, China.

white pterostigmas and shining black, orange-tipped abdomen is a lovely insect and aptly named 'Firetail'. It can be found at most altitudes wherever there is swiftly flowing water running through forested areas. Despite such habitat, Firetails are sun-lovers and must continually be on the move flying from one perch to another as it is warmed by a travelling beam of sunshine.

Members of the oriental genus *Calicnemia* are of medium size (India's *C. eximia* has a wingspan of 45 mm). They appear to prefer high altitude montane areas where they are associated with waterfalls and China's blood-red *C. sinensis* seemed to be no exception. Keith Wilson, who had found it in streams draining the highest peaks of Hong Kong and in Guangdong Province of China, later reported finding a colony at sea-level on 'a drowned mountain at Big Wave Bay, Hong Kong Island'!

When visiting Malaysia's Cameron Highlands, Graham Vick was delighted to find two species in totally different habitats: '*Calicnemia rectangulata*, a strikingly marked species with a red and black abdomen, was found on a small stream that flowed fairly rapidly over a bed of flat rocks — not really a waterfall at all. The water depth was only a few millimetres in most places and the water

Coeliccia albicauda in Shenu Province, Thailand.

The endemic Risiocnemis serrata (male) at Mt Makeling, Luzon, Philippines.

A female Coeliccia werneri in Palawan, Philippines.

Michael Samways

A male Mesocnemis singularis on the banks of the Vaal River, South Africa.

temperature at midday was 19.5°C. Males were perching on overhanging branches.'

The other species, the rare *Calicnemia chaseni*, he found opposite a huge waterfall on an almost vertical rockface, with just a few seepages of water trickling down it. 'There were clumps of vegetation and some woody creepers which had managed to secure a hold on the vertical surface. The bright red *chaseni* males were settling on these clumps and appeared to be waiting for females to come to the seepages to oviposit.'

The largest genus in the subfamily, *Coeliccia* with over 40 species, has representatives in most of South-East Asia and contains a number of

endemics. In species from Hong Kong, Thailand and the Philippines the thorax is decorated with a varying display of small coloured spots or slashes. However, this is not always the case and a number of species in the Indian subcontinent are not so adorned. They occur in montane areas beside fast-moving forest streams.

The genus *Risiocnemis* with at least 12 species, is entirely confined to the Philippine islands and some of them to a single island. Matti Hämäläinen is certain that there are many more of these interesting species waiting to be discovered in the fast-dwindling rainforests of this archipelago.

The two species belonging to *Mesocnemis* are confined to Africa, *M. robusta* to the Nile valley and *M. singularis* to southern and western parts of the continent where they inhabit wide open stretches of running water.

The South-East Asian genus *Indocnemis* is one of a handful in the subfamily to be monotypic and *I. orang* is one of the largest of this subfamily known (abdomen: 51 mm, wingspan: *c.* 80 mm).

Subfamily Platycnemidinae (Featherlegs)

The subfamily consists of just two genera and occurs in Europe and Asia. The name Featherlegs (translated from the German *feder-libellen*) is a good one; the tibiae on the males' legs and, in some instances, on the females' too, are considerably more distended than in the previous subfamily. In addition, the lower distal angle of the discoidal cell is not quite as acute.

The genus *Copera* has some 10 good species and several subspecies, all of which occur within South-East Asia. The tibiae on females' legs are never distended. Typical habitats are lowland streams, ditches and well-vegetated margins of lakes and ponds. They will often be found perched close to the ground in long grasses beside tracks and footpaths, sometimes at considerable distances from their breeding area. F. C. Fraser divides the genus into two groups: the *marginipes* group with coloured legs and tibiae only moderately distended, which breed in streams; and the *annulata* group with white legs and greatly dilated tibiae which breed in ponds and lakes. In a number of species, tenerals are almost white: a feature that has led to confusion in the past. The most widespread species is *C. vittata*, which has no fewer than seven subspecies occurring in different parts of South-East Asia.

The other genus, *Platycnemis*, occurs widely throughout Asia, Europe and Africa. They are delicate-looking insects that appear to be wafted by the breeze rather than move of their own

Male *Copera vittata vittata* in Shenu Province, Thailand.

volition. Like the previous genus, there are many species with numerous subspecies and there are no fewer than 10 that are endemic to Madagascar. Three species occur in Europe but only one, *P. pennipes* breeds in Great Britain. In many species, females as well as males have distended tibiae on their middle and hindlegs (*P. acutipennis* is an exception). The area on top of the head is transversely enlarged with strongly projecting eyes.

Platycnemi pennipes occasionally breeds in ponds and lakes but more often in slow-moving streams or in those reaches of larger rivers that are close to the embankment and outside the main current. They can sometimes be observed in great numbers on the banks and in the

A male *Platycnemis pennipes* in Surrey, England. Note the distended tibia on the hindleg.

meadows beside them. Males exhibit a fluttering courtship flight but show little sign of territorial behaviour and a pair will mate in the company of many others. Oviposition, which can take several hours, is performed in tandem and eggs are laid in stems floating on the surface of the water. While his horizontally positioned mate is busy, the supporting male holds himself vertically above her with his legs pressed against his thorax. He will threaten an approaching rival by waving his legs to display the enlarged, white tibiae.

Family Platystictidae (Forest Damselflies)

The species within this tropical forest-dwelling family possess long, slender bodies and short wings with a distinctive cramped venation. They seldom travel far from their breeding sites. The base of the wings appear to have no space for the usual number of veins: the arculus is difficult to identify, the length of the cubital vein varies according to subfamily and the anal vein is generally absent.

Found only within the tropics, one of the two original subfamilies (Palaemnematinae) is restricted to the New World and the other (Platystictinae) to the Old. A third (Sinostictinae) has been erected by Keith Wilson to contain a single genus, *Sinosticta*.

Subfamily Palaemnematinae

There is only one genus in this subfamily and its 40 or so species are spread around Central and South America, extending as far south as Peru where they inhabit rainforests. They are shade-loving and often found at rock-bottomed streams where they spend most of their time perched on snags or leaves close to the ground. Rosser Garrison and Enrique Gonzalez Soriano recorded (in 1988) that most species appear to have small geographic distributions and that,

Sidney Dunkle

ZYGOPTERA

COENAGRIONOIDEA

Platystictidae

Male *Palaemnema desiderata* in Belize.

within their range, they are localised and exhibit extreme site fidelity. They are small, fragile looking damselflies with hyaline wings decorated with black or brown tips.

In 1982, E. Gonzalez Soriano, R. Novelo-Gutierrez and M. Verdugo Garza reported on the reproductive behaviour in *Palaemnema desiderata*. They observed that mating and ovipositing commenced each morning before 6 a.m. Such early activity is very unusual among odonates. Males, who were very aggressive to each other, held small vertical territories in trees used by females for oviposition and appeared to use wing-clapping as both a territorial declaration and to attract approaching females. Eggs are laid on twigs, branches and leaf petioles of various non-aquatic woody plants hanging over the water.

Subfamily Platystictinae

This is a somewhat colourless collection of small to medium sized damselflies found throughout eastern areas of Asia. They are set in three genera, the largest being *Drepanosticta* with more than 70 species, and the smallest *Platysticta* with three species. Most have long, dark abdomens and relatively short wings. The abdomen may be coloured at the tip and between the segments.

Members of the subfamily are generally

ZYGOPTERA

COENAGRIONOIDEA

Platystictidae

Protosticta beaumonti in
Hong Kong, China.

Keith Wilson

slightly built, very inconspicuous and easily over-looked. It is therefore to be expected that new species are not infrequently being discovered.

They inhabit woodland streams, generally with mossy banks (or swampy areas feeding the streams) in moist tropical rainforests, and they seldom fly far from the breeding area. Bert Orr reports that he has never found any of the Borneo species more than about 50 m from water: 'Drepanosticta rufostigma was common at Kuala Belalong on one of the small streams although, even here, it was restricted to an area (50–80 m of stream) between two waterfalls. Males, which showed no sign of territorial behaviour, rested on vegetation at the side and a female was seen ovipositing (alone) onto the leaf rib of a plant overhanging the stream just before the second large waterfall'.

According to F. C. Fraser, Indian species belonging to the third genus, *Protosticta,* are extremely local in distribution and 'in some cases have been found confined to one spot for years, streams close by never rendering a single specimen.' Robert Kemp was delighted, in 1990, to encounter a good population of *P. kinabaluensis* in Malaysia's Mt Kinabalu National Park. The population, was confined to a couple of adjacent pathways which were a fair distance from the nearest stream and Kemp deduced that breeding took place within the 'tiny, persistently wet, gullies near

these paths' and adds that many individuals were very newly emerged. The species, which is only known from Mt Kinabalu, was described, from the male only, by Laidlaw in 1915 and still awaits description of the female. Kemp continued: 'Very much a shade-loving damsel, on disturbance it will rarely fly high or far before settling again; its black body with fine yellow markings renders it difficult to see against the various colours of the forest floor and low vegetation.' Matti Hämäläinen also records seeing this species in 1994 at the side of a trail following the Silau-Silau stream; they were hanging on a 'nearly vertical shad-owy and moist slope'.

Subfamily Sinostictinae

Surprisingly, this newly erected Chinese subfamily has features that are closer to the New World subfamily Palaemnematinae than to the Asian subfamily, Platystictinae. The most striking difference between the Palaemnematinae and Sinostictinae is in the superior appendages. Keith Wilson records that: 'The superior appendages of *Palaemnema* are spindly, complex structures, which are similar to many species of *Drepanosticta* and *Protosticta*. The superior appendages of *Sinosticta* are quite different being stout, broad and relatively simple in structure.'

Keith Wilson

Sinosticta ogatai in Hong Kong, China.

Family Protoneuridae (Pinflies)

Protoneuridae is a large and varied family with more than 230 species. They are spread throughout the tropical forests of the world but are exceptionally difficult to find as they are very secretive, making it likely that many more species await discovery. They are mostly small although some, especially in the Old World, are medium-sized, and the abdomen of most species is pin-thin. Wing venation is basically coenagrionid but characterised by very long rectangular discoidal cells (at least three times as long as they are wide).

The colour markings of the males, which range throughout the spectrum, are usually concentrated at both ends of the body, on the head and thorax and at the tip of the abdomen; females are usually an inconspicuous brown or black. The majority of Pinflies have clear wings but those of a few Old World species are sometimes marked with black or yellow.

Larvae look like those of the Coenagrionidae, with leaf-like caudal gills varying in shape from wide and blunt to narrow and pointed, while larvae of the Old World genus *Disparoneura* have gills which are triangular in cross section. Pinfly larvae are usually brown, but may be green or black. Whilst most cling to pieces of submerged debris, a few live on the underside of rocks in fast currents or on the underside of floating leaves.

Pinflies are divided into three subfamilies, two (Caconeurinae and Disparoneurinae) in the Old World and one (Protoneurinae) in the New. However, it is now generally accepted that they are too similar to warrant such separation.

The habitat of most Pinflies is semi-shaded flowing water, from seepages to rivers, but a few breed in still or sluggish water such as lakes or ponds. The Australian genus *Nososticta*, despite its diminutive stature, likes fast-running water and can cope well with deep water. Allen Davies tells us of the interesting speciation in this genus. There are 11 species in Australia and a number of others in New Guinea and other islands to the north. Each has very different coloration: one, *N. solida,* is widespread and widely known; two, *N. solitaria* and *N. coelestina,* are confined to northern Queensland; and the rest are endemic, each to its own isolated locality across the 'Top End' of Australia. Most species have patches of yellow or brown in the wings. All of them breed in streams or riverine pools. John Trueman suggests *N. solida* may be the most widespread because it will also breed in lakes. They are great hoverers and can be seen, often in tandem, hanging in beams of sunlight penetrating the canopy.

Southern Africa's *Elattoneura glauca* haunts long grass beside open footpaths and is seldom found in shady conditions.

ZYGOPTERA

COENAGRIONOIDEA

Protoneuridae

Ian Endersby

Nososticta solida in Wangaratta, Victoria, Australia.

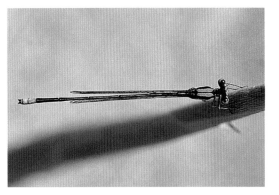

Male *Elattaneura glauca* in Kwa-Zulu Natal, South Africa.

On the other hand the brightly coloured Philippine endemic *Prodasineura palawana* is shade-loving and was found in deep rainforest bordering a shallow fast-moving river on the island of Palawan. The Malayan peninsula species *P. collaris* with its brilliant blue and black thorax, has a very similar habitat. Bert Orr has made observations on the behaviour of *P. verticalis* in Borneo streams: 'the males fly over the water at the edge of shadows where they are very inconspicuous and females oviposit in tandem in exposed roots in the river bank just above the water.'

Pinflies mate at the water or in trees and they come to the water in tandem. Eggs are usually laid while the pair is still in tandem, generally in rootlets just under the surface of the water or else in floating leaves and twigs. Sometimes many pairs can be seen ovipositing simultaneously in a mass of floating debris caught in a whirlpool. A few Protoneurinae have been seen ovipositing in other kinds of places, for instance in moss, stems and leaves a little above the surface of the water (*Protoneura*), in leaves on damp sandbars (*Neoneura joana*), or in mud at the water's edge (*Neoneura bilinearis*). While a pair is ovipositing the male balances erect on the thorax of the female, from which viewpoint he can see predators approaching and can hoist the female into a quick take off.

Prodasineura collaris, from Bori Phut, Thailand, is coloured brightly enough to show up in shade.

Male *Protoneura cupida* in Belize.

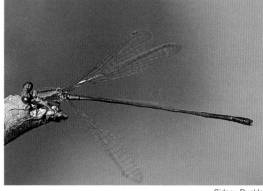

Male *Neoneura amelia* in Belize.

During the 1980s, V. K. Srivastava and B. S. Babu studied the reproductive behaviour of the Indian species *Chloroneura* (*Disparoneura*) *quadrimaculata*. They tell us that the male has an orange-red body and a wide black band across each wing: when he hovers his body seems to be surrounded by a thick black circle.

Another species whose behaviour has been examined in some detail in Brazil by A. B. M. Machado is *Roppaneura beckeri* (Becker's Pinfly). The larvae of this species live in the water held at the leaf bases of an unusual plant, *Eryngium floribundum*. The plant looks like a *Yucca*, *Aloe* or *Agave*, with a rosette of spiky leaves originating at ground level but it is actually a member of the Carrot Family (Umbelliferae).

Their extremely thin abdomens, together with small, round, widely spaced eyes make identification easy and the name Pinfly is an apt one. However, the extreme thinness of their abdomens is matched by that of the Isostictidae (Narrow-wings) and perhaps the two groups should once again be reunited in a single family. A proposal to this effect was made by Günter Bechly in 1996.

Family Pseudostigmatidae (Forest Giants)

This New World family is confined to the rainforests of Central and South America with just a single species found in Trinidad. It contains the largest known members of living Odonata, with bodies of up to 21 cm in length and a wingspan of up to 16 cm.

The family has intrigued odonatists for many years due to the fact that individuals can be seen flying in forests far from any obvious breeding place. Although adults were collected and studied, larvae and their habitats remained unknown until the 1980s. In 1984, O. M. Fincke reported that *Megaloprepus caerulatus* spent three to seven months as a larva; the maximum recorded adult lifespan of this species is 165 days. As their name (Pseudostigmatidae) suggests, many of them do not bear pterostigmas on their wings but the species of one genus, *Mecistogaster*, has very large ones, ones that actually protrude beyond the leading edge of the wings. They have a sophisticated control over their wing movements, demonstrated by their ability to pluck small spiders from their webs while fluttering in front of them. Peter Miller described how, having plucked them out, the damselfly will fly backwards, carefully avoiding contact with the web. This behaviour has also been observed in *Megaloprepus*.

Their great length (some species have a total length of 21 cm) was originally attributed

Sidney Dunkle

ZYGOPTERA

COENAGRIONOIDEA

Pseudostigmatidae

A male *Mecistogaster lucretia*, in Loreto Dpt, Peru, has a body length of 150 mm and a wingspan of 125 mm.

to the need to reach down into the axils of bromeliads to deposit their eggs but, in 1981, A. B. M. Machado and A. Martinez recorded *Mecistogaster jocaste* 'throwing' individual eggs into water-filled tree holes. This is undoubtedly exophytic oviposition and not endophytic as used by other zygopterans. Machado and Martinez studied the apical abdominal segments of three *M. jocaste* specimens and found that the ovipositors were of the usual zygopterous type, recording that, 'on morphological grounds, one could never guess that the oviposition of *M. jocaste* would be exophytic'.

Today, the 'flicking' of eggs by female Forest Giants is well recognised behaviour and, in addition to tree holes, some species flick their eggs into the leaf base of certain plants. It would seem that a long abdomen is more efficient than the more usual zygopteran one for flicking eggs into small water-filled receptacles. Indeed, it seems probable that the long body is an adaptation for this method of oviposition as well as for penetrating the depths of

ZYGOPTERA

COENAGRIONOIDEA

Pseudostigmatidae

plant axils in order that eggs may be deposited endophytically therein. Clearly both exophytic and endophytic oviposition can be used by many of these pseudostigmatid damsels.

In 1911, P. P. Calvert recorded that *Mecistogaster modestus* breeds in the water accumulated in the leaves of epiphytic bromeliads and, in 1981, N. D. Santos found the larvae of *Microstigma* species in the water accumulated in the pods of brazil nuts that had fallen onto the forest floor. The males of all species aggressively defend oviposition sites.

In 1996, Fincke and Yanoviak carried out experiments to determine the population dynamics of odonates and their mosquito prey in tropical treeholes. Two interesting facts emerged. Experiments with *Megaloprepus caerulatus* revealed that the larvae kill their conspecifics even when well fed. When other prey is scarce, such cannibalism reduces the odonate larvae to just one or two per litre, thus allowing maximum larval growth and increasing the likelihood that the surviving larvae will emerge before the water in the tree hole seasonally dries out. In a 'seasonal Panamanian forest', the most favoured prey of *M. caerulatus* was mosquito larvae and the surprising discovery was made that the number of these actually increased as the season wore on, suggesting that 'this predator may chemically attract ovipositing mosquitoes'.

It is generally accepted that Pseudostigmatidae evolved from Coenagrionidae and recent studies by A. Ramirez support the theory. The larvae of those coenagrionids that breed in phytotelmata are unlike those that do not do so, but they are very similar to pseudostigmatid larvae: among other features, they have smooth bodies, short legs and modified leaf-like gills.

Female *Microstigma rotundata* in Loreto Dpt, Peru, has a wingspan of 132 mm.

Sidney Dunkle

SUBORDER ANISOZYGOPTERA
SUPERFAMILY EPIOPHLEBIOIDEA

Family Epiophlebiidae

This is the only extant family in the suborder Anisozygoptera. It holds just two species, classified in one genus, which are the only known living members of a once widespread group. Their basic features, which are described on pages 7 and 8, are partly zygopterous and partly anisopterous. In addition to these the discoidal cell in the forewing is uncrossed and four-sided while, in the hindwing, the outer crossvein is long making the cell wide distally, and sometimes an oblique crossvein develops in the centre. The arculus is situated between the primary antenodals. The body colour of both species is similar to that of gomphids, being dark brown to black with yellow mark-

ings. Larvae are anisopterous in almost every feature.

The habits of the two species also show a mixture of zygopteran and anisopteran characteristics. For example, at rest they hang vertically like dragonflies but their wings are positioned like damselflies. On first settling, the wings are held half open like Reedlings (Lestidae) but shortly afterwards they close over the top of the abdomen. Apart from this, their habits are more of an anisopterous nature than zygopterous.

The best known species, *Epiophlebia superstes*, is distributed through the islands of Japan (where it is called Mukashi-tombo) and seems confined to habitats with ancient underlying rock strata. The adult was described by Selys in 1886 from specimens sent from Japan by a young English butterfly specialist H. J. S. Pryer, whose name lives on in the specific names of more than one Japanese dragonfly. The larvae

ANISOZYGOPTERA

EPIOPHLEBIOIDEA

Epiophlebiidae

Atsushi Sugitani

The 'living fossil',
Epiophlebia superstes,
egg-laying.

ANISOZYGOPTERA

EPIOPHLEBIOIDEA

Epiophlebiidae

were first described by T. Esaki in 1932, although specimens collected as early as 1927 have been found in an American collection.

Epiophlebia superstes breed in fast-flowing, cold rivers and streams in remote and undisturbed steep-sided valleys in hilly and mountainous country. The larvae act rather like stonefly larvae, holding on to the underside of stones in fast highly oxygenated water. It emerges very early (in mid-April) and its flight period is over by the end of May, before most insect predators have appeared. The temperature is generally low at this time of the year but *E. superstes* is adept at conserving its energy. Georg Rüppell, who is an expert on the flight of Odonata, feels that energy conservation depends more on economic flight action than on any other activity. It takes short feeding flights and spends a lot of its time suspended vertically from low shrubs with its wings closed above the abdomen, thus sheltered from the cold within its surrounding cover.

Less is known about *Epiophlebia laidlawi*, which is confined to the eastern Himalayas in

Nepal and was, until recently, considered an endangered species. It has a strange history, being described in 1921 by R. J. Tillyard from a single larva collected in 1918 by a man named Kemp from a stream near Darjeeling. It was not until 1958 that more larvae were located and a paper was published by S. Asahina. It was Asahina who later had the pleasure of describing the long sought adult, from a mature pair collected near Chittrey in eastern Nepal in 1963. In 1988 Peter Northcott (as part of a Cambridge University team) found larvae on the north side of Mt Shivapuri. In 1992, Allen Davies found them flying in a clearing, within a dense bamboo forest, 'above the clouds and rain', at 3500 m. Further exciting news of the species became known in 1996 when reports were received from Subodh Sharma of one or two larvae having been found in each of four new sites, one north-east of Kathmandu in central Nepal and the others in the Solokhumbu region (south of Everest).

The larval period (according to Davies) appears to be longer than that recorded for any other odonate. A fast-growing larva, in perfect conditions, would require five years to complete its development (six years is normal). A slowly developing specimen however may not emerge until the spring of its ninth year. According to Stephen Butler the larvae of both species stridulate vigorously when disturbed. It is well recognised that neither species is able to use the anisopteran 'jet propulsion' method of escape, but they do make rapid 'walking' movements. A photograph of an *E. laidlawi* larva can be found on page 17.

Emergence is of the 'hanging back' type seen in the anisopterans. The adults of both species fly high above the breeding area during the maturation period. The flight of *E. superstes* is swift with rapid wing movement and they appear never to glide; that of *E. laidlawi* is

Specimens of
Epiophlebia laidlawi
exuvia and imago.

Collection of Allen Davies

slower and rather uncoordinated. Having attained maturity, males return to running water in order to find females, who will be skulking amongst the riverside plants. While thus engaged, the flight pattern changes to a characteristic slow flight, low down and close to the water.

Having found a mate, the male grasps her by the back of her head, thus showing another example of anisopteran behaviour. Copulation is probably carried out while the pair is settled.

The female is unaccompanied during egg-laying. Clinging to the stem of a plant growing at the water's edge, she uses her ovipositor to insert her eggs, one by one, into the plant tissue. Starting from the bottom and moving upwards, the eggs are arranged in a regular zig-zag pattern. A number of plant species have been recorded as being used, with a bias towards bryophytes.

It is interesting to speculate how these 'living fossils' have survived for so many millions of years. As is the case with any long-surviving creature, the vital ingredient of success is the ability to occupy and hold a particular niche. Not a lot is known of *E. laidlawi* but the fact that it flies between 3000 and 3650 m in the Himalayas means that it has a negligible number of predators and virtually no competition. In 1992, Davies reckoned that they probably bred in waterfalls above 2000 m, the adults then flying up to the mountain tops. The altitudes at which breeding sites have recently been found are even lower than this. In 1988 Peter Northcott quoted 1860–2380 m and Stephen Butler found larvae on Shivapuri at approximately 1800 m, probably the lowest altitude recorded. The species would now appear to be quite widespread, almost common and, given the necessary protection of habitats, safe.

ANISOZYGOPTERA

EPIOPHLEBIOIDEA

Epiophlebiidae

Allen Davies

Epiophlebia superstes, collected on Japan's Mt Fuji, survived a journey to England in a matchbox!

ANISOPTERA

AESHNOIDEA

Aeshnidae

SUBORDER ANISOPTERA SUPERFAMILY AESHNOIDEA (ANGLE WINGS)

Most of the larger, swift-flying dragonflies belong in this superfamily. They are strong fliers and can often be found at long distances from their breeding grounds. The group is considered a primitive one. With the exception of Gomphidae and one species of Neopetaliidae which use exophytic oviposition, females use their functional ovipositors (structurally similar to those found in zygopterans) to insert eggs into slits made in vegetable matter above or below the level of the water (endophytic oviposition).

Eyes either touch on top of the head or, in case of Gomphidae and Petaluridae, are well separated. Triangles in fore- and hindwings are equally distal from the arc; the primary antenodals are the only crossveins aligned with those below them. The base of the male's hindwing is usually angulated and auricles are present on segment II. Larvae are long; the labial mask is flattened and rarely bears setae (hairs).

Robert Thompson

A typical aeshnoid larva, *Aeshna caerulea.*

A typical aeshnoid imago, *Anaciaeschna isosceles.*

Family Aeshnidae (Hawkers)

Representatives of this family occur in every continent and the family is considered to be one of the most archaic, evidenced by the fact that, like damselflies, females possess well-developed ovipositors with which they insert their eggs into plant tissue. Larvae, which spend their time climbing among the 'jungle' of water-plants, are long and smooth; their labia, long and flat. Imagos are large to very large and, following emergence, may fly many miles from their emergence site. Wings of males are, in many species, angulated at the base and those of both sexes bear elongated, crossed triangles which are of similar shape in fore- and hindwings.

Hawkers live up to their name and will fly tirelessly up and down a stretch of ground, hunting and catching the smaller insects on which they live. A cutting or an open glade in a wooded area can sometimes be alive with hawkers and such an occasion will bring infinite delight to the interested observer. When they alight they usually take up a vertical position, hanging from a twig or the bark of a tree. Interestingly, in North America, *Aeshna* and *Anax* species are known, colloquially, as Darners, the name probably originating from the old one of 'Devil's Darning Needles'.

Subfamily Aeshninae

Some of the largest species in the world belong in Aeshninae, a subfamily which contains 20 genera. Triangles on the wings bear several crossveins, and R4 and the anterior median gradually converge. The subfamily is split into three tribes: Aeshnini, Anactini and Gynacanthini.

Spread worldwide, members of Aeshnini tribe 'catch the eye' and are probably the most noticed of all dragonflies. R3 is not bent towards the pterostigma and there is an anal triangle at the base of the hindwing. The tribe is centred on the large genus *Aeshna* whose members, with one or two exceptions, are species of temperate climes. A few, such as *A. juncea* (see page 49) and *A. subarctica*, are Holarctic occurring in northern Europe and Canada, while *A. mixta* (see page 29) and *A. caerulea* are found throughout the Palaearctic region. *A. caerulea* is one of just a few odonates occurring within the Arctic Circle. British Columbia is home to no fewer than 13 species of *Aeshna*: *A. palmata* (see page 60) is one of the most widespread, ranging from Alaska through British Columbia and the Rocky Mountains of Alberta to California, Utah and Colorado. Robert Cannings tells us the species tolerates a wide variety of larval habitat, ranging from shaded woodland ponds to warm springs. *A. sitchensis*, on the other hand, is a small species confined to Alaskan and Canadian northern bogs. The genus is represented by only a handful of species in Africa. *A. minuscula* is common in the south, whereas *A. scotias* is recorded only very rarely in parts of West and East Africa although an expedition in 1999 to Cameroon found a number of larvae, representing several instars, in a rather insalubrious stream. These larvae are interesting in that their abdomens are decorated in many different patterns, some are very dark and almost unmarked, some have pale horizontal bands and some pale longitudinal stripes. However, identification is ensured by the presence of a pale spot on Segment VIII and stripes on all three anal appendages.

Aeshna brevistyla is the only member of the genus to occur in Australasia, where it has a wide distribution, but Allen Davies questions its place within the genus.

ANISOPTERA

AESHNOIDEA

Aeshnidae

Female *Aeshna cyanea* (Southern Hawker) is a well-known visitor to English gardens.

Male *Aeshna affinis* (Mediterranean Hawker). Photographed in France.

There are just two species of *Indaeschna*, one a Philippine endemic and the other, *I. grubaueri*, occurring in that part of South-East Asia that includes Malaysia and Borneo. The latter species is known, occasionally, to breed in tree holes.

The genus *Coryphaeshna* is confined to the New World where they are known as Pilot Darners. They are long bodied and short legged; the female *C. ingens* is remarkable for her very long anal appendages, which by the time she is fully mature have generally been snapped off short.

The Anactini tribe is widespread over much of the world. R3 bends abruptly towards the pterostigma and there is no anal triangle. Several anactinis approach the world's largest dragonfly: the African *Anax tristis* (length *c.* 115 mm, wingspan 130 mm) is one and America's *A. walsinghami* another. The size of the widespread *A. imperator* (see pages 13 and 19)

ANISOPTERA

AESHNOIDEA

Aeshnidae

Robert Kemp

The very striking male *Indaeschna grubaueri*, in Sabah, Malaysia.

Anax speratus (Orange Emperor) in South Africa is deep rusty orange from front to tip!

David Pryce

A juvenile female *Coryphaeschna ingens*, in the Everglades, Florida, USA.

Carlo Utzeri

Anax longipes (Comet Emperor or Darner), wingspan 90 mm, with its green thorax and red abdomen.

depends on subspecies: in Europe, *A. i. imperator* has a body length of just 78 mm and a wingspan of 106 mm; however, in the southern African *A. i. mauricianus*, the length is *c.* 85 mm and the wingspan 128 mm.

A. junius provides another example: Nick Donnelly tells me that F. C. Kennedy, in 1929, wrongly stated that the Hawaiian representatives are indistinguishable from mainland specimens. 'In fact,' says Donnelly (unpublished data), 'the insular specimens have consistently shorter abdomens and they have apparently been in the islands long enough to have evolved a distinguishable insular race.'

Most *Anax* species are coloured blue or green and their thoraces are generally unmarked green. There are, however, several exceptions: for example, the South-East Asian *A. immaculifrons* male has a reddish brown, ringed abdomen and his yellowish thorax bears black lateral stripes; *A. speratus* (Orange Emperor) is a southern African species which is distinguished by the fully mature male having a body that is deep rusty orange from the front of his face to tip of his abdomen, including the thorax; immature males and females have the more usual apple-green thoraces; and a species with an even more unusual colouring is the widespread southern

United States *Anax longipes* (Comet Emperor), which is interesting in that its abdomen is brilliant red, thus invalidating the theory that only libellulids (among anisopterans) have evolved the red pigment.

The genus *Anax* contains species that are renowned for their territoriality. Ponds, lakes and marshes over much of the world are likely to have at least one male incumbent. On a visit to The Gambia in 1996, we observed three or four male *A. imperator* each patrolling their own section of a large marsh, while flying some 2.5 m above them was a lone *A. tristis.* He majestically patrolled the whole area, and a stunning sight he was. Even ignoring his impressive size, his body markings made misidentification impossible: a dark abdomen with a large pale cream patch covering the second segment and several smaller marks running down the side were unlike anything else flying. We visited the site two days running. On the first day there was no *A. tristis* flying but we found a drowning male and, on rescuing him, we were able to make a close examination. We returned the following day and were delighted to observe another individual patrolling the marsh. It would appear that when one male, for any reason, relinquishes his territory, it is taken over immediately by an opportunist successor.

The genus *Anaciaeschna* contains 10 species all of which are confined to Eurasia. *A. isosceles* (Norfolk Hawker) only just makes it to Britain where it is that country's sole listed species although, over the past few years, the number of its breeding sites has increased encouragingly. Although most *Anaciaeschna* are diurnal, Japan's *A. martini* flies well after dusk and before dawn, and is oblivious to even the hardest rain.

There are two species of *Hemianax* and it is a genus with a strange distribution. *H. ephippiger* (Vagrant Emperor) (see page 28) is basically an African species that extends its breeding range

into south-west Asia and southern Europe. A compulsive migrant, it is the only species ever recorded from Iceland. *H. papuensis*, (see page 43) is common in Australia, Papua New Guinea and the western Pacific islands. It enjoys a particularly long flight period and is one of only a few species that can be seen in the winter. In Queensland, it is probably the commonest aeshnid and the one that greets travellers as they walk out of the Brisbane Airport building! Neither species shows any sign of territoriality and, where present, they will often occur in large numbers. Both *Hemianax* species frequently oviposit in tandem.

Although most members of the tribes Aeshnini and Anactini are daytime flyers, many of those occurring in Japan are recognised as crepuscular. According to Kiyoshi Inoue, even species of *Anax* can be crepuscular in Japan but also fly in daylight. Indeed, Europe's *Aeshna cyanea* will often be found hunting midges after dusk.

The tribe Gynacanthini are crepuscular aeshnids and, among them, are some of the real giants among Odonata. They are spread throughout all continents except Europe, occurring in the tropics and subtropics. Their name comes from the Greek *gnaikos* meaning 'woman', and *akantha*, meaning 'thorn' — very apt as females possess two, three or even four

ANISOPTERA

AESHNOIDEA

Aeshnidae

This male *Anax tristis* (Giant Emperor) (wingspan 130 mm) was rescued from drowning in a marshy area of The Gambia.

ANISOPTERA

AESHNOIDEA

Aeshnidae

stout spines projecting ventrally from Segment X which they use to penetrate the vegetation into which they insert their eggs.

It is generally possible to identify *Gynacantha* (or other species belonging to the tribe) by their exceptionally large, head-enveloping eyes. Their wing venation is similar to Aeshnini. Generally speaking their body colouring is shades of brown, sometimes with green or blue on the thorax. Eyes, though often brown, can be blue or, more rarely, green. The wings of most species are hyaline, often slightly dusky but, in some, the costal area is heavily marked with dark brown.

Generally speaking, members of the tribe are difficult to spot, partly due to their crepuscular habits and partly to their dark coloration; being generally brown or even almost black (Australia's *Austrogynacantha heterogena* for instance) and generally perching on the brown bark of a forest tree does not make it easy. Although the period of their greatest activity is during the period between dusk and dawn, *Gynacantha* do fly in daylight hours, particularly in cooler weather.

Keith Wilson records that males of *Gynacantha japonica* (which has only recently been recorded from Hong Kong) have been observed, during the middle of the day, holding territory by patrolling short beats over an area of weedy swamp and actively seeing off intruding males of the same species, and the same

David Pryce

The rare *Heliaeschna lanceolata,* male (top) and female (bottom) in Cameroon.

behaviour was witnessed with *G. subinterrupta* in Thailand. Sidney Dunkle tells us that (in *G. nervosa*) mating occurs while the pair hangs from a twig in forest undergrowth and that females oviposit, warily, into the soil near the edge of pools or even into depressions which will later fill with rainwater.

Other notable genera belonging in this tribe are the South-East Asian *Tetracanthagyna* and *Polycanthagyna*, the Central and South American *Triacanthagyna* and *Neuraeschna*, and *Heliaeschna* which is spread around Africa and South-East Asia. Among them is the magnificent *Tetracanthagyna plagiata* (see page 37), the female of which, with a wingspan of 160 mm, vies with a couple of other giants for the honour of being recognised as the world's

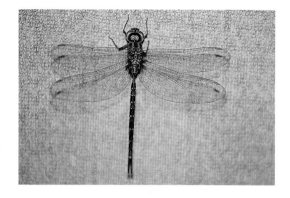

Male *Gynacantha subinterrupta* from Tong Nja Chang in southern Thailand.

Kiyoshi Inoue

Polycanthagyna melanictera, **a Japanese endemic.**

largest known living dragonfly. Important information comes from Keith Wilson who, on the subject of *Tetracanthagyna waterhousei*, tells us that 'the larvae grow at an incredibly rapid rate, given ample feed, and are capable of achieving the mature larval stage within a few months of hatching'. They breed in a variety of slow-moving water beside forest, and other, streams. A mating pair of the rare *Heliaeschna lanceolata* provided one of the highlights of a recent expedition to Cameroon.

The genus *Polycanthagyna* is sometimes placed into a fourth Aeshninae tribe, Polycanthagynini. According to Wilson, the female *P. erythromelas* has a bright coppery red body and is thus another species that confutes the 'no-red-pigment-in-aeshnids' theory. The male's abdomen is predominantly black. *Polycanthagyna melanictera* ('Yabu-yamma' which means 'thicket aeshnid') is another of Japan's crepuscular species. During hot weather they roost during the daytime and can be found hanging from shady twigs in the forest but, on cooler days, according to Kiyoshi Inoue, males are more active and may be seen patrolling the forest ponds. Larvae inhabit small, shady and often stagnant pits and ponds in low mountain areas. According to Inoue, females lay their eggs 'into wet moss or earth near or some 1 m distant from ponds'.

Subfamily Brachytroninae

This is a smaller subfamily of 16 genera whose members, with a few exceptions, are mostly confined to the Old World. They differ from aeshnines in that R3 and the anterior median run almost parallel to each other, diverging slightly at the distal end. The genera are divided between two tribes, Brachytronini and Gomphaeschnini.

The Brachytronini tribe can only be separated from the Gomphaeschnini by a really close look at the wing venation: i.e. whether or not a vein called IR3 (an extension of the radial sector) is forked or not; in Brachytronini it is forked.

Brachytron pratense is the only species of its genus but it takes different forms in different parts of Europe. It appears to be rapidly extending its range in the British Isles. Some of the most unusual looking dragonflies are

Female *Brachytron pratense* (Hairy Hawker) in County Antrim, Northern Ireland.

A female *Aeschnophlebia anisoptera*, with a body length of 77–83 mm and wingspan of 96 mm.

ANISOPTERA

AESHNOIDEA

Aeshnidae

ANISOPTERA

AESHNOIDEA

Aeshnidae

contained in the genus *Cephalaeschna* which occur as high as 4100 m in Nepal and at similar altitudes in parts of China: they bear a hugely inflated frons, the reason for which is not known. *Aeschnophlebia anisoptera* is one of the Japanese crepuscular anisopterans that has been observed flying, in teeming rain, from about 4.30 a.m. in the morning. There are very few members of the tribe in the New World, *Epiaeschna heros* is one and *Nasiaeschna pentacantha* another.

In Australia the tribe is represented by the genus *Austroaeschna* holding 21 species (strangely, there is a 22nd which occurs in Assam). They all breed in streams and rivers, many of them confined to those in rainforests or montane areas. The red-legged *A. multipunctata* is well named: the thorax and abdomen are covered in a multitude of small pale markings. *A. weiskei* is a crepuscular species and draws attention to itself as it disappears into the forest: the apex of the abdomen glows in the dark and looks like the tip of a burning cigarette. *A. hardyi* (wingspan 88 mm) is a rarely seen Tasmanian endemic.

Within the tribe Gomphaeschnini, the genus *Boyeria* contains five species, two in the New World, one in Europe and two in the Far East. *Boyeria irene* is a crepuscular species which has

been seen flying in unlit town streets just 23 cm from the ground. During daylight hours they are still active but retreat from the towns, making for the streams and small rivers in which they breed.

The South-East Asian genus *Oligoaeschna* is a fairly large one with one or two species that are endemic to such islands as Luzon and Mindanao in the Philippines and Ryu Kyu in Japan. It is an interesting genus and F. C. Fraser considered it contained the most primitive of Indian aeshnids and that it was closely related to the Neopetaliidae. The male's inferior anal appendage is deeply bifid and females bear an unusual shaped genital plate and a large ovipositor, suggesting that they oviposit in dry earth. This suggestion is corroborated by Kiyoshi Inoue who says that *O. pryeri* larvae are mostly terrestrial: 'they are found under fallen leaves on wet ground, sometimes in caves made by themselves'.

The Australian genus *Telephlebia* contains six species, all of which are crepuscular and all of whose wings are marked with brown lines or patches along the costal edges. *T. tillyardi* (see page 33) flies well after dark, keeping to the centre of wide dirt tracks; they cannot be seen but, in the deep stillness of a Queensland rainforest, they can actually be heard approaching.

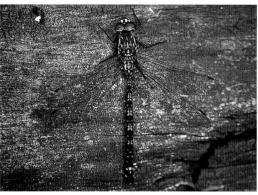

Allen Davies

Austroaeschna hardyi **is a rare Tasmanian endemic.**

Robert Kemp

Male *Boyeria irene* **in France.**

Family Gomphidae (Clubtails)

Keith Wilson

Gomphids are an ancient family with very high species richness and their classification at sub-family level has yet to be fully agreed. The family probably originated in South-East Asia but, over the millennia, it has spread all over the world.

Gomphid adults and larvae are distinct from all other dragonflies. Adults are characterised by transversely elongated heads with widely separated eyes (a feature shared with the Petaluridae) and, in females, an ovipositor which is absent or reduced to a simple structure originating in abdominal segment VIII and rarely extending beyond segment IX. Since widely separated eyes are a feature of zygopterans, it is considered to be an archaic character. Despite their colloquial name, not all members of the family have clubbed tails. The ground colour of the adult is yellow or green (never metallic), marked with black or dark brown. Some desert forms are predominantly yellow or pale but for others, including many forest dwellers, black is usually the dominant colour.

Wings are clear or, very rarely, darkened at their bases. With a few exceptions (*Anisogomphus* is one) the base of the male hindwing is excised and strongly angulated. Gomphids are the most primitive dragonflies to possess a subtriangle; the discoidal cell of the hindwing is more elongate than that of the forewing.

Most species prefer streams and riverine habitats and have short seasons as adults. In the tropics the majority of species emerge, over a period of a few weeks, shortly after the onset of the rainy season but in temperate areas they generally do so in spring or early summer. Those species preferring pond and lake habitats, tend to have a less synchronised pattern of emergence and longer seasons on the wing. Gomphid flights are usually short hops or occasional patrols along stream watercourses or lake shorelines. During dull weather their activity is much reduced and they seldom fly after dusk or before dawn.

The larval stage for most species lasts from one to three years but some species may take as long as five, or even more, before they are ready to emerge. Larvae have fairly precise habitat requirements and are intolerant of organic pollution. As adults, many species depend on nearby forest in which to mature and losses in riparian and nearby woodland may be responsible for declines in many gomphid populations. In species-rich areas in the tropics and warm temperate latitudes, they are excellent indicators of pollution and riverine habitat quality. In northern climes the number of gomphid species found is greatly reduced when compared with tropical regions, reflecting the likely origin of the group.

Gomphids usually emerge in the early morning and immediately disappear into nearby scrub or woodland where young adults remain until matured. Adults feed voraciously: the North American *Hagenius brevistylus* has

ANISOPTERA

AESHNOIDEA

Gomphidae

Male *Dromogomphus spinosus* in Bays Mountain Park, Tennessee, USA.

ANISOPTERA

AESHNOIDEA

Gomphidae

been reported taking smaller gomphids and butterflies; I have observed *Labrogomphus torvus* dart out and seize the much smaller gomphine, *Burmagomphus vermicularis*; and I have frequently seen *Ictinogomphus pertinax* take small libellulids such as *Brachythemis contaminata*.

At maturity, most males return to their emergence site to await the arrival of females. Males of many species will settle on stones or gravel shoals within the stream watercourse whilst others will perch on adjacent banks or bankside vegetation, including prominent sticks and overhanging branches. Once a male has grasped a receptive female, coupling takes place. Pairing initially occurs in the air but most species soon retreat to the safety of bankside vegetation or forest canopy where they remain coupled for several minutes. A number of Lindeniinae species pair briefly in the air without settling at all.

Females oviposit, unattended by the male, by striking the water's surface with their abdomens. Eggs are dropped as individual eggs or in bundles of eggs. The female of the southern United States species *Dromogomphus spinosus* (known as Black-shouldered Spinyleg) takes an unusual course: according to Sidney Dunkle, females fly fast figures of eight low over the water, dropping the abdomen at intervals to touch the surface and deposit eggs.

Philip Corbet reckons that, in general, the most primitive dragonflies can be found near the source of a watercourse and that, towards the mouth and neighbouring plains, the characteristic species become progressively more advanced. Applying this principle to the Gomphidae, the most primitive members would be expected to be found amongst the Onychogomphinae and Gomphinae subfamilies and the most modern forms in the Lindeniinae. Most lindeniines prefer pond and lake habitats,

have long flight periods, wide distributions and wide dispersal behaviour following emergence: all traits typical of the modern libellulids. This contrasts with many montane Gomphinae and Onychogomphinae which have short flight periods, very small distributions and adults which return faithfully to their breeding sites.

Subfamily Gomphinae

This subfamily is poorly defined and the differences between the two tribes into which it is divided (Gomphini and Octogomphini) are slight. The triangle of the forewing is deeper and narrower than on the hindwing and there is no anal loop. Within the subfamily, a wide variety of larval body forms can be found. Most are either round bodied (mud, sand and gravel burrowers) or slightly flattened (shallow mud burrowers).

The Gomphini tribe contains numerous genera with representatives in all major zoogeographic regions. Although there are a number present in Europe, only *Gomphus vulgatissimus* breeds in the United Kingdom; *Notogomphus praetorius* (see page 38), which has an unusually slender abdomen and no club at the tip, is one of many African examples and the genus *Stylurus* is widespread over North America and the Far East. The tribe includes several genera whose larvae have developed elongated abdomens to assist in the uptake of oxygen in soft muddy sediments, for example *Arigomphus* (North America), *Stylurus* (Holarctic and Oriental regions) and *Gastrogomphus* from China. There are a few extreme examples, such as *Labrogomphus* and *Lestinogomphus* that have dramatically extended abdominal segments (see page 20).

The Octogomphini tribe contains genera from all major zoogeographic regions except Africa. The genera *Lanthus*, *Stylogomphus* and *Trigomphus* are widespread but only one genus, *Neogomphus*, is known from the Neotropical

Keith Wilson

Male *Stylurus clathratus* in Guangdong, China.

Atsushi Sugitani

***Leptogomphus yayeyamensis* is a very rare Ryu Kyu Island endemic.**

Keith Wilson

***Trigomphus carus* in Guangdong, China.**

Keith Wilson

***Leptogomphus perforatus* in Guangdong, China.**

ANISOPTERA

AESHNOIDEA

Gomphidae

region and only one from Australia: the endemic *Hemigomphus* species. These last are small clubtails which are widely distributed along the eastern coastline. The South-East Asian genera *Leptogomphus* and *Heliogomphus* are examples of Epigomphinae, a proposed subfamily that has been largely rejected.

Subfamily Onychogomphinae

The hindwings in this subfamily have a two- or three-celled anal loop. The genus *Onychogomphus* is known from the Palaearctic, Ethiopian and Oriental regions but, of the 19 onychogomphine genera, 15 occur in Asia. The European *O. uncatus* breeds in shallow, fast

flowing riffles of streams and rivers. The brown-tipped genus *Paragomphus* is widespread with species occurring in Europe, Africa and Asia. The North American *Ophiogomphus rupinsulensis* has a very un-Clubtail colouring, the thorax being a bright emerald green and the abdomen a dark, rusty brown with yellow spots. It has been graphically described by Matt Holder as 'a gleaming green ball of light zipping over fast rivers'. The large genus *Davidius* occurs over much of the Oriental region, from China to the Himalayas.

A few members of this subfamily attain impressive sizes. Members of the genus *Megalogomphus*, as the name suggests, are very

ANISOPTERA

AESHNOIDEA

Gomphidae

This male *Onycho-gomphus uncatus* was photographed in Italy.

Megalogomphus sommeri is amongst the largest gomphids with a total length (male) of 80 mm and a wingspan of 106 mm.

Keith Wilson

large and occur in the Oriental region. The larvae of China's *Megalogomphus sommeri* (up to 50 mm in length) can overcome a sizeable fish by grasping and pulling it, by a series of strong jerks, into the coarse sand and gravel until just the tail of the fish is visible, protruding above the substrate surface. The larvae then proceed to feed on the immobilised victim.

Subfamily Hageniinae (Dragonhunters)

These very impressive dragonflies occur in North America (a single species) and the Oriental region. They are characterised by uncrossed sub- and hypertriangles in both wings and a three- or four-celled anal loop. *Sieboldius albardae* from Japan has a large abdomen, 53–66 mm in length (male), and hindwing 47–56 mm. According to Hidenori Ubukata, it has a very short flight period from the end of July to the end of August.

Hagenius brevistylus, an inquisitive, 'friendly' beast, is the sole representative of the subfamily in the New World. It is a large insect with robust, powerful-looking legs. Its favourite food is said to be other dragonflies and, according to Sidney Dunkle, they will take large aeshnid dragonflies and swallowtail butterflies. In Canada they have been observed carrying out true cannibalism by devouring their own species. In Florida, the species has a very long flight period, from April to November. The large flattened larvae sprawl on the surface of the slower sections of moderately fast streams and rivers amongst uprooted roots, leaf debris and vegetation.

Male and female *Sieboldius japonicus*, in Thailand, unusually coloured black and white.

The male *Hagenius brevistylus* has a wingspan of 106 mm.

Subfamily Lindeniinae (Tigers)

Jill Silsby and Sidney Dunkle

Tigers' wings have all sections of the discoidal cell crossed by at least one vein. (In the Gomphoidini tribe, the hypertriangle is uncrossed.) Of the two tribes within the sub-family, the Lindeniini tribe contains species from all major regions except the Nearctic. *Gomphidia* is one of the most widespread genera with representatives in the Palaearctic, Ethiopian and Oriental regions. *Gomphidia kelloggi* is a medium sized species from southern China with a total length (male) of 71–74 mm. *G. quarrei* was originally known

Keith Wilson

Male *Gomphidia kelloggi*, length 71–74 mm, in Hong Kong, China.

only from the Congo but its range is more extensive than this.

Ictinogomphus is another widespread genus with representatives in the Oriental, Ethiopian and Australasian regions. Many members of this genus and of *Sinictinogomphus* have prominent leaf-like foliations from abdominal segment VIII. *S. clavatus* is easily recognised by the large yellow half-moon shaped spots on these foliations; it is a magnificent, large-bodied, bright yellow and black species with a wide range over Indo-China, southern China, Korea, Russia and Japan. *Cinitogomphus dundoensis*, which had not previously been recorded south of the Sahara, was found in Botswana's Okavango Delta in 1991.

Most species breed in streams with moderate flows or ponds, lakes and reservoirs. Many *Gomphidia* species frequent gravel, sandy shoals and pools of submontane streams, while *Ictinogomphus* and *Sinictinogomphus* occur in lakes, ponds and slow flowing sections of streams and rivers. The males of these genera select prominent perches adjacent to the stream, pond or lake, such as sticks, reeds or even the prow of a small boat and will defend their territory against intruding males of the same species. In 1990, Peter Miller recorded

ANISOPTERA

AESHNOIDEA

Gomphidae

Male *Gomphidia quarrei* (Scarce Tiger) in the Okavango Delta, Botswana.

Male *Cinitogomphus dundoensis* (Okavango Tiger) in the Okavango Delta, Botswana.

interesting behaviour in *I. rapax*: 'during a visit to Jodhpur (India), several pairs were making brief aerial copulations, sometimes followed by guarded ovipositions — both unusual features for gomphids.' Probably the rarest *Ictinogomphus* species is one of Tasmania's endemics, *I. dobsoni*.

Many genera of the Lindeniini tribe have limpet-shaped larvae, for example *Gomphidia* and *Ictinogomphus*. The larvae nestle in the substrate surface rather than burrow. The broad flat abdomen would provide greater stability in the flowing currents which are the preferred habitat of many *Gomphidia* species. Interestingly, in Hong Kong, early instars of *G. kelloggi* are found in streams with gravel riffles but mature larvae are found in muddy sand pool sections and coarse sandy shoals.

Europe is home to just one member of the Lindeniinae, *Lindenia tetraphylla*. It has several colour forms; one almost black and, at the other extreme, one which occurs in the Arabian desert that is very pale cream or almost transparent.

Male *Ictinogomphus australis* (Australian Tiger) in a typical posture for the genus.

The Gomphoidini is a group which is currently treated as a tribe of the subfamily Lindeniinae. They have short legs and wing venational features in common but are otherwise a somewhat heterogeneous assemblage. Most members of the tribe occur in the tropical regions of the New World, where they constitute about three quarters of Clubtail species. However, more than 20 species range south into Argentina, while nine species in three genera range north into the United States, some almost to Canada. The only Clubtails on the Caribbean Islands (Cuba, Jamaica and Hispaniola only) belong to this tribe.

The majority of tropical Gomphoidini probably live in the rainforest canopy and many are known from only one or a few specimens. Most are small and furtive and little is known of them. The larva of *Desmogomphus tigrivensis* is the only Clubtail larva known to have two rows of dorsal hooks on its abdomen instead of one. *Cacoides latro* of Brazil, a large mostly black species that inhabits lakes, is the only New World Clubtail which has been found to be truly territorial (males defend territories about 9 m long from perches on the tips of reeds in the lake in the same manner as the few Old World territorial Clubtails). More is known

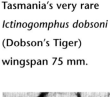

Tasmania's very rare *Ictinogomphus dobsoni* (Dobson's Tiger) wingspan 75 mm.

Allen Davies

Sidney Dunkle

Male *Phyllogomphoides stigmatus* (**Four-striped Leaftail**), with a wingspan of 85 mm.

about the three genera in the United States which have acquired English names: the Sanddragons (*Progomphus*), Forceptails (*Aphylla*) and Leaftails (*Phyllogomphoides*).

The larvae of some *Progomphus* species are the champion burrowers among dragonfly larvae. Their prowess is described on page 18.

Progomphus perithemoides, with a wingspan of only 30 mm, is the smallest Clubtail known and the genus includes some of the few gomphids with coloured (yellow or brown) spots on the wings. The most interesting features of Sanddragons, though, are adaptations used in mating. The males of most species have a split epiproct (ventral abdominal appendage); the two appendages thus created are similar in function to the two paraprocts of damselflies — a remarkable parallelism.

Three genera: *Phyllogomphoides*, *Aphylla*, and *Phyllocycla*, each with well over 20 species, show a fascinating evolutionary progression. Males of these genera have curved, pincer-like cerci (dorsal abdominal appendages). In *Phyllogomphoides* (Leaftails), the male epiproct is reduced compared to most Clubtails but is still functional in gripping the top of the female's head during mating. *Aphylla* (Forceptail) males have a vestigial epiproct but

possess posterior-lateral projections on the ventral corners of abdominal segment X which catch the upper rear rim of the female's head. The male cerci are membranous on their medial surfaces, allowing a more secure grip on the female's prothorax. In *Phyllocycla*, males have lost the functional corners of abdominal segment X and grip the female only with the cerci. However, they have sculptured ventral edges on abdominal segments VII, VIII and IX which fit against the contours of the female's face during mating.

Females of several species of Leaftails and Forceptails have been observed laying eggs by hovering or flying slowly above the water and dropping their eggs like miniature bombs. In this way they stay out of the reach of predatory fish and frogs. Lastly, the larvae of *Aphylla* and of *Phyllocycla* are unusual in that abdominal segment X is elongated into a tube that may be as long as the rest of the abdomen. This functions like an underwater snorkel, allowing the larvae to burrow deeply while breathing clean water above a mucky bottom.

ANISOPTERA

AESHNOIDEA

Gomphidae

Male *Aphylla williamsoni* (**Two-striped Forceptail**), wingspan 90 mm.

Sidney Dunkle

ANISOPTERA

AESHNOIDEA

Neopetaliidae

Family Neopetaliidae (Redspots)

This is a small family of just nine species, very uniform in wing venation and in overall aeshnoid appearance. Their eyes just touch at the top of the head; the triangles in fore- and hindwings differ only a little. All are readily identified by a series of bright red or reddish-brown spots along the costal borders. Six species in three genera (*Neopetalia*, *Phyllopetalia* and *Hypopetalia*) are known from Chile, and three species in two genera (*Austropetalia* and *Archipetalia*) from south-eastern Australia. Presumably the family predates the break-up of Gondwanaland. In size, they vary considerably: for instance, Tasmania's *Archipetalia auriculata* has a wingspan of 66 mm, while Chile's *Hypopetalia pestilens* has one of 97 mm.

There are considerable differences of opinion regarding the most suitable slot for this family and the taxonomic history of Redspots is very complex. The latest suggestions by F. C. Carle redistribute the neopetaliid species between four subfamilies, a number of tribes and several new genera. However, since these

A cold, wet *Archipetalia auriculata* in Tasmania.

Gerhard Jurzitza

***Phyllopetalia apollo* in Valdivia, Chile.**

taxonomic changes have not been generally accepted, they are not being used here.

All species inhabit cold, wet, mountainous regions and the adults fly at temperatures down to about 9°C. *Austropetalia patricia* (Waterfall Redspot) emerges in late winter when the ground is still covered in frost. *Archipetalia auriculata* (Tasmania Redspot) lives in cool highlands where mists and fog are common at any time of the year. Neopetaliid adults fly and feed together without the aggressive behaviour often noted in aeshnids. Observations on the Chilean genus *Phyllopetalia* suggest that the larval stage may last about three years.

There appear to be no published accounts of mating behaviour, and oviposition has been observed only in *Neopetalia punctata* and *Austropetalia patricia*: Carle records that he observed a single female *N. punctata* ovipositing into a small stream below a dense cave-like understorey: 'She hovered momentarily close to the water surface, turned to face shore and smacked the water surface with the apex of her abdomen, she then slowly rose while intermittently stopping and turning to navigate upward through the dense understorey.' He reckons that females may build up a large cluster of eggs before ovipositing. According to John Trueman, *A. patricia* females oviposit into moss in the

Norman Moore

splash zone around torrents and waterfalls. The eggs are worked well down into the rhizome mat but are not inserted into the plants themselves.

Information on eggs, larvae and imagos of *A. patricia* also comes to me from John Trueman: 'The eggs are sausage-shaped, like those of most Aeshnidae, and are covered for about a third of their length with a fine hexagonal patterning. They hatch to a spindle-shaped larva, about 2 mm long, with short legs. These larvae appear never to swim and, in the laboratory, will move cautiously across the bottom or sides of a dish, raising one leg at a time and testing each new grip several times before letting go with the next leg, just as if living on slippery rocks in a raging torrent. In their natural habitat, mature larvae have been seen to crawl out onto mossy rocks to feed at night and, on occasion, have been captured in pitfall traps set for terrestrial insects beside streams. Adult Waterfall Redspots spend much of their time cruising in clearings on hilltops overlooking the streams in which they breed, or resting vertically in low vegetation, but they can be remarkably fast and agile when a net is nearby!'

Family Petaluridae (Petaltails)

The family is generally considered to be the most primitive of the Anisoptera. Fossils, which some researchers identify as Petaluridae, are known from the Jurassic (195–136 mya). Today

11 living species, classified in five genera, are known. All but one (North America's *Tachopteryx thoreyi*) occur round the edges of the Pacific Basin: *Petalura* (five species in Australia); *Uropetala* (two species in New Zealand); *Phenes* (one species in South America); and *Tanypteryx* (one species in North America and one in Japan). The circum-Pacific distribution of Petaltails suggests that this family has its origin in the days when the Pacific was vastly less extensive than it is today.

Petaltails can be recognised by their large size, their well-separated eyes and by the males' anal appendages which, in the majority of species, take the form of large petal-shaped foliations. The triangles in petalurid wings are of totally dissimilar shape and the pterostigmas are exceptionally long. In colour all species are subdued black, grey or brown with nondescript markings of cream or yellowish-green. Colours are fully developed and stabilised on emergence, the dragonfly becoming progressively duller as it ages. *Tachopteryx thoreyi*'s ability to merge into its background is illustrated on page 53. In all species, the sexes are similar in colour and marking.

Petaltails are confined to lowland and mountain bogs and areas in woodland where there is extensive ground water seepage. *Petalura hesperia*, the smallest species in its genus (female wingspan 130 mm), was once

ANISOPTERA

AESHNOIDEA

Petaluridae

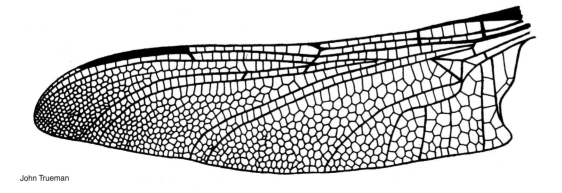

John Trueman

The hindwing of
Petalura gigantea.

ANISOPTERA

AESHNOIDEA

Petaluridae

common along creeks, seepages and bogs in the Perth area of Western Australia but, according to Allen Davies, it could have been ousted by the overuse of stream water, housing estates and, especially, stream-head orchards. It appears to be confined to a handful of colonies and even these may not survive for long.

Petalura ingentissima is probably the largest living dragonfly with, in the male, a wingspan of 145–150 mm (female 158–162 mm) and a length of 110 mm.

Another very rare Petaltail is *P. pulcherrima*. It was discovered by R. J. Tillyard in 1913 but has hardly been seen since although, after a lengthy search in all possible areas, Allen Davies finally sighted two individuals in 1990. Fortunately its last recorded sightings have been in forests which are not being logged. The New Zealand species, *Uropetala carovei* must have managed to survive the long period when the islands were covered

with ice. Davies presumes there were refugia of the kind that enabled the present flora to survive.

Females possess functional ovipositors, structurally similar to those found in zygopterans. They lay their eggs alone, often into mossy clumps on shaded stream banks or at the edge of seepages. In most species, larvae construct burrows in the substrate of such areas and can spend long periods out of water. They are large, strongly built creatures which start digging a burrow with their strong front legs and continue by bulldozing the loose soil out with their heads. Burrows are not easy to find: they are deep and descend to below stream level, even if their entrances are some distance from the stream or bog themselves (see page 19).

The burrowing, semi-aquatic state of Petaltails is thought to be the last link with the supposed fully terrestrial larvae of the Protodonata and this makes the Petaltails

A male *Petalura ingentissima* in north-east Queensland, Australia. Note the petal-shaped appendages that give the family its name.

Robert Kemp

Gerhard Jurzitza

Phenes raptor in Valdivia, Chile.

Gerhard Jurzitza

Female *Phenes raptor*, **feeding.**

unique. The long larval period, of five to six years (or perhaps considerably longer), is spent covered in mud, feeding at the mouth of the burrow on terrestrial creatures, such as spiders and cockroaches, which wander within range of the labial strike. An exception to the burrowing habit is recorded by Sidney Dunkle who made a study of *Tachopteryx thoreyi* in 1981. He found that the larvae dwelt in depressions in the soil or under wet leaves but never in burrows, nor were there any burrows in the vicinity. Interestingly, it has recently been confirmed (by Muzon and Garrison) that *Phenes raptor* is another species that does not burrow. In corroboration, Sidney Dunkle has found that the morphological structure of *P. raptor* larvae is intermediate between *T. thoreyi* and the burrowing species.

Emergence of the adult petalurid is of the 'upright' type found in all damselflies and in Gomphidae and not the 'hanging back' type of other anisopterans.

The adult petalurid seldom travels far from its breeding ground but, although recognised as sedentary insects, in flight they are powerful, elegant and swift. Indeed the largest of them, *Petalura ingentissima*, reminds one of a miniature cruise missile as it approaches and then powers away. In contradiction to this, Richard Rowe informs us that *Uropetala* are particularly vulnerable to predation by birds because they 'lack the agility in flight displayed by the smaller species and their rather poorly sclerotized structure allows easy penetration by any predator that catches them.' Petaltails remain settled a great deal of the time, some genera (e.g. *Petalura*) with their long bodies hanging at an angle of 45 degrees from the tips of branches, and others (e.g. *Tachopteryx*) which press themselves flat against boulders or tree trunks. Some species can be closely approached and there are several records of motionless observers being used as perches.

A female *Tachopteryx thoreyi* in Tennessee, USA, has settled on a pair of jeans!

ANISOPTERA

AESHNOIDEA

Petaluridae

SUBORDER ANISOPTERA SUPERFAMILY CORDULEGASTROIDEA (GOLDEN RINGS)

The superfamily displays a mixture of aeshnoid and libelluloid features. The female oviposits by stabbing her long, blunt, non-functional 'ovipositor' (an enlarged vulvar plate that extends well beyond the tip of the abdomen) into wet ground, releasing eggs with each stab. Eyes meet at a point on the top of the head. Larvae are long; the labium is spoon-shaped and carries setae. There is just one family.

Robert Thompson

A typical cordulegastroid larva, *Cordulegaster boltonii.*

Robert Thompson

A typical female cordulegastroid imago, *Cordulegaster boltonii.*

Family Cordulegastridae (Goldenrings)

Graham S. Vick

Goldenrings are presently split into two subfamilies, Cordulegastrinae and Zoraeninae and these aptly named dragonflies form a very distinctive family. All the species are large, with thorax and abdomen black, or dark brown, marked with yellow; there are never any blue, green or red body markings. The eyes are either green or blue according to species. Females are especially distinctive as they possess an enlarged vulvar lamina (plate) which is a development of the ventral surface of the eighth abdominal segment and this 'ovipositor' frequently extends beyond the tip of the abdomen. In males the peg-like outer spines on the tibia of the mid and hind legs are believed to assist them achieve the copulatory position in flight. The tibiae on the forelegs of the males bear a small apical flange which is quite different from the long keels of the superficially similar Chlorogomphidae. Close examination of the wing venation will show that the median space is uncrossed (unlike in Chlorogomphidae) and that the pterostigma is extremely long, being about eight times as long as wide. The family is unique in possessing an extra supplementary sector arising near the bridge crossvein.

The distribution of Goldenrings is almost confined to the Nearctic and Palaearctic regions. In the Americas, the family occurs from Canada to Costa Rica, but the greatest diversity is in the south-eastern USA. In Europe and Asia, many often very local species occur and two species are found in North Africa. In Asia, there is a significant region of diversity which stretches from Nepal and Assam to southern China and Japan: the family therefore just extends its range into the montane parts of

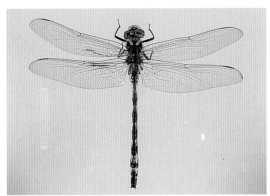

Collection of Allen Davies

Male *Zoraena diastatops*, wingspan 78 mm.

the Oriental region. As the most primitive species (those in subfamily Zoraeninae) are found in America, Heinrich Lohmann believes the origin to be there. After the break up of Laurasia about 65 million years ago, two groups of genera have survived and speciated: one in the Americas and the other in Eurasia, with an especially rich speciation in the Himalayas and in China.

All members of the family breed in running water and, in temperate regions, small woodland streams with sandy or silty beds are preferred by many species. Certain species are specialists and prefer cool springs and shallow seepages. In the Himalayas, for example, members of the genus *Neallogaster* are found up to the tree-line, and they breed in small streams and trickles of water which flow through the montane forests. In 1984, a male *N. latifrons* was seen as high as 4100 m in the Buri Gandaki of Nepal. Members of *Neallogaster* are distinctive in that they bear a hugely inflated frons, rather like that of the Himalayan *Cephalaeschna* species which occurs with them, but the reason for this is not known.

The genus *Anotogaster* also occurs in the Himalayas and in other montane regions of South-East Asia. These species are more typical of the wooded streams of the warm-temperate

regions, such as one finds in the Kathmandu Valley, where *A. nipalensis* breeds. The genus is unusual in that the males do not have angled hindwings but rounded ones as found in the libellulids; accordingly there are no auricles on the abdomen. Some species of *Anotogaster* are massive, as large as all but the largest petalurids.

In southern Europe and adjacent parts of Asia, several smaller species occur and, in Greece for example, it is possible to find four species of the family. *Thecagaster bidentata* breeds abundantly in the cool mountain streams while, in the slower more silty woodland streams, the large *Cordulegaster heros* occurs; in the north (Macedonia) its place is taken by *C. picta*. At springs in the limestone mountains, breeding in less than a centimetre of water, another small species, *Sonjagaster helladica*, can be found and this genus, which occurs between Greece and Iran, contains several very local species.

Cordulegastrid males are believed not to be territorial. Most of the stream-dwellers patrol the water and react aggressively towards other males but they do not delimit and defend territories. Females visit the stream

Female *Anotogaster sieboldii* (wingspan 135 mm) at Takeshima in Japan showing the long 'ovipositor' possessed by all female cordulegastrines.

infrequently and a patrolling male will attempt to pair with any female he sees while on patrol. If successful, the pair fly off into the treetops, or into thick cover nearer the ground, to mate.

In the primitive *Archaegaster sayi* of northern Florida and Georgia, males perch in low scrub near the breeding site which is often a densely shaded trickle. They do not patrol the water to find females but intercept them as they fly towards the stream.

Female Goldenrings behave elusively when they come to water to lay their eggs. Hovering over shady, shallow parts of the stream and holding their abdomen almost vertically, they stab the sandy or silty substrate repeatedly with their elongated 'ovipositors', thereby drilling holes in the stream-bed. The internal stylets (probes) of the organ push eggs into the newly created holes.

The very hairy larvae are dwellers in the sand and silt, especially where there is much overlying leaf litter and other detritus. They burrow into the sand by kicking debris backwards or over their backs with their powerful mid- and hindlegs. They bury themselves, with just the eyes, antennae and 'tail' protruding. Initially they live in the shallows but, as they mature, they appear to move towards somewhat deeper water. The larval stage probably never lasts less than two years and, possibly, up to five years will be required in cold, northern habitats. When more than one species occurs on a stream, it is usual for them to partition the habitat. For example, where *Thecagaster bidentata* coexists with *Cordulegaster heros* in Greece, the former occupies the cold springs and seepages, while *heros* favours the open stream. However, in areas where *bidentata* occurs alone, it will occupy the entire stream.

A mating pair of *Cordulegaster boltonii* (Goldenring) in Scotland.

SUBORDER ANISOPTERA SUPERFAMILY LIBELLULOIDEA (DIPPERS)

Regarded as the most evolutionarily advanced, this superfamily forms the dominant group and, almost everywhere in the world (tropical and temperate) they will be found in large numbers wherever there are suitable habitats. Females have non-functional ovipositors: some, while in flight, dip the tip of their abdomens into the water, releasing eggs as they do so; others flick the eggs on to surrounding herbage or even into tree holes.

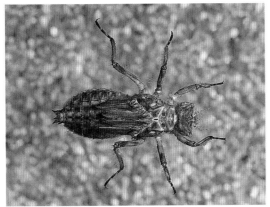

Robert Thompson

A typical libelluloid larva, *Libellula depressa*.

A typical libelluloid imago, *Crocothemis erythraea*.

Eyes are often broadly confluent. Triangles in the forewings are elongated and situated well distal to the arc; subtriangles are present in forewings only; triangles in the hindwings are situated close to the arc and are not elongated. Larvae are generally short-bodied and sturdy; the larval mask is spoon-shaped and bears setae. There are five accepted families.

Family Chlorogomphidae (Tiger Bodies)

These very large, spectacular dragonflies are confined to mountainous areas in South-East Asia and the Far East. Their wings, particularly in the case of females, are very striking being coloured to varying degrees with patches and whorls of orange, yellow or black. The abdomen is black with golden rings, although the rings are fewer and less prominent than those of the cordulegastrids.

The name of the family, and of its species, is misleading: there is no relationship to Gomphidae. Until recently the genus *Chlorogomphus* was placed in a subfamily (Chlorogomphinae) within Cordulegasteridae. However, the subfamily has been promoted to family status and moved to the superfamily Libelluloidea. Although there are many features similar to cordulegasterids (the body colour is one), there are clear differences: the shape of the triangle differs between fore- and hindwings, the former being equilateral and the latter transversely elongated; the median space is crossed; the hindwing is broadened and possesses an anal loop. Most importantly, females do not possess the long distinctive non-functional 'ovipositors' that are such a feature of female cordulegasterids.

Tiger Bodies are very large and very spectacular. Their eyes are large and meet, or barely meet, at a point on the top of the head. Wings, particularly in the case of females, are their

ANISOPTERA

LIBELLULOIDEA

Chlorogomphidae

ANISOPTERA

LIBELLULOIDEA

Chlorogomphidae

most striking features: the wings of a female *Chlorogomphus papilio* from China are hyaline with whorls of orange and yellow; another species has wings of bright amber and another of orange, bordered with black. So intense is the colour of the wings of a female *C. xanthoptera* (an Indian species found in the Western Ghats) that a yellow shadow may be seen on the white roads as it passes overhead. One of the smartest is undoubtedly *C. nakamurai* from Taiwan and there is reputed to be another, unnamed, species somewhere in the same country with bright orange and brown wings.

In most species it is only the female whose wings are brightly coloured, those of the males being generally hyaline although, in one or two cases, the males' wings are equally colourful.

The genus *Chlorogomphus* contains some 40 species recorded from mountainous areas in South-East Asia and the Far East: India, Myanmar, Assam, Nepal, Sikkim, Thailand, Japan, China, Taiwan, Malaysia, Indonesia and Vietnam. They are found at high altitudes, generally between 2400 and 4260 m and never below approximately 900 m. According to

As in most members of the genus, the male *Chlorogomphus brunneus* has hyaline wings.

Fraser, who made a study of three of the Indian species, they soar hundreds of feet above the treetops where, with the aid of binoculars, he saw them 'performing the most graceful evolutions, not unlike the soaring, wheeling flight of vultures'. At other times, both sexes will patrol mountain roads, apparently mistaking the glistening sunny surface for rivers. Their flight is slow and they appear to glide rather than fly. They are exceedingly difficult to find, have proved hard to capture and almost impossible to photograph. Again, according to Fraser, mating takes place in the jungle, far from water and males probably never return to their parent streams after emergence. The larvae develop in the deep pools of fast running, sometimes torrential, mountain streams and burrow deeply in sand, often at the foot of a small waterfall.

Allen Davies records that, in 1993, a friend of his 'rediscovered' the amazing dragonfly *Chlorogomphus papilio* (female wingspan 145 mm) somewhere close to the borders of Vietnam, Laos, Thailand, Myanmar and China. It has been described as the 'greatest' of all living species, being only about 20 mm less in wingspan than the two monsters (*Petalura ingentissima* and *Tetracanthagyna plagiata*) but with much broader wings'.

Female *Chlorogomphus nakamurai* (wingspan 124 mm) from Vietnam.

Collection of Allen Davies

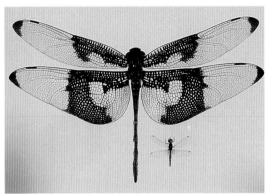

Collection of Allen Davies

Female *Chlorogomphus papilio* (wingspan 145 mm) with *Nannophya pygmaea* to provide a comparison.

Family Macromiidae (River Emeralds)

This group of dragonflies has been elevated from subfamily level within Corduliidae to a family in its own right. Members of the family are best known for their long, spidery legs. With the exception of the genus *Didymops*, which have brown bodies, the thorax is dark metallic green, usually marked with yellow humeral and/or dorsal stripes; wings are long and relatively narrow (clearly adapted for fast, sustained flight); abdomens are generally glossy black, each species marked with a distinctive pattern of golden patches and rings. Males' wings are angled at the base. Larvae also have very long, spidery legs which they use to clamber about in the roots and weeds at the water's edge. In Borneo, Bert Orr witnessed the spidery larvae of *Macromia orientalis* rising to the surface of a quiet backwater and plucking its prey therefrom. There are three genera: *Didymops* (Brown Cruiser) which is confined to North America; *Epophthalmia*, containing very large species that are present in South-East Asia; and the big cosmopolitan genus, *Macromia*, with over a hundred species.

Males are fast, tireless fliers and cover long stretches of shady rivers and streams, or the shorelines of lakes and large ponds. Females spend little time at the water, only appearing there to mate and lay their eggs. Oviposition is carried out on the wing, the female tapping the water with the tip of her abdomen to release her eggs as she flashes by.

Like corduliids, River Emeralds settle by hanging almost vertically in the manner of aeshnids (apart from *Didymops*, which, according to Sidney Dunkle, hang obliquely). As evening approaches *Macromias* make for the tops of nearby conifers. Early in the morning at Cape Vidal in northern Natal we observed *M. bifasciata* flying out from the treetops and engaging in frenetic activity as they broke their fast before moving on to their watery beats. At Lake Biwa, the largest of Japan's lakes, the large *M. amphigena* was seen skimming just inches above the gently lapping water. In Hong Kong, Keith Wilson has watched *M. urania* soaring at about 5–10 m, usually in sheltered spots close to woodland. One of the rarest members of the genus is *M. euterpe*, a northern Borneo endemic. Matti Hämäläinen records watching females laying their eggs in a torrential stream below the Langanan Fall and,

ANISOPTERA

LIBELLULOIDEA

Macromiidae

This male *Macromia bifasciata* in South Africa, with its long, narrow wings, is one of very few *Macromia* to have settled long enough and low enough to be photographed.

Male *Epophthalmia elegans* (wingspan c. 110 mm) in Yunnan, China.

Allen Davies

on another occasion, 'saw a female corduliid, most likely this species, laying eggs on the wet wooden balcony of the Old Fellowship Hostel after a heavy downpour.'

The female of Australia's *M. tillyardi* is one of the few Macromias to have colour on the wings: her wings are suffused with amber from nodus to tip. F. C. Fraser recorded that this species frequently patrolled along railway cuttings. China's *M. berlandi* is another species with coloured wings: both sexes have amber at the base. There is one word that describes Macromias: splendid — and Europe's *M. splendens* takes its name from it.

The genus *Epophthalmia* has five species distributed over South-East Asia of which the most widespread is *E. elegans*. This is a magnificent creature of mighty proportions, with a body length of 75 mm (males), 81 mm (females). Its exceptionally fast and apparently ceaseless flight makes both capture and photography almost impossible.

Family Synthemistidae (Southern Emeralds)

This ancient family peaked about 80 million years ago and still has 32 representatives (placed in just four genera) living in Australia, New Guinea and New Caledonia. One New Caledonian species, *Synthemis macrostigma*, just makes it into Fiji. Habitats vary from boggy seepages and swamps, through stagnant riverine pools and sluggish streams to, in one or two cases, faster streams and rapid rivers. The four genera are not easily distinguished from each other and, indeed, the key in J. A. L. Watson *et al*'s *The Australian Dragonflies*, runs direct from subfamily to species, avoiding the present generic boundaries.

Most Southern Emeralds are rather small and lightly built though there are exceptions. The thorax is furry and the abdomen is as narrow as many of the larger Australian damselflies: from a distance they look as though they might be one of those damselflies which rest with the wings held out away from the body. Abdomens are generally green with yellow at the sides.

Larvae are broad, hairy and hold the mask up in front of the face. John Trueman suggests the last feature (which is shared by the neopetaliid *Neopetalia punctata*) is 'just an adaptation for living in boggy seepages or some other equally muddy situations'. The larva of *Synthemis eustalacta*, a bog dweller, buries itself in dry sand and is capable of withstanding considerable loss of body fluid. At the beginning of the dry Australian summer, female *S. leachii* lay their eggs in drying mud, the eggs apparently not hatching until the water level is sufficient to provide suitable larval habitat.

At close quarters adults can be simply separated from corduliids by two features: first, the antenodals on their hindwings are alternately thick and thin and, second, the median cell is crossed with from one to five veins. The first feature is strikingly evident in Western Australia's *Synthemis macrostigma occidentalis*: because of the very dark streaks running from the base of the wings, the thick antenodals show deep yellow while the thin ones are barely visible. This particular species is

Female *Synthemis macrostigma occidentalis* (wingspan 85 mm) showing the alternate thick and thin antenodals in the hindwings.

Male *Eusynthemis nigra* in Paluma Forest, near Townsville, Queensland, Australia.

also unusual in that the large pterostigmas are deep red and the abdomen is non-metallic brown. The beautiful *Eusynthemis nigra* from Queensland is more typical in colour with a lot of green dorsally and bright yellow at the sides; the species occurs in rainforest and appears able to survive in small ponds of dubious purity.

Synthemis regina is of particular interest because of the way the female uses a secondary, or neo-ovipositor, formed by the extended valves of Segment VIII to lay her eggs, after the manner of a cordulegasterid. John Trueman records: 'The female hovers over shallow water

at the edge of a muddy bottomed pond, with the abdomen pointing vertically downward. Instead of dropping eggs onto the water or simply washing them off as most libelluloids do, the female *S. regina* plants the eggs into the bottom mud by dropping vertically and spearing the rearmost 2–4 abdominal segments into the ooze. This is done repeatedly for a minute or so, then the female flies off to a tree and rests.' The unusual egg of *Synthemis regina* is shown on page 15.

Choristhemis flavoterminata, only found in eastern parts of Australia, has a very narrow abdomen, a very weak flight and the habit of sometimes resting with its wings half closed: it looks so much like a zygopteran that it is readily mistaken for one until caught and the wings examined. *Synthemiopsis gomphomacromioides*, a Tasmania endemic, is small (wingspan 60 mm) and has a dark abdomen with pairs of tiny yellow dots and a broader yellow patch near the tip; the hindwings bear unusual short, club-shaped, diverging black marks at the base and small black spots at the nodus. As its name suggests, it is very similar to the South American genus *Gomphomacromia*.

ANISOPTERA

LIBELLULOIDEA

Synthemistidae

The Tasmanian endemic *Synthemiopsis gomphomacromioides* (wingspan 60 mm).

Allen Davies

ANISOPTERA

LIBELLULOIDEA

Corduliidae

Family Corduliidae (Emeralds)

This is a family of small to large dragonflies which generally have metallic green or black bodies and emerald eyes (often brown in immature specimens). In some species the bodies are marked with shades of yellow. Their features are something of a mix between Cordulegastroidea and Libelluloidea, showing a few characters of the former but more of the latter: most corduliid males have angled hindwings and auricles on the second abdominal segment, though a few genera (e.g. *Epicordulia, Hemicordulia, Procordulia*) do not. There are no primary antenodals in the hindwing, all being of equal thickness; there are no cross veins in the basal space; the triangles in fore- and hindwings are of dissimilar shape. The female's nonfunctional ovipositor is short. When perched, Emeralds generally hang suspended vertically in the manner of cordulegastrids and aeshnids. The family is divided into six subfamilies and their members are distributed around the world.

Subfamily Cordulephyinae

These small dragonflies are found in the east and north-east of Australia and are contained in just one genus, *Cordulephya*. They are particularly interesting in that they hold their wings closed over the top of the body, in the manner of damselflies. They breed in smallish rivers, streams or creeks in very out of the way locations and, consequently, little has been written about their behaviour.

Cordulephya montana is the biggest species with a wingspan of 54 mm, that of the other three being about 40 mm (*C. pygmaea* 45 mm). The thorax and abdomen have a background of shiny green marked with a variety of yellow stripes and rings between the segments. Wings are rounded at the tips and (another similarity

Ian Endersby

Male *Cordulephya pygmaea*, wingspan 45 mm, in Melbourne, Australia.

to zygopterans) the base of the hindwing is not broader than in the forewing; triangles in all wings are angled on the costal side and the anal loop has two to three cells.

Cordulephya montana is a late spring and summer species but the three others emerge in late summer and autumn; *C. pygmaea* emerges in late March and is known to fly until the first frosts of late June. According to John Trueman: 'The only dragonflies likely to be on the wing here in Canberra [in June] are a few aeshnids and coenagrionids which overwinter, and those peculiar *Cordulephya pygmaea* no doubt perched on the trunks of trees, wings tight together, feeling the cold but enjoying every minute of it!'.

This species is widespread and common all over the south-east of the Australian mountain region and down to the coast. It is little known because, as Trueman puts it: 'people don't go looking for small dragonflies 20 ft up the trunks of trees at this time of the year'. *C. divergens* is another species which flies very late.

Subfamily Corduliinae

This, the largest of the subfamilies with 21 genera, is a trans-global group of medium sized, metallic green, brown or black species which are sometimes scantily adorned with yellow (most *Epitheca* species are nonmetallic brown although the species that occurs in Eurasia, *E. bimaculata* is black with bright yellow marking). In most genera the wings are hyaline; there are less than three crossveins in the cubital space; the sectors of the arc diverge from the origin; and the anal loop is well developed. Habitats include both running and stagnant waters.

There is confusion in the naming of a number of genera: *Epitheca* used to be confined to the Eurasian *E. bimaculata* but today most, if not all, of the American *Tetragoneuria* species are generally known as *Epitheca*, as is the former *Epicordulia princeps*. America's 'Baskettails' (*Tetragoneuria*, or *Epicordulia* and *Epitheca*) are unusual in that, in almost all cases, the costal edge of all four wings is strikingly marked with brown. Some of the latter species are so similar to each other that Sidney Dunkle likens them to the 'little brown jobs' (LBJs) well known to birdwatchers! The large and spectacular Prince Baskettail, *Epitheca princeps*, presented a majestic sight as it leisurely flew up and down over a large lake in Bays Mountain Park — a few beats of the wings alternated with short glides on slightly raised wings. The Eurasian *Epitheca bimaculata* is also a lake dweller and equally tireless and elusive (a female is on page 14).

The niche of the rare and very beautiful north Australian species *Pentathemis membranulata* (wingspan 57 mm) is a little unusual — rapidly flowing water, about one to three feet deep, running through reeds and sheltered by pandanus palms. Allen Davies found them in a side runnel between two falls on the Katherine

river in the Arnhem Land area and describes how they flew ceaselessly over the water with great rapidity in 'zigzag circles'. They appeared to fly only when the temperature was above 40°C and Davies never saw one perched.

The Northern hemisphere genus *Somatochlora* contains the largest number of species (some 40 or so), with a Palaearctic and Nearctic distribution and a small number penetrating into the Oriental. Some of them, e.g. *S. arctica* and *S. alpestris*, are boreo-alpine, being found in the Alps and the northern regions of Europe and Asia. *S. sahlbergi* has the most northerly breeding range of any odonate and is more or less confined to Lapland, Siberia,

ANISOPTERA

LIBELLULOIDEA

Corduliidae

Male *Epitheca princeps* (Prince Baskettail), wingspan 90 mm.

Somatochlora semicircularis was common by mountain ponds in British Colombia, Canada.

Alaska and the Yukon in north-western Canada. Breeding in cold, deep water (according to Sydney and Robert Cannings), it is a little known species and considered a rare one, but this could well be due to the inhospitable regions in which it occurs. Europe's *S. metallica* is illustrated on page 60.

Hemicordulia is another large genus, this time with a distribution covering East Africa, Mauritius and Madagascar, South-East Asia, Australia and the islands in between. The Australian *H. tau* is a species that can be encountered in the most urban areas and Ian Endersby has had their larvae climbing the walls of his house prior to emergence. Female *H. australiae* have often been recorded ovipositing on shiny cars and Endersby has witnessed one attempting to do so on the shiny tiled floor of the Norfolk Island airport!

Much work has been carried out in England to discover the exact breeding requirements of *Cordulia aenea*. It appears to prefer the shallow edges of acid ponds with plenty of broad-leafed woodland nearby to provide the substrate of leaf-litter in which the larvae like to hide. The closely related *C. shurtleffi* is present in Canada in areas where the same conditions prevail. Although most members of the subfamily are daytime flyers, at least one species is known to be crepuscular: *Neurocordulia virginiensis* which breeds on the Santa Fe River.

Cordulia aenea (Downy Emerald) on Thursley Common, Surrey, England.

Subfamily Gomphomacromiinae

Despite its name, this subfamily is not closely related to macromiids and even less closely to gomphids. There are 13 genera spread around Australia, South Africa, Madagascar, South America and one, *Oxygastra curtisii* (Orange-spotted Emerald), which is found in south-western Europe. As usual, wing venation distinguishes them from other corduliids: there are less than three crossveins in the cubital space; the anal loop is long and narrow, two cells wide; the costal border of all triangles is straight; and the triangles and subtriangles are uncrossed. They generally fly fast and low over the water making the acute turns that are recognisably corduliid.

Gerhard Jurzitza

Neocordulia setifera in Parque Nacional Iguazu, Argentina.

One of the Australian species, *Lathrocordulia metallica* was aptly named by R. J. Tillyard in 1911: 'lathro' means 'secretive'. A few years ago Allen Davies found a colony of them in south-west Australia near an almost inaccessible stream at the bottom of a very steep cliff which was completely deprived of sun by overhanging trees.

Another member of the subfamily, *Syncordulia venator* (Ferruginous Emerald) is unusual for a corduliid. Most of the family are

The very striking female *Syncordulia venator* at Hermanus, Cape Province, South Africa.

A female *Oxygastra curtisii* in the Dordogne, France.

metallic green or black but this species is basically reddish with intrusive tongues of metallic green on the thorax and pale yellow spots and black bands on the abdomen. This striking insect is only recorded from south-western Cape Province in South Africa.

The western Mediterranean species *Oxygastra curtisii* (Orange-spotted Emerald) enjoys a fragile extension into other parts of Europe, where it is very local and susceptible to extinction. It disappeared from Belgium, the Netherlands and southern England in the 1950s but was later rediscovered in the first two countries. The species requires unpolluted running water in which to breed and is found

in slow-moving, tree-lined rivers with muddy bottoms. At a well-reeded reservoir in the Dordogne region of France, adults were flying in the shallow borders of the lake close to where the feeding stream entered. A female was actually laying her eggs among the dense reeds at the side and not in the stream itself.

Subfamily Idionychinae (Asian Emeralds)

This is a subfamily of typical metallic emeralds that is confined to eastern Asia where they inhabit deep jungle or well wooded hill streams. The main differences between these and other corduliids is that they have unusually large heads and small thoraces. The first two or three postnodals in fore- and hindwings are not always continued into the space below. There are just two genera, *Idionyx* and *Macromidia*.

There are some 26 species of *Idionyx* most of which are very local, the exception is *I. yolanda* which has a wide range over East Indies, Malaysia and Thailand. They are small, elusive corduliids (abdomen *c.* 30 mm) with a weak, erratic flight and they are seldom seen far from deep virgin jungle. In Hong Kong, according to Keith Wilson, *I. victor* may be seen at most

ANISOPTERA

LIBELLULOIDEA

Corduliidae

Idionyx burliyarensis, wingspan 72 mm.

Collection of Allen Davies.

times of the day, including dawn and dusk, and in fine or cloudy conditions, flying high in the forest canopy. During the low light periods, 'The adults become hyperactive, flitting around in shady areas in short erratic beats a few feet above the ground or water. The proportion of females caught in these aggregations appears to be far higher than the number of males.'

Macromidia species appear on the wing only on cloudy days. They are larger than their cousins and, in most species, their flight is rapid and more direct. They are said to be crepuscular, most often flying at dusk and early dawn for brief intervals. Referring to *M. donaldi*, Fraser comments on their 'brief, wild and extremely rapid evolutions in the air, before vanishing again to their retreats in the jungle canopy'.

Bert Orr, who spent several years working in what was then North Borneo, saw the endemic *M. fulva* on only one occasion: 'an hour before dusk a swarm of tenerals suddenly appeared and flew low over the water near a rapid for about 20 minutes and then, as suddenly, disappeared'.

In 1995 Keith Wilson described a new species, *M. ellenae*, from a very small, restricted area in the New Territories, Hong Kong. He found adults

Macromidia ellenae is unusual among this genus in having yellow spots on the thorax.

Keith Wilson

roosting 'over or adjacent to their well-shaded stream breeding sites or flying erratically over the water's surface or in adjacent clearings'.

Subfamily Idomacromiinae (Central African Emeralds)

This is a small subfamily represented by one genus, *Idomacromia*, which is found only in the forests of Central and West Africa. Just two species are currently known: *I. proavita*, found throughout the rainforests of Zaire, Gabon, Cameroon and the Ivory Coast and the smaller *I. lieftincki* which appears to be restricted to Gabon and Senegal but, according to Graham Vick, is almost certainly more widespread. They are small metallic emeralds and hard to find, although being specialist rainforest insects, it is probable that they are underrecorded rather than rare.

The wing venation of *Idomacromia* differs from *Macromia* in that the anal loop is narrow and elongate, with a midrib; like *Macromia*, the discoidal cell in the hindwing is distal to the level of the arculus whereas in other corduliids found in the region, it is situated at the level of the arculus. According to Graham Vick and David Chelmick: 'The general appearance of the imagos is strongly reminiscent of the genus *Somatochlora*. In *I. proavita* the males have a strongly iridescent green thorax and green eyes; the abdomen is darker and duller, although the hint of iridescent green is still present. The female is similar, if duller, than the male but possesses extensive dark markings at the base of the wings and strong yellow coloration on the underside of the abdomen. She bears an unusual 'pseudo-ovipositor' which is a development of the sternites of segment VIII and reaches almost to the end of the abdomen; it consists of two large triangular plates which touch at their bases but diverge markedly at their tips. We observed a female ovipositing in a

David Chelmick

Idomacromia proavita (length 58 mm, wingspan 86 mm) on Mount Kupe, Cameroon.

Collection of Allen Davies

Neophya rutherfordi, wingspan 54 mm.

damp seepage in upland rainforest at an altitude in excess of 1200 m. A male was seen patrolling a small shaded stream, with a sandy bed, in lowland forest, at an altitude of approximately 300 m. Both insects were observed in the middle of the day.'

In the past, observers have mentioned the erratic flight of *Idomacromia* males; and this is now confirmed: 'Prior to capture the male was observed flying in a most erratic manner along the stream, in deep shade'.

Subfamily Neophyinae

This final subfamily consists only of *Neophya rutherfordi*, a species which is said to resemble the Asian *Idionyx* but, according to Allen Davies, 'looks like nothing we are familiar with'. It is a small, very elusive and very untypical corduliid but known from a number of west African countries where it appears to be confined to the indigenous rainforest belt and probably has a similar distribution to that of the previous subfamily. The base of the hindwing is broad and amber-coloured to the fifth or sixth postnodal. The triangle, in all wings, may be angled on the costal side, making it four-sided (and perhaps may be mistaken therefore as a candidate for a libellulid Tetrathemistinae).

Family Libellulidae (Perchers)

This is the largest anisopteran family and several attempts have been made over the years to divide it into a meaningful set of subfamilies. With over 1000 species, they dominate the odonate fauna in most parts of the world and many individual species are widespread, occurring in more than one zoogeographical region. Representatives flourish in tropical, subtropical and temperate climes, and they come in a wide variety of shapes, sizes and colours. Most Perchers rest in a horizontal position, although there are exceptions, and the majority dart off to capture food and immediately return to the same perch. They are seldom metallic (members of Zygonychinae (Cascaders) are an exception). Males often pruinose red or blue as they attain maturity as do, in some cases, females if they survive into 'old age'. The hindwings of all Perchers are rounded at the base and there are no auricles on the second abdominal segment.

Subfamily Tetrathemistinae (Primitives)

Primitives are so called because their wing venation has characters of primitive odonata. The subfamily contains the libellulid genera in which the forewing discoidal cell (triangle) is

ANISOPTERA

LIBELLULOIDEA

Libellulidae

four-sided. A dragonfly's discoidal cell (see page 11) is divided by a strong crossvein into Hypertriangle and Triangle, making the latter three-sided. In Tetrathemistinae, however, this strut vein separating the two portions does not run straight, but at a tangent, so that it meets the anterior median vein before the apex, thus making the 'triangle' four-sided!

It is by no means a certainty that all libellulid genera with four-sided triangles are closely related to each other. Previous authors, including F. Ris (1909–19) and Fraser (1957), battled with the problem of linking triangle four-sidedness with other wing and body features in order to produce a workable taxonomic scheme, but with little success. John Trueman suggests that a plausible hypothesis might be that there have been three separate origins of four-sidedness: one in Old World *Tetrathemis* and its allies, one in Old World *Bironides* and *Microtrigonia*, and one in the New World *Nannothemis* group. A rival hypothesis might be that four-sidedness was the primitive condition for Libellulidae.

Tetrathemis species are of moderate size but *Nannophlebia* are small (about 20 mm long). All the latter are black, brown or olive with

yellow markings and could be mistaken for small corduliids, particularly for *Cordulephya*, if they did not perch with their wings held well away from the body. Five tetrathemistine species in two genera (*Tetrathemis* and *Nannophlebia*) occur in Australia though only *N. risi* is at all well known. *N. eludens*, named by R. J. Tillyard in 1908, 'for its peculiar elusive zigzag flight', occurs sporadically in northern Queensland while the remaining *Nannophlebia* species have localised distributions in the far north-west. The only Australian *Tetrathemis* is *T. irregularis*, a common species in New Guinea which just makes it into the extreme north of Queensland.

Hypothemis hageni is an interesting species that is endemic to the Fijian island of Vanua Levu. Ris considered it to be the most primitive libellulid but this hypothesis is questioned by Nick Donnelly. Its closest relative is *Tapeinothemis boharti* of the Solomon Islands.

Only two genera (*Tetrathemis* and *Notiothemis*) occur in southern Africa although others occur in west, central and east Africa and several more in Madagascar. Although *Tetrathemis polleni* is fairly widespread in East and southern Africa, it is not easy to find. Its chosen habitat seems invariably a small, dirty piece of water overhung by a large broad-leafed tree. Mature males (totally pruinosed pale blue and with smoky-black patches on their wings) hold territory on the tip of a particular twig of a tree or of a particular blade of reedmace. On the approach of a female (black and yellow with, generally, hyaline wings) there is a flurry of male activity ending in one of the males being successful and transporting his captive mate to his own territory where a very brief copulation takes place. Females eject their eggs in the normal libellulid fashion but, instead of releasing them over water, they deposit them in clutches on the underside of the piece of

Male *Tetrathemis polleni* (African Primitive), wingspan 57 mm, in Mpumalanga, South Africa.

vegetation upon which copulation took place, that is on the underside of leaves in overhanging branches, or of the blade of reedmace in the centre of the pond, or even (according to Jochen Lempert when writing about *T. godiardi* in West Africa) onto the thread of a spider's web. On hatching, the tiny larvae drop into the water below.

The other southern African member of the subfamily, *Notiothemis jonesi* has a slightly different habitat: shaded streams or heavily vegetated ponds leading off them. A small colony has been present on such a pond in the centre of the Botanical Gardens in Pietermaritzburg for several years but are seldom noticed by visitors due to their subdued colouring, retiring habits and general immobility. On being disturbed by the flash of a camera they retire to the top of sheltering trees and will only return after an hour or two. The East African species *N. robertsi* was observed by Philip Corbet 'hovering just above the surface of a pool and placing its eggs on an exposed stone'.

Micromacromia species, which are restricted to more central areas of Africa, can be mistaken for small corduliids with their green eyes and greenish bodies.

Of the Asian members of the family, *Tetrathemis irregularis* is the most widespread but *T. platyptera*, a forest species, is the most well known. The latter is a unusual looking little dragonfly, bearing scant resemblance to its African congeners. Fraser records that females 'deposit their eggs on objects overhanging water from which the newly hatched larvae drop into their future habitat' and adds that he had seen 'a mass of eggs deposited on a leaf and, on other occasions into moss covering logs or trunks of trees standing well out of the water'. He describes the species' watery habitat as 'small, often dirty and stagnant pools in the submontane areas of India and Burma'.

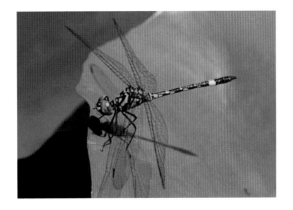

Male *Notiothemis jonesi* (Jones's Primitive), wingspan 46 mm, Pietermaritzburg, South Africa.

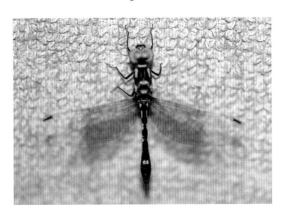

Male *Tetrathemis platyptera* in Thailand.

ANISOPTERA

LIBELLULOIDEA

Libellulidae

Subfamily Brachydiplacinae (Dwarves)

The 25 genera making up this subfamily are spread around Africa, eastern Asia, Australia, Central and South America and many of the islands in between. They are a somewhat heterogeneous collection of genera that Allen Davies suggests includes several unrelated groups which are presently placed together until they can receive the expert study needed to sort them out.

Dwarves are very small to medium sized species which retain most of the primitive venational characters although the arc is between antenodals 1 and 2, the triangle in the hindwing is distal to the arc and a small anal loop is present.

ANISOPTERA

LIBELLULOIDEA

Libellulidae

Keith Wilson

The tiny *Nannophyopsis clara* in Hong Kong, China.

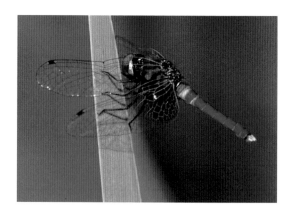

Male *Nannophya pygmaea* in Japan.

Female *Nannophya pygmaea* in Japan.

Nannophyopsis clara of China is the world's smallest known dragonfly. This rare creature has an abdomen of about a thumbnail's length (15 mm) and the span of its forewing, which is longer than the hindwing, is 34 mm. Unlike most libellulids, *N. clara* has a body of metallic green and eyes that are brilliant green: it resembles a midget corduliid. The wings are suffused with amber at the base. According to Keith Wilson the male's genitalia are corduliine too.

Other small species belong to a widely spread genus, *Nannophya*, in which there are four species, with a number of subspecies. They inhabit areas of swamp and marsh and the brilliant red (in Old World species) males

are conspicuous as they perch on the tips of low-lying grasses. The brown and yellow females appear to mimic wasps in colour, in their mode of flight and even to the extent of 'buzzing' as they fly. I have seen two *Nannophya* species: *N. pygmaea* in Japan and *N. australis* in Australia. Obviously closely related is the North American species *Nannothemis bella*, the male of which pruinoses pale blue but which inhabits very similar calcareous pieces of marsh and bog.

There are a few larger members of the subfamily, including a number of the 35 species of *Micrathyria*. Most of these occur in Central and South America but three make it into the south of the United States: *M. aequalis* occurs from southern Texas to Ecuador and is present in the West Indies; *M. didyma*, according to Sidney Dunkle, was first found in the Miami area in 1985 and has not yet spread further; it also occurs in the West Indies and from northern Mexico to Ecuador. It is a dark species and, since males perch over water in the shade, they are inconspicuous. The third species, *M. hageni* occurs in Central America and extends into Texas. *Uracis imbuta*, also from South and Central America does not perch horizontally but suspends itself like a ramrod down the stem of tall grasses.

A female *Uracis imbuta* in the Amazon Camp, Peru.

Tyriobapta torrida in Bori Phut, southern Thailand.

ANISOPTERA

LIBELLULOIDEA

Libellulidae

Female *Hemistigma albipuncta* at Cape Vidal in northern Kwa-Zulu Natal, South Africa.

An almost mature male *Chalcostephia flavifrons* at Cape Vidal in northern Kwa-Zulu Natal, South Africa.

South-East Asia's *Tyriobapta torrida* is the size of a medium sized *Sympetrum* and is a striking dragonfly with a blue body, deep black patches at the base of the hindwings and very unusual eyes. *Brachydiplax chalybea*, from the same area, is catholic in its habitat requirements and is one of only a few species that will tolerate brackish water. Australia's *B. denticauda australis* is similarly catholic and generally found in still sluggish water.

There are not many members of the subfamily in southern Africa but those that do occur are generally easy to recognise. There are two species in the genus *Hemistigma*, one in Madagascar and the other which I have seen in Botswana's Okavango Swamp and in The Gambia where they were very common. Both sexes are yellow and black as immatures and pruinose blue as they mature but, at all stages, they can be recognised by their pterostigmas which are neatly and exactly divided into two halves, one black and the other white. The monotypic *Chalcostephia flavifrons* is another species that is fairly widespread in tropical and subtropical Africa (Nigeria, Cameroon, Malawi, Mozambique, Botswana and Kwa-Zulu Natal). The male is a blue species which can be recognised by its short body, narrow wings and yellow face below a shining green frons.

ANISOPTERA

LIBELLULOIDEA

Libellulidae

The widespread *Leucorrhinia dubia* (male) in Scotland.

A female *Leucorrhinia dubia* in Cheshire, England.

A male *Leucorrhinia glacialis* in Kananaskis, British Columbia, Canada.

The very different-looking *Leucorrhinia caudalis* in central France.

Subfamily Leucorrhininae (White-faces)

Members of this subfamily, except *Austrothemis* (southern Australia and Tasmania), are confined to the northern hemisphere. They are mostly medium to small, with white faces. The venation is open; the sectors of the arculus separate at its base; the base of the triangle in the hindwing is at the level of the arculus; and the cubital space is crossed. Eggs generally take several weeks to hatch and larval development takes two years to complete.

Members of the genus *Leucorrhinia* are circumboreal. They are widely distributed, although most species inhabit northern bog pools with an acidic base. *Leucorrhinia dubia* is one of the most widespread, occurring from Britain, through Siberia to Japan. Exceptionally, according to Robert Cannings in his *Dragonflies of British Columbia*, *L. intacta* is 'not at home in northern ponds and lakes; it is an insect of warm waters' and is known as far south as California. He also tells us that *L. glacialis*, when the sun shines, 'will fill the air but, should a cloud obscure the sun, even for a minute, the insects will alight in long, closely packed lines on fallen logs.' They are delicate and very pretty little insects, most of them black with red (mature males,) or yellow (immature males and females) markings on the abdomen and with a dark triangular patch at the base of the hindwings. There are exceptions to the above colour scheme: for example, Europe's *L. albifrons* and *L. caudalis* are black, but as they mature, they pruinose pale blue or white at the base of the abdomen. The latter is unusual in that the pterostigmas are creamy white above but dark brown on the underside. White-faces are renowned for their unwariness; they are among the easiest of species to approach and photograph.

The genus *Celithemis* contains some very beautiful species. Although they do not have white faces, they somehow look like members of this subfamily and they are remarkable for their attractively marked wings. *C. ornata*, for instance, could well be taken for a *Leucorrhinia* at first glance, with its black and red body and small dark area at the base of the hindwing. They occur in much warmer climes, in eastern and southern parts of the USA. Interesting information on the behaviour of *C. elisa* (Calico Pennant), comes from Sidney Dunkle: males await females, facing away from the water with the object of intercepting them before they reach open water; females will deposit a total of 700–800 eggs during a single session.

The Australian endemic genus *Austrothemis*, with the single species *A. nigrescens* is, according to Allen Davies, unlikely to be related to the other genera in the subfamily although it has structural similarities. It is, as he puts it, 'needing a new place in the classification'.

Male *Celithemis elisa* (Calico Pennant) in Tennessee, USA.

Subfamily Libellulinae (Chasers)

This is a totally cosmopolitan subfamily made up of 275 species within 29 genera. The genus *Orthetrum* alone, which is confined to the Old World, has more than 80 species and *Libellula*, found only in the northern hemisphere, has 37. They provide material sufficient to fill a book in themselves and it is certainly impossible to do them justice here.

In size they are mostly medium to large. Venation is a mix of primitive and recent: the triangle in the forewing is short on the costal side; there is an anal loop. The distal antenodal is variable, sometimes extending into the sub-costal space and sometimes not.

It appears that true blue pigmentation is not present in these insects, but red in all its shades and brilliance is evident in many of them. Males sometimes pruinose red but more often blue. Most male *Orthetrum* (Skimmer) species gain pruinescense as they mature (the transformation of *O. cancellatum* is illustrated on page 26). In Europe and Africa we are accustomed to them turning blue and the sight of *O. pruinosum* in India, with its purplish bloom, comes as a complete surprise. Even redder red species (*O. chrysis, O. testaceum*) occur in various parts of South-East Asia. In Australia, too, although there is one species of blue *Orthetrum* (*O. caledonicum*), there is also the brilliant red *O. villosovittatum*. The widespread *O. sabina* occurs throughout most of Asia and also in Australia and its somewhat larger but similar-looking relative *O. trinacria* (Hawker Skimmer) takes its place in Africa. Both of these are renowned for feeding on other odonate species, sometimes of greater size than their own.

ANISOPTERA

LIBELLULOIDEA

Libellulidae

ANISOPTERA

LIBELLULOIDEA

Libellulidae

Orthetrum pruinosum **in Kodaikanal, India.**

Keith Wilson

Orthetrum poecilops **in a tidal mangrove swamp in China.**

Orthemis ferruginea **(Roseate Skimmer) in Amazonian Peru.**

O. icteromelas (Cannibal Skimmer) is another member of the genus with strong cannibalistic tendencies. (A female is illustrated on page 42.) The males of Asian *Orthetrum*, due to distinctive abdominal colours, are not too difficult to separate but this cannot be said of their African congeners: the African continent boasts a considerable number of pruinosed blue Skimmers, most of which can only be separated by close examination and careful consultation with classification keys. Females of this genus usually oviposit alone, often with their mates hovering above to repel usurpers.

The beautiful *Orthemis ferruginea* (Roseate Skimmer), a South American species that just reaches southern USA, has two distinct male colour forms: one deep pink and the other carmine red, the latter being more common in the southern parts of its range. The species also occurs on the islands of the Bahamas.

Although a number of libelluline abdomens bear spots or stripes of a different colour to the background, there are not many clearly divided into two colours. One is the interesting looking Australian *Notolibellula bicolor* whose four apical abdominal segments are bright red, while the rest of the abdomen and the thorax are powdery blue. *Diplacina braueri* which is endemic to the Philippines could almost be said to be tricoloured: the entire body is turquoise blue and black apart from a very conspicuous red spot near the base of the abdomen. This species is very wary, generally settling on the side of a large boulder in the middle of a fast flowing stream. It took an unusual amount of patience to photograph one. Its bright emerald eyes are unusual for a member of this subfamily.

Apart from the widespread Holarctic species *Libellula quadrimaculata* (4-spotted Chaser), only two other members of this genus occur in Europe and there are five in Asia; the rest are New World species. Some of the North American Chasers (confusingly called skimmers) are very striking to look at:

Diplacina braueri **on the Philippine island of Mindanao.**

Libellula julia **is known as 'The Corporal' in the USA.**

L. pulchella (wingspan 85 mm) has a series of large black and milky white splashes on all four wings. *L. auripennis* (Golden-winged Chaser) has vermilion pterostigmas and the same colour on the anterior veins. The lovely *L. luctuosa* is illustrated on page 36, the female *L. depressa* (Broad-bodied Chaser) on page 54, *L. fulva* (Scarce Chaser) on page 62 and *L. incesta* (Slaty Chaser) on page 1. Another closely related American species whose territorial behaviour is described in Chapter 7, and illustrated on page 55, is *Plathemis lydia* (Common Whitetail). Interestingly, the Madagascar endemic *Thermorthemis madagascariensis* could very easily be mistaken for an American *Libellula*.

There are few libellulids that are truly at risk but the Japanese *Libellula angelina* is one that is. Its habitat consists of old ponds and marshes with rich vegetation of reeds and/or water oats, leaving plenty of open water surface; grassy fields close to the breeding area seem necessary for immature adults. According to Kiyoshi Inoue: 'Such places are most suitable for turning into housing lots and factory areas. We have destroyed their habitats in this way and the numbers of the species have been much diminished. *Libellula quadrimaculata asahinai* occurs in very similar habitats and, in fact, most habitats of the former are inhabited by the latter

Libellula pulchella **(Twelvespot) in Upper New York State, USA.**

though the converse is very far from being true; but *L. quadrimaculata* is adaptable while *L. angelina* is very sensitive.' Attempts have been made to introduce *L. angelina* larvae to sites where *L. quadrimaculata* are strong but, to date, with no success at all: Inoue says, 'we have not found the delicate needs of *angelina* yet'.

The genus *Lathrecista* has just one species, *L. asiatica*, with subspecies in Thailand, Malaysia, India, Australia and the Moluccas; the shape of its long, narrow wings bears little similarity to that of other members of the subfamily.

The majority of libellulines breed in still water of one kind or another and one or two species are able to do so in phytotelmata.

Kiyoshi Inoue

A female *Libellula angelina*. The species is the first Japanese odonate to be listed as 'Endangered'.

Bert Orr

Cratilla metallica in Brunei.

Lathrecista asiatica in Thailand.

According to Bert Orr, the South-East Asian species *Lyriothemis cleis* (see page 14) probably breeds exclusively in tree holes. The larvae of *L. elegantissima* are known to dwell in tree holes but, according to Keith Wilson, females can also be observed ovipositing in pools beside forest streams; and, according to Kiyoshi Inoue, the same is true of *L. tricolor* which inhabits Iriomote Island, the furthest south-western part of Japan. Another species that occasionally breeds in tree holes is *Cratilla metallica* although, according to Orr, this is probably a secondary habitat; they have also been observed ovipositing 'in a shallow permanent pool in a hollow in a rock beside the stream bed'.

Subfamily Sympetrinae (Darters)

This is another large cosmopolitan subfamily with 24 genera. The arculus is between antenodals 1 and 2; the distal antenodal is incomplete; an anal loop is present; the cubital space is crossed and the nodus is almost halfway between base and apex of the wing. The nominate genus, *Sympetrum*, has members in almost all regions of the world except the Australasian. In a number of cases an individual species occurs in more than one region. For example *S. fonscolombei* (Red-veined Darter) can be found in Asia, Europe and Africa; *S. danae* (Black Darter) in Asia, Europe and North America; and Europe's *S. striolatum* (Common Darter) (see page 62) has a subspecies, *kurile*, endemic to the island of that name (lying between the Japanese island of Hokkaido and the Kamchatka Peninsula), and another, *pallidum*, found only in Turkestan. On the other hand there are species that are confined to one particular part of the world: *S. ambiguum* (Blue-faced Darter) only occurs in North America; *S. commixtum* is confined to north and north-west India; and *S. sanguineum* (Ruddy Darter) is a European species.

Sympetrum are on the wing until late in the season. North America's very late-flying

Sympetrum sanguineum (Ruddy Darter) (male) is expanding its range in the UK.

Crocothemis nigrifrons in Townsville, Queensland, Australia.

ANISOPTERA

LIBELLULOIDEA

Libellulidae

Female Crocothemis erythraea in Le Pinail, France.

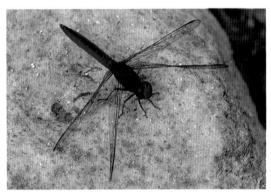

Crocothemis servilia on Luzon, Philippines.

S. vicinum remains on the wing until early December in New Jersey and is thus routinely exposed to unusually cool temperatures.

Most members of the genus can be found in large numbers in suitable breeding areas but eastern Asia's S. kunckeli is, as Kiyoshi Inoue puts it, 'a somewhat delicate and sensitive insect' and finds it difficult to become established in a particular environment. S. danae is different from most others in that the colouring of adult males is black and not red.

Oviposition is almost invariably carried out in tandem. Most females release their eggs by striking the surface of the water with the tip of their abdomens, some ovipositing close to the shore, others further out. A few species (S. flaveolum and S. sanguineum are examples) drop their eggs into vegetation some distance from the water's edge in the expectation that the area will later become inundated.

The genus Crocothemis is another genus that is spread around the world. Most species are brilliant red: for example, C. erythraea (Scarlet Darter) (see page 56) which occurs in Europe, the Middle East and Africa, and C. servilia which was introduced accidentally into the United States from Asia. But C. sanguinolenta is clear orange and, in Australia, C. nigrifrons is blue.

Brachythemis leucosticta belongs to a genus with representatives spread over southern

ANISOPTERA

LIBELLULOIDEA

Libellulidae

An immature *Brachythemis leucosticta*. **The mature male is shown on page 33.**

Brachythemis lacustris. **Note the bicoloured pterostigma on both these South African species.**

The unusually shaped *Acisoma panorpoides ascalaphoides* (Pintail) in South Africa.

Europe, Asia, the Middle East and Africa. In many parts of Africa the ground is literally teeming with '4-square Groundlings', perhaps never more so than in The Gambia. Mature males of this species have black bodies and black patches on the wings but most other Groundlings (India's *contaminata* and Africa's *B. lacustris* for example) have bright red bodies and orange coloration at the base of the wings; in all cases they can be separated from other similar looking darters by their bicoloured pterostigmas.

Philonomon luminans has been named the Barbet because of its multicoloured body (see page 41). When this species thinks it is threatened, it will collapse to the ground, lose a lot of its colour and very realistically feign death. When the danger has passed the insect rights itself, flies off to the centre of its pond and, in a few seconds, the brilliant colours will have reappeared. Perhaps the most unusual looking species is the cryptically patterned *Acisoma panorpoides* (Pintail) which has one subspecies (*A. p. panorpoides*) occurring in Asia and another, *A. p. ascalaphoides* in Africa. This species has a very weak flight; it seldom flies higher than a few inches from the ground and is almost invariably found in low vegetation close to its breeding sites.

Among the smallest members of this subfamily are those belonging to the genus *Diplacodes* which occur in Africa, Asia, Australia and the Middle East. The smallest member of the genus is Africa's *D. deminuta* (length 24 mm) and the male *D. lefebvrei* is the only totally black-bodied dragonfly found in that continent. In stark contrast is Australia's *D. haematodes* which is a bright blood red; and, somewhere in between, there is India's *D. trivialis* in which the male is pale blue.

Diplacodes deminuta in Kwa-Zulu Natal, South Africa.

Diplacodes haematodes in Queensland, Australia.

The lovely *Neurothemis ramburi* on the island of Mindanao, in the Philippines.

Neurothemis tullia is strikingly different from most members of the genus.

Some of the most spectacular species belong in the genus *Neurothemis*. Most of these occur in Asia but one or two make it down to New Guinea and the most northerly parts of Australia. In some cases (*N. tullia* is one) the wings are predominantly black but in others (*N. ramburi* for example) the wings of mature males are dark, velvety red, while those of immatures and females are golden to brown, according to age. The flight of these species is generally weak and fluttery and they are seldom found far from their breeding sites which are, generally, cultivated areas such as paddy fields, or slow moving streams. The genus is a difficult one and Matti Hämäläinen considers that the taxonomy of *N. fluctuans/N. ramburi/N. fulvia/N. terminata* is very uncertain. In the Philippines *N. ramburi* and *N. terminata* often occur together and, since the coloured area of the wings in both species is very variable, separation is difficult; the wings of female *N. terminata* can be coloured or totally hyaline, even in the same population.

Erythrodiplax is another large genus, most of whose members occur in South and Central America although four species do just make it into the southernmost states of the USA. One species, *E. connata* (Blue Dragonlet) must hold the record for the shortest time needed to complete copulation:

ANISOPTERA

LIBELLULOIDEA

Libellulidae

Sidney Dunkle tells us the act can be accomplished in 3–15 s. Another interesting species is *E. berenice* (Seaside Dragonlet) which, again according to Dunkle, is the only truly saltwater dragonfly in North America; its habitats are salt marshes and mangrove swamps along the coasts. Spread over the same general area is the genus *Erythemis* (Pondhawks). According to Dunkle, *E. simplicicollis* is probably America's most ferocious odonate, attacking all types of insect including newly emerged dragonflies even larger than themselves. A bright green abdomen is not usual among anisopterans but females and immature males of this species are so coloured (see page 50). Finally, also from Central and North America, the lovely monotypic *Pachydiplax longipennis* (see page 15) deserves a mention: the species is on the wing throughout the year and its size varies greatly, generally with the largest individuals occurring in the Spring and the smallest in the Autumn.

Female *Neurothemis ramburi*.

Trithemis pallidinervis (Dancing Dropwing) in Madurai, southern India.

Subfamily Trithemistinae (Dropwings)

There are 13 genera in this subfamily, which are distributed around Africa, Asia, New Guinea and the Americas. On landing, many species within the group will almost immediately lower their wings, behaviour that is responsible for their English name.

An exception is South-East Asia's *Trithemis pallidinervis*. This species seldom drops its wings and it perches in an almost unique fashion. Bunching its long spidery legs together like a stalk, it takes up the posture of a ballerina performing a pirouette. It is not uncommon to find a party of Dancing Dropwings perched on tall blades of grass — and all facing into whatever breeze there may be.

The *Trithemis* genus (containing over 50 species) is, essentially, an African one but, as Allen Davies put it, 'five have 'escaped' into Asia and made a great success of it'. Certainly the small, dark *T. festiva* (Indigo Dropwing) must be the most abundant dragonfly from western Asia to the Philippines, and the plum-coloured *T. aurora* (Dawn Dropwing) is equally successful over much the same area. The common African *T. annulata* (Plum-coloured Dropwing) has managed to cross the Straits of Gibraltar and has become well

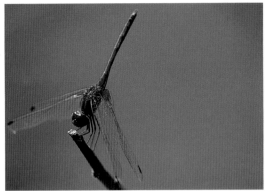

Male *Trithemis festiva*.

Male *Trithemis arteriosa* (Red-veined Dropwing) in Gauteng, South Africa.

Trithemis aurora (Dawn Dropwing) on the island of Mindanao, in the Philippines.

Female *Trithemis arteriosa* (Red-veined Dropwing) in Mpumalunga, South Africa.

ANISOPTERA

LIBELLULOIDEA

Libellulidae

established in Spain, where it is rapidly extending its range. The lovely *T. stictica* is illustrated on page 32.

Trithemis arteriosa is abundant over the whole of Africa and the Middle East. Henri Dumont tells us it is widespread in desert environments and that 'Larvae have been found buried in damp sand at depths of about 30 cm, in beds of temporary pools in the Sahara. Estivation (summer diapause, compare hibernation) is evidently adaptive in areas where rainfall is erratic.' Interestingly, in the Middle East, the females' wings bear brown patches at the tips and at the nodus: these are not present in forms found in other parts of their range. The genus does not reach the New World but *Dythemis rufinervis* is a doppelganger (translated as 'a ghostly duplicate of a living person')! Its posture as well as its shape and colour appear identical to Africa's *Trithemis arteriosa*.

New Guinea and other islands in the Bismarck Archipelago are home to some 20 species belonging to the genera *Huonia* and *Lanthanusa*; these are very poorly studied because, to quote Allen Davies again: 'who is lucky enough to be able to go there?' The Far Eastern species *Pseudothemis zonata* is a very unusually coloured dragonfly which generally

Male *Pseudothemis zonata*, near Osaka, Japan.

perches on a piece of vegetation just out of range for a photographer. When a party of males 'dances' up and down over a piece of water, in and out of dappled sunlight, it is a sight not soon forgotten.

Subfamily Onychothemistinae

There is just one genus, *Onychothemis* (with five species) in this tropical subfamily. They are found in South-East Asia and the various species have different subspecies in different areas. For example, *O. testacea* has distinct

Male *Onychothemis testacea testacea* in southern Thailand.

subspecies in Thailand (*O. t. testacea*), Sri Lanka and India (*O. t. ceylanica*), and China, Vietnam and Taiwan (*O. t. tonkinensis*). They are of medium size and robust build. Wing venation shows them to be advanced libellulids: they have numerous antenodals, the last one being incomplete. A unique feature is found on the legs: their claws are without hooks. Otherwise they are characterised by their dark, metallic thoraces and brightly coloured abdomens. *O. testacea* has a black abdomen with reddish and citrus-yellow markings. Another, *O. culminicola*, from Myanmar, Thailand and Malaysia, has a bright rust-red abdomen with restricted yellow markings.

According to F. C. Fraser, they are bold, strong fliers, although their flights are usually of short duration. They are of shy and retiring habits and can only be found in really dense jungle, where they flash up and down the borders of fast submontane streams. They take frequent rests and strenuously attack all other large dragonflies that invade their territory. Females oviposit in shallow water under the shade of overhanging vegetation, threading their way through thick vegetation in order to do so.

Subfamily Palpopleurinae (Widows)

This is a subfamily of just four genera found over much of Asia, southern and central Africa, and the Americas. Widows are stout, broad-bodied perchers with wings that, in many species, are coloured and often heavily marked with black. The shape of the wings is unique among libellulids, the base of the forewing being strongly convex on the leading edge. The arc is between the first and second antenodals and the most distal antenodal is incomplete.

Courtship behaviour is not common among anisopterans but males of this subfamily show

A female *Palpopleura lucia* in Kenya.

Palpopleura deceptor in The Gambia.

ANISOPTERA

LIBELLULOIDEA

Libellulidae

it to a marked degree. In the case of zygopterans, it is the males of species with distinctive features (legs, wings or tips of abdomens) that perform courtship displays; in the case of the anisopteran palpopleurines, many of them have distinctive patterns on their wings and this feature would seem to justify courtship display. In *Palpopleura* the display is often intricate and always fascinating to watch. For example, the courting male of Africa's *P. lucia* or of Asia's *P. sexmaculata* hovers in front of a perched female with his body almost vertical and his wings flapping slowly so that the markings are clearly visible to his prospective mate. Peter Miller reckoned that the frequency of this wing flapping was only about one-fifth of that used in normal flight.

Norman Moore gives us a vivid description of the dance of a party of male *P. lucia* in West Africa: 'They were over a stream which flowed through the forest by the edge of the River Gambia and fluttered in and out of an intricate pattern of brilliant light and deep shade. Spots of sun on golden brown water and on the dark markings of the dragonflies made regular patterns which varied continually like chips of glass in a kaleidoscope.' The species has two distinct forms: *P. l. lucia* and *P. l. portia* (see page 52).

At the breeding site males of this genus will aggressively hold their small territories but, away from the water, large mixed-sex parties are locally common, with individuals perched on the tip of pieces of grass in close proximity to one another. As dusk approaches they will fly up to the tops of trees or tall bushes where their distinctively marked wings are clearly visible against the gradually darkening sky. Females and immature males are unusually conspicuous with broad yellow and black bodies and strongly marked wings; males, as they mature,

A mature male *Palpopleura lucia lucia* (African Black Widow) in Kwa-Zulu Natal, South Africa.

ANISOPTERA

LIBELLULOIDEA

Libellulidae

develop a pale blue pruinosity. The species *P. deceptor* is well named as its appearance is indeed deceptive; it does not look like a *Palpopleura*: it is larger but slimmer than the other species; the wings are narrower, less convex between base and nodus and they only bear one or two small dark streaks. *P. sexmaculata*, which is an Asian species, has its wings suffused with orange-red, bearing little or nothing in the way of black markings.

Males of the New World genus *Perithemis* show equally intricate territorial and courtship behaviour. A male holding territory will make a dash at an intruder and then flap his wings slowly to display their colour. The territorial behaviour of *P. mooma* and the courtship behaviour of *P. tenera* are discussed in Chapter 7. Although not always the case, when a female accepts the advances of a male she will find a nearby perch and settle on it, thus announcing herself ready to mate.

Male *Perithemis tenera* (Eastern Amberwing) in Upper New York State, USA.

Many researchers have examined the reproductive behaviour of different species in this genus, and many conflicting conclusions have been reached. It would appear that behaviour patterns vary considerably according to different environmental factors, and with regard to male density.

Female *Palpopleura sexmaculata* in Kerala, India.

Gerhard Jurzitza

Zenithoptera lanei **with his wings closed.**

Gerhard Jurzitza

Zenithoptera lanei **displaying the vivid colour of his opened wings.**

Gerhard Jurzitza

Diastatops obscura **in Brazil.**

The genus *Diastatops* is confined to South America and one of its most widespread species is the beautiful *D. obscura*. An unusual piece of thermoregulatory behaviour performed by a *Diastatops* species in Surinam is described by Marcel Wasscher in Chapter 4.

Another South American genus, *Zenithoptera*, contains the interesting Brazilian species *Z. lanei*; this species inhabits swampy areas and, unusually for libellulids, males generally rest with their wings closed, thus presenting an inconspicuous appearance. However, on the approach of an intruder, signs of territorial behaviour are exhibited and the perched dragonfly will spread his wings wide open to display the vivid blue of the upper surface.

Subfamily Trameinae (Gliders)

This subfamily has, for convenience, been divided into three tribes: Rhyothemistini, Trameini and Zyxommatini which all share the distinctive features of an unusually broad base to the hindwings, pointed at the tips. This feature is responsible for their characteristic flight: although most of them can fly quite fast, they are proficient gliders. Venationally, they are among the most advanced species: the arculus is between the first and second antenodals; the most distal antenodals are incomplete; the triangle in the forewing is long with a very short costal side and the triangle in the hindwing is level with the arc. Their eyes are broadly touching on the top of the head.

(i) Rhyothemistini

There is a single genus, *Rhyothemis,* in this very lovely group which occurs in Asia, Australasia and Africa. The body shape is distinctive: the abdomen, in many cases, being only about half the length of one of the forewings. Wings are spectacularly adorned with patches of colour which, when the sun shines on them, glisten with rich, metallic purples, violets, blues and

Male *Rhyothemis fenestrina* (known by the local naturalists as 'Double-wing') in Botswana's Okavango.

***Rhyothemis semihyalina* in South Africa.**

***Rhyothemis phyllis phyllis* in southern Thailand.**

***Rhyothemis phyllis chloe* in Townsville, Australia.**

greens. In some species, both wings are liberally adorned in this way (e.g. the Japanese *R. fuliginosa*, the Australian *R. princeps* and the African *R. fenestrina*). In others the wings are suffused with an amber background and decorated with spots and patches: the Australian *R. graphiptera* (illustrated on the cover) which looks like a gold filigree brooch, set with amethysts is an example. In yet others, the colour, which may or may not be metallic, is confined to the base of the hindwings, as in the case of the African *R. semihyalina* (metallic) and the widespread *R. phyllis* (not metallic). When the sun goes behind a cloud, the metallic colours disappear, leaving the wings with

patches of dingy black (apart from *R. phyllis* where the yellow and black are not affected by lack of light). This last example has a number of subspecies which can be identified by varying amounts of black and yellow: for example *R. p. phyllis* in Thailand, *R. p. dispar* in Hawaii and *R. p. chloe* in Queensland.

They are generally found flying low over large ponds; their flight is slow and fluttering and they frequently settle on the tips of waterlily buds or reeds growing in the water. As night falls, they fly high to roost in the tops of nearby trees. In the morning they fly down again and warm themselves on lower branches before returning to the water.

Tramea lacerata (Black-mantled Glider) in Florida, USA.

Camacina othello, wingspan 93 mm.

Allen Davies

Tramea limbata, in India.

Female *Pantala flavescens*. The male is shown on page 5.

ANISOPTERA

LIBELLULOIDEA

Libellulidae

(ii) Trameini

This is a group of trans-global, tropical species set in nine genera. They are generally of medium size although *Hydrobasileus brevistylus* (South-East Asia down to northern Australia) and *Camacina* (with a similar distribution) are considerably larger than the others; *C. gigantea* has a wingspan of 108 mm. The chief differences between species in this tribe and the previous one are that their flight is stronger and more sustained, they are more inclined to hover, and the abdomen is not as short relative to the length of the forewings. The wings are said to be more pointed, but this is not easy to determine. The broad-based hindwings, in some genera, are strongly marked with red, red and black or black.

When flying over the water, *Tramea* males are very aggressive to males of their own and other libellulid species. They spend a relatively short time over water and parties of both sexes will congregate above patches of grass some distance from water or in forest clearings, often in company with *Pantala flavescens* (the Globe Skimmer). When they do come to the water, it is to mate. Copulation can take a long time and mating pairs may be observed using an unusual, fast, somewhat clumsy, switchback flight. Due to the heavy basal patches on the wings, they appear large and heavy in the

ANISOPTERA

LIBELLULOIDEA

Libellulidae

thoracic area. Females lay their eggs alone among waterlily plants.

The best known species within this group is undoubtedly *Pantala flavescens*. This is a reddish-brown dragonfly with only a small yellowish patch at the base of the hindwings but identifiable at close quarters by the fact that the pterostigma on the forewing is longer than that on the hindwing. It is a migrant which disperses enormous distances from its breeding place, capable of crossing oceans as it does so: monsoon fronts and the associated winds are often instrumental in carrying them these colossal distances. They appear in Africa, North and South America, Australia and all over Asia It is well named the Globe Skimmer. Its larvae are also known to develop rapidly, an ability that allows the use of temporary pools (including swimming pools) as breeding places. Michael Parr reminded me that this species was one of the very first insects (of any Order) to re-colonise Bikini Atoll in the Pacific after the cessation of atomic testing.

At some time the Globe Skimmer alighted on Easter Island in the mid-Pacific and settled there. The colonies found on the island were

investigated by H. J. Dumont and D. Verschuren in 1990. It appeared that adults had abandoned their long-distance dispersal behaviour and had become relatively poor flyers. A possible reason given for this was the extreme scarcity of larval prey material: 'dragonfly larvae might find just enough food to complete development but may be incapable of building up the fat reserves required for long-distance flight'.

(iii) Zyxommatini

Although this tribe shares the same wing characteristics as the previous two, the abdomen of most species is longer than the wings, a feature that is particularly noticeable in *Zyxomma* itself. In the male of this genus the long abdomen becomes very slim after the swollen first three segments. Members of the tribe are of medium size and, in habit, differ from the others in that they are crepuscular. The chief venational difference is that the borders of the anal loop run to the wing border which means that the apex is open. The tribe consists of nine species arranged into four genera which occur in tropical regions of Asia, Africa and the Americas, as well as in northern Australia and the islands to the north.

One of the most interesting of these species is *Tholymis tillarga* which can be found in tropical and subtropical Asia and Africa. The mature male of this species is easily recognised by two patches on the hindwings: one an orange/brown antenodal patch and the other an opalescent milky-white post-nodal patch which shows up well in reflected light. It is extremely catholic in its habitat requirements: females will lay their eggs into treated sewage lagoons in South Africa; into shallow, scummy water at the edge of falls-base pools in Thailand; into village water tanks and into marshes bordering large lakes in India. The method of egg-laying is probably unique: the female dips alone but

Male *Tholymis tillarga* (The Twister) in Madagascar.

Kay Thompson

Female *Zyxomma petiolatum* in a Manila garden, Philippines.

generally with the male guarding her from a few inches above. Between each dip, she twirls her body round 180 degrees which makes it appear an extremely frenetic activity. Egg-laying is often difficult to observe because it seldom takes place before dusk and, also, because, whenever the site allows, the female will chose an area of water immediately under the bank. Their crepuscular habit means that both sexes appear on the wing shortly before dusk and continue to fly over the breeding area until long after dark when, particularly if there is moonlight, the opalescent patches on the males' wings produce, as E. C. G. Pinhey aptly puts it, 'a ghostly effect as he skims the water'. During the day they disappear, presumably lying up in nearby shrubs and other such vegetation.

There are five species of *Zyxomma* spread around West Africa, the Seychelles, Australasia and South-East Asia. They are a somewhat drab collection, their abdomens being decorated in various shades of brown and their hyaline wings tinted yellowish-brown at the tips. The species is the most crepuscular of all in the subfamily, rarely being seen during daylight hours unless it is very overcast. They are attracted to lights and at least one species (*Z. petiolatum*) will frequently make its way into lighted buildings.

Subfamily Urothemistinae (Baskers)

Some authors consider this subfamily sufficiently individual to warrant it being classified as a family on its own: Macrodiplacidae. It is characterised by a very open wing venation, a small number of antenodals among which there are two weak primary ones, and a well developed anal loop. Most species perch in conspicuous places and the name Basker is an apt one.

The subfamily is small with around 20 species set in four genera. They come in many shapes and sizes and most are brightly coloured. The genus *Aethriamanta* occurs in South-East Asia, Australia, Madagascar and much of tropical Africa; it includes *A. rezia* whose male is a small, bright crimson dragonfly that is difficult to approach. *Macrodiplax* is a genus with just two species, one, *Macrodiplax balteata*, occurring in South America and southern United States, and the other, *Macrodiplax cora*, in the Far East and Oceania. *M. cora* is a small species and a particularly active one; males perch briefly on the top of bare twigs or posts and make frequent dashes after prey, almost always returning to the perch from which they had taken off.

ANISOPTERA

LIBELLULOIDEA

Libellulidae

Male *Macrodiplax cora* in the Philippines.

ANISOPTERA

LIBELLULOIDEA

Libellulidae

Male *Urothemis edwardsi* (Blue Basker) in Kwa-Zulu Natal, South Africa.

Robert Kemp

The dark form of *Selysiothemis nigra*.

Male *Urothemis assignata* (Crimson Basker) in The Gambia.

The genus *Urothemis* contains species occurring in Africa, Asia, Australia and New Guinea. The two dominant species, *U. edwardsi* and *U. signata* each have a number of sub-species. *U. e. edwardsi* (Blue Basker), whose male is deep blue with black markings, is widespread over the whole of Africa and *U. e. hulae* occurs in Israel. *Urothemis signata* (male is deep blood red, also with black markings) and *U. s. insignata* occurs in Malaysia, *U. s. yiei* in Taiwan, *U. s. aethiopica* in Somalia and *U. s. aliena* in New Guinea and northern Australia. The male *U. assignata* (Crimson Basker) is a striking insect that, between periods of strong flight over the breeding area, makes frequent pauses to perch on the tip of a reed or point of a waterlily; females like to oviposit among floating plants such as waterlilies and the males will generally hover above them while they do so. At other times, both sexes like to perch conspicuously on the topmost branches of trees and tall shrubs, sometimes at considerable distances from water.

The monotypic *Selysiothemis nigra* is a Mediterranean species which is known in various types of habitat throughout the Middle East; surprisingly, it was also observed near Jodhpur in India by Peter Miller in 1990. A pair was ovipositing in tandem into a 'temporary lake'. The species has two distinct colour forms: it is described in the literature as black (nigra) in wet parts of its range but creamy-yellow in dry, desert areas (e.g. Arabia). However, the colour of the male shown here is greyish blue rather than black. Habitat selection of the species is very catholic, almost anything seems acceptable: brackish lagoons, salt marshes, desert regions, and ponds at altitudes of over 1000 m.

Subfamily Zygonychinae (Cascaders)

Cascaders are robust dragonflies with the most advanced libellulid venation. Mature males in prime condition have green eyes and shining green or black bodies, the thorax in particular being marked with yellow. As they age, much of the colour disappears and the shiny green becomes blackish. In colour and in many of their habits they are similar to corduliids and macromiids; females are duller in their back-ground colour but are often more generously adorned with yellow. At rest they hang almost vertically in the manner of aeshnids. Larvae are unique in possessing twin claws, a feature that helps them to survive in their particular habitat: waterfalls and cascades.

Zygonychines form an Old World group containing four genera, two of which are monotypic: *Zygonychidium gracile* is endemic in Africa's Ivory Coast and *Celebothemis metallica*

ANISOPTERA

LIBELLULOIDEA

Libellulidae

Zygonyx torrida in The Gambia, unusually at a site far from any fast-running water.

on the Indonesian island of Sulawesi. The latter is reputed to be a curious species, superficially unlike those in the other genera in shape, and in being highly metallic. *Zygonyx* breed in fast running water. Immatures assemble in large mixed-sex parties, flying high, above tree level, in forest clearings.

Female *Zygonyx natalensis* (Natal Cascader) in Eastern Province, South Africa.

ANISOPTERA

LIBELLULOIDEA

Libellulidae

Zygonyx iris malayana (Iris Cascader) in Song Khla, Thailand.

In southern Africa, mature *Zygonyx natalensis* males come to the breeding sites where they will fly with great speed over and beside waterfalls, swerving away with the greatest of ease from a waiting net. It is easy to mistake some of the large green-eyed *Z. torrida* for a corduliid or macromiid. A similar mistake is easily made with *Z. iris*. This species has nine subspecies, a different one occurring in different Asian countries. The largest, *Z. i. insignis* occurs in China, including Hong Kong, and the smallest, *Z. i. errans*, in Malaysia. Graham Vick found both *Z. ida* and *Z. iris* on submontane streams in western Malaysia: *Z. ida* appeared to prefer the shady forest-stream waterfalls and *Z. iris* the rapids in broader more open rivers.

Larvae, with the twin claws mentioned above, are able to cling to the vertical rock surfaces behind waterfalls and, thanks to these and to their long powerful legs, they are able to survive in the fastest currents.

The fourth genus is *Olpogastra* and again, because of the bright green eyes, from a distance it is possible to misidentify its three species. They sit uncomfortably under the name of Cascaders since their habitat differs totally from the rest of the subfamily. *O. fuelleborni* has been seen perched beside a wide and particularly slow-moving stretch of the Sabie River in Mpumalanga, South Africa; *O. lugubris* (Mock Emerald) on papyrus bordering the hippopotamus channels in the Okavango swamps, Botswana; and, more recently, in a paddy field not far from the River Gambia.

Olpogastra lugubris (Mock Emerald) in Botswana's Okavango Swamp.

10
Evolutionary riddles

JOHN TRUEMAN

Animals with backbones first took to the land during the Devonian period, some 400 million years ago. A few wingless insects (Apterygota) already existed at that time. Flying insects (Pterygota) appeared about 70 million years later. They are found in the earliest of the Upper Carboniferous (335–285 mya) coal deposits. By this time the insects which can fold their wings (Neoptera, the subclass to which the majority of modern insects belong) were already distinguished from the non-folding-winged insects, Palaeoptera, and these were separated into three clearly recognisable major lineages: superorders Ephemeropteroidea, Palaeodictyopteroidea and Odonatoidea.

The three superorders of Palaeoptera

Ephemeropteroidea is the Mayfly lineage. It consists of the single order Ephemeroptera, which always has been a small and distinct group. Fossils can be recognised by a strongly curved vein near the base of the wing as in all modern mayflies.

The second superorder, Palaeo-dictyopteroidea, once were very common.

During the Upper Carboniferous and Permian this was the dominant superorder as measured by either species number or family-level diversity. There were several orders and many families, each with a unique wing venation but all with similar, distinctive sucking mouthparts superficially like those of true bugs belonging to neopteran order Hemiptera. However, the Palaeodictyopteroidea died out at the end of the Permian, 245 mya.

All of the remaining palaeopteran fossils show wing vein fusion to various degrees and on this basis are grouped as Odonatoidea.

A reconstruction, by Carsten Brauckmann, of the beautifully preserved palaeodictyopteran, *Homoioptera vorhallensis* (Namurian, Lower Carboniferous) which was taken from the Hagen-Vorhalle beds in the Ruhr Valley, Germany. [Fuhlrott Museum, Wupertal, Germany.]

The oldest such fossil is *Eugeropteron lunatum* from the lowermost Upper Carboniferous (Namurian) strata of Argentina. Several families and orders now placed in Palaeodictyopteroidea were previously regarded as Odonatoidea, before evidence for sucking mouthparts was discovered in some species. Some of the early odonatoid fossil species may be more closely related to the palaeodictyopteroids than to modern Odonata.

Unfortunately, the fossil record of early insects is somewhat sparse and the timing of key evolutionary events is not well known. It can be inferred that Odonatoidea separated from other Palaeoptera some time before 335 mya, but evolutionary relationships amongst the three palaeopteran superorders are not very well established.

The orders of Odonatoidea

Superorder Odonatoidea comprises two orders, Protodonata and Odonata. The Protodonata (sometimes referred to as Meganisoptera) are confined to the Upper Carboniferous and Permian periods, while Odonata are known from the early Permian to the present day.

Protodonata, as currently circumscribed, comprises the three families Meganeuridae, Paralogidae and Eugeropteridae.

As with the superorders, the evolutionary relationships of Protodonata to Odonata are disputed. It seems most likely that the immediate ancestor of the modern order Odonata was a species of small meganeurid dragonfly that lived at some time in the Upper Carboniferous period. Evidence for a meganeurid origin of Odonata can be found in the odonate wing venation, which is quite close to that of Meganeuridae. As well, an unpublished (and as yet unconfirmed) report suggests that some meganeurid larvae were armed with a grasping labium (labial mask) just as larval dragonflies and damselflies are today.

The Meganeuridae are sometimes referred to as 'Palaeozoic giant dragonflies'. They include the largest and heaviest insects ever known to fly. The Permian species *Meganeuropsis permiana*, with a wingspan of 72 cm, was more than four times as broad and hence approximately 64 times as heavy as the largest modern dragonfly. A number of other species also were huge by modern standards. Extremely large species

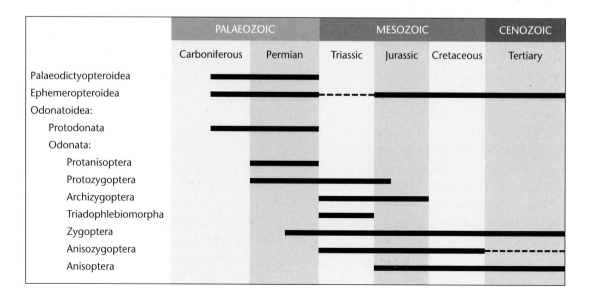

The geological periods from which palaeopteran fossils have been found.

occur in the Upper Carboniferous genus *Meganeura* and in Permian genera *Tupus* and *Oligotypus*. However, other meganeurid fossils are known which spanned only 3–5 cm from wingtip to wingtip, not at all an unusual size for a dragonfly. Although the late Palaeozoic era (Upper Carboniferous and Permian) is renowned for its huge, primitive dragonflies, many ordinary-sized odonatoids occurred at that time as well.

Whether or not it arose from within Meganeuridae, the order Odonata had become well established by early in the Permian period. True odonates, with apparently five main stem veins at the base of the wing and a fully formed nodus, but still with the arculus open basally, flourished at this time. Meanwhile the ancestors of dinosaurs and mammals were two quite undistinguished reptiles living somewhere among ferns and giant club-moss trees in the ancient coal-measure forests.

The suborders of Odonata

The Permian period closed suddenly, with a huge mass extinction far worse than the better-known event at the end of the Cretaceous. This was about 245 mya. Many well-established groups, including Palaeodictyopteroidea and Protodonata did not survive. The Odonata by this time had differentiated into several major lineages. Three are recognised in the fossil record as suborders Protanisoptera, Protozygoptera and Archizygoptera.

Also, during the Permian, either some protozygopteran species took on a very zygopteran appearance or else a fourth distinct suborder, the modern Zygoptera, was already established. In particular, the fossil species *Permagrion falklandicum,* from the Falkland Islands, has been interpreted as a protozygopteran by some workers but as a true zygopteran by others. Some even have argued that Protozygoptera and

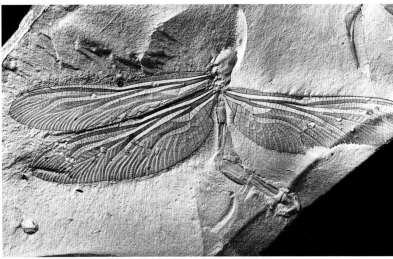

Ed Jarzembowski

Zygoptera form a continuous series and should be regarded as a single suborder.

During the Triassic period (245–210 mya) another suborder, Triadophlebiomorpha, made a brief appearance. Given the unusual way in which the nodus is formed in this group, and that the wings lack a pterostigma, it is possible this is really a protodonatan suborder which survived the end-Permian extinction. However, most systematists regard Triadophlebiomorpha as a short-lived suborder of the Odonata.

The suborder Anisozygoptera also appears for the first time in the Triassic. This suborder is represented today by a single genus, *Epiophlebia.* The Triassic anisozygopterans were, for the most part, even more anisopteran-like in wing venation than are the two extant species.

The final suborder, Anisoptera (modern dragonflies), first appears in the Jurassic period (210–145 mya), coinciding in time with the beginning of the Age of the Dinosaurs.

The intermediate nature of Anisozygoptera has led to much debate about how Zygoptera (modern damselflies), Anisozygoptera, and Anisoptera (modern dragonflies) are related. The most likely scenario is that despite the earliest fossil record for Anisozygoptera predating

Valdaeshna surreyensis (130 mya) is the best preserved Cretaceous odonatan found so far in southern England.

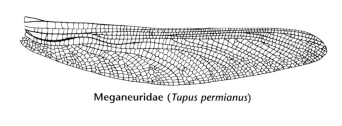

Meganeuridae (*Tupus permianus*)

Protanisoptera (Ditaxineuridae: *Polytaxineura*)

Protozygoptera (*Kennedya mirabilis*)

Archizygoptera (Protomyrmeleonidae: *Triassagrion*)

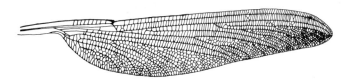

Triadophlebiomorpha (*Triadophlebia madygenica*)

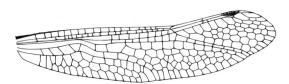

Zygoptera/Protozygoptera (?) fossil *Permagrion falklandicum*

Representative wings from the fossil suborders.

that for fully modern Zygoptera, it is Zygoptera which includes the original stock from which all modern Odonata are descended. According to this hypothesis, Anisozygoptera are a derived lineage within the Zygoptera, and Anisoptera in turn are derived from within Anisozygoptera. A consequence is that the subordinal names and conventional taxonomic classification fail to match the true evolutionary relationships of the groups.

The superfamilies of Odonata

The modern superfamily Aeshnoidea first appears in the Jurassic. Narrow-winged damselflies (Coenagrionoidea) arguably are found in the Permian but broad-winged damselflies (Calopterygoidea) do not appear until the Cretaceous period (145–65 mya). The Cretaceous saw the rise of the flowering plants and ended with the sudden demise of the dinosaurs (excepting those feathery ones which we now call birds). Almost all the modern odonate families plus two or three others now

extinct are known from before the Cretaceous/Tertiary (K/T) boundary. The exception is anisopteran superfamily Libelluloidea. Families Corduliidae and Libellulidae do not appear in the fossil record until more than five million years into the Cenozoic era (Eocene epoch, 60–35 mya).

Evolution of the odonate wing

Although one group of systematists regard Zygoptera as being a continuation of Protozygoptera and hold that Anisozygoptera is derived from a zygopteran ancestor and Anisoptera, in turn, from an anisozygopteran, another group regard Triassic Anisozygoptera as the 'stem group' from which modern Anisoptera and modern Zygoptera arose as two separate lineages.

These two scenarios imply totally different histories for the evolution of the odonate wing. Either an almost-anisopteran venation is primitive and the narrower damselfly wing is derived by reduction, or else damselflies show the primitive condition and the wings of Anisozygoptera and Anisoptera are derived. Rival wing-vein-naming systems rely on one or other of these phylogenetic histories but no system is consistent with both. Because no one has yet clearly demonstrated that one history of wing evolution is right and the other wrong, no agreement has been reached about the relationships of the suborders. Likewise, because no one has yet shown which of the plausible patterns of evolutionary relationship is correct, the proper identification of wing veins across the suborders remains uncertain.

The Zygoptera-first hypothesis is the most consistent with the fossil record, provided only that *Permagrion* is interpreted as a zygopteran. This scenario allows *Epiophlebia* to be placed near Zygoptera rather than near Anisoptera and allows a consistent explanation of odonatan wing veins in terms of those observed in other insects.

The Zygoptera-first hypothesis also suffices to explain the curious differences in larval gill development and overall larval shape between Zygoptera and the other surviving suborders. Suppose that Anisozygoptera, and hence Anisoptera, are descended from a zygopteran ancestor (Permian/Triassic) which adopted a near-terrestrial lifestyle. Some modern anisopteran larvae are terrestrial and others semi-terrestrial, living under logs in rainforest or making permanent tunnels above water level in sphagnum bogs. Out of the water, the caudal gills would be useless as gills and might well have become reduced to short spines. At the same time, these larva would have become more robust and stocky than in typical Zygoptera. If, at some later time, a descendant species took to water again, it would have had to invent a new gas-exchange system, and what better than the unique rectal gills of the Anisozygoptera and Anisoptera, derived from the much weaker folds in the rectum of Zygoptera? The rival

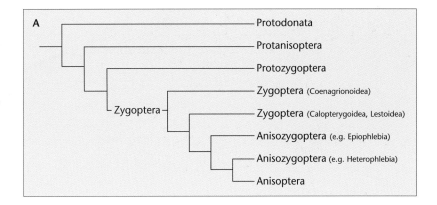

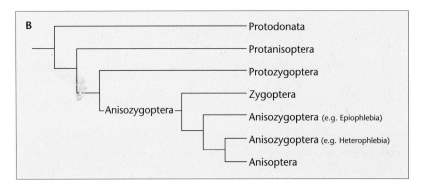

'Anisozygoptera-first' hypothesis offers no explanation for loss of the three primitive caudal filaments or gills in Odonata, as compared to Protodonata, nor for the remarkable coincidence that exactly three such gills would later re-evolve in Zygoptera, in exactly the same positions.

Rival hypotheses of relationship amongst odonate suborders: (A) 'Zygoptera-first' hypothesis; (B) 'Anisozygoptera-first' hypothesis.

Classification of Anisoptera and Zygoptera

Anisoptera traditionally are divided into two main superfamilies, Aeshnoidea and Libelluloidea, with the somewhat modified but broadly aeshnid-like Cordulegastridae regarded as a third superfamily, Cordulegastroidea. The modern Aeshnoidea are divided into four families (Aeshnidae, Gomphidae, Neopetaliidae and Petaluridae). Superfamily Libelluloidea comprises just two main families, Corduliidae and Libellulidae, but these together contain more than half of all anisopteran species.

A number of alternative classifications of Anisoptera have recently been proposed. One is to raise the large family Gomphidae to superfamily level. A second is to break up the small family Neopetaliidae, with one species to remain in Aeshnoidea while seven are transferred to Libelluloidea. A third proposal would raise both Gomphidae and Petaluridae to superfamily level but reduce Cordulegastroidea to a family within the Libelluloidea. A fourth (followed in this book) splits the family Cordulegastridae into two parts, one subfamily remaining as Cordulegastroidea while the other is raised to family status and transferred to the Libelluloidea.

In Zygoptera, the main taxonomic division is between the narrow-winged and broad-winged forms. The two typical superfamilies commonly are named Coenagrionoidea and Calopterygoidea, respectively. Lestoidea are a third superfamily and a second group of narrow-winged damselflies. However, some genera of the Lestoidea are quite robust or have an unusually complex wing venation and there has been much disagreement about where the boundaries of Lestoidea and Calopterygoidea should be set. A fourth superfamily, Hemiphlebioidea, is used for a single, peculiar species, *Hemiphlebia mirabilis*, found only on a few small swamps in south-eastern Australia. Hemiphlebioidea most likely is more closely related to Lestidae or Synlestidae than to any other extant family (though it has been separated from either at least since the mid Cretaceous). However, at one time it was considered to have diverged from other odonates even before the modern suborders split from each other. *Hemiphlebia* often is called a 'living fossil', as is *Epiophlebia* (Anisozygoptera). But then, in reality, aren't they all?

From 1890 until about 1950 a great confusion in zygopteran classification was caused when several odonatologists took a view that the correct name for *Calopteryx*, which is a genus of broad-winged damselflies and the genus from which Calopterygoidea takes its name, should be *Agrion*. The cause of the confusion was that for a century or more this name had been applied instead to the type genus of the narrow-winged forms. In reading the literature of this period, whenever the name *Agrion* or any of its derivatives occurs, it is necessary to establish from the context whether it refers to broad-winged or narrow-winged damselflies. In modern literature the genus name *Agrion* and the confusing and obsolete family-level names Agrionidae and Agrionoidea are rarely used. Coenagrionidae and Coenagrionoidea are the preferred names for the narrow-winged forms.

A very radical proposal for reclassification of the whole order appeared in the early to mid 1990s, associated with the German odonatologist G. Bechly. This detailed scheme is based on the 'Anisozygoptera-first' hypothesis but follows a particularly extreme school of systematics in which every hypothesised node on the tree of life has to be separately named, even before any evidence for its reality has been accumulated. As a result, the proposal involves numerous changes to the meaning of commonly used names and creates many new taxa at above the family level, together with at least 20 new family names and 13 new subfamilies. Among other things, the ordinal name Odonata itself would disappear to be replaced by the new name Odonatoptera. Fortunately, this strange and inherently unstable classificatory system has not been widely adopted.

No one denies that there are anomalies in the current system of classification, but until either the wing venation nomenclature or phylogenetic relationships among suborders and families have been properly sorted out these cannot satisfactorily be resolved.

11
Artificial rearing

STEPHEN BUTLER

It is probable that a high percentage of the world's odonate larvae can easily be reared out by artificial means although some species, because of the nature of their habitats and behaviour, will present more of a problem.

In certain countries, legislation forbids the import, export or movement of odonate larvae internally, so it will be important to check this should the transfer or collection of larvae be attempted abroad. In such countries (Australia is one and Germany another) it is important to obtain the necessary permits to collect and transport. In most countries, however, there are no such restrictions, except for Red Data Book species.

To begin with, larvae of local species should be reared out in order to become familiar with methods and problems. More success will be experienced with common species inhabiting still water; these require very little in the way of equipment and can be released into the environment after successful rearing. It is always best to choose a larva that is mature and close to emergence so that the minimum of feeding and attention will be needed. Much can be learned from regular observation and even the most amateur beginner should have a notebook handy so that observations can readily be recorded.

The following basic equipment will be needed at this stage: a suitable container, chemically untainted water, material for the larva to emerge on and, finally, a supply of food.

A variety of containers can be utilised (depending on the species involved), ranging from jam jars to aquaria. The latter are more suitable however, as they produce a greater surface area for the exchange of oxygen. If larvae are immature, then it is important to create a stable environment for them to live in

A container in the form of an aquarium.

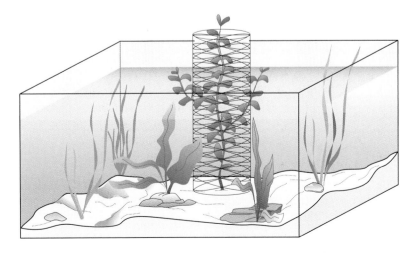

and so the introduction of suitable detritus, oxygenating plants and live food will be necessary. Overcrowding can be a problem even for small zygopterans and the only guarantee against cannibalism is to have one individual per container. A sad fact of life is that common species always eat rare species, never vice versa!

As most larvae emerge vertically, a simple stick or plastic mesh can be introduced, preferably in the centre of the container so that there is no contact with the side, thus preventing accidental escape and probable death. Many larvae, particularly those of the family Cordulegastridae, are inveterate explorers even at an immature stage and will take advantage of any opportunity to wander. Some individuals close to emergence will periodically climb out of water and conditions must be created for them to spend several hours per day in this state. Significant changes in barometric pressure appear to trigger both ecdysis (the periodic moulting between instars) and emergence in most species. Many gomphid larvae emerge on horizontal supports such as shingle or rocks and these can be incorporated into any tank system, or larvae can be induced to climb up an angled mesh support.

Gomphids often emerge on horizontal supports.

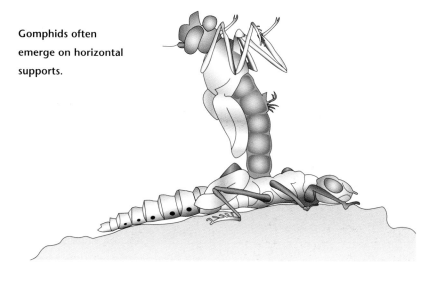

The current popularity of Aquatic Centres has made it possible to obtain a variety of live food that will survive for several days in water and will not foul up the environment by dying prematurely. Daphnia, brine shrimp, white worm and bloodworm can be obtained in this manner and it is possible to culture the latter two, and also to obtain mosquito larvae from containers placed outside in the summer. It may be important for larger individuals to exercise the gut, and larger treats such as garden worms should be provided periodically. Aeshnids will actively stalk and devour both tadpoles and water snails and will also wrestle vigorously with worms many times their own size. It is vital that any undigested remains should be cleared out afterwards to prevent decay and subsequent poisoning of the water. Most larvae reared artificially appear to produce smaller adults than those which have developed naturally and investigations on diet would be a worthwhile study. Richard Rowe, in his *Dragonflies of New Zealand* (1987) includes an invaluable chapter on methods and ideas, covering the feeding of early instars, right through to the adult.

Many aspects of behaviour can be studied using these basic conditions, including territorial behaviour and feeding habits. Any moults obtained can be preserved by immersing them in acetone for several hours in order to produce a hard specimen suitable for display or study. If the adult is required for any reason, it must be remembered that the specimen will be soft and may not have acquired its mature colouring, and that feeding larvae over a long period can be a demanding task. The final exuvia can easily be extracted from its perch without damage, if both are sprayed with water; this will soften the surface and enable the tarsal claws to be freed with a minimum of damage; the jaw can be extended and both antennae and lamellae set for examination whilst the exuvia is still soft.

For larvae which live in running water, there are many sophisticated modern aquatic systems, incorporating both air and water pumps with filtration systems. Tanks can be divided into sections, each with a slight fall to the next lower division thus producing turbulent and well oxygenated conditions as required by stream dwellers such as euphaeids and epiophlebiids. If this seems daunting, it may be a relief to know that some calopterygids, platycnemids and gomphids from lowland rivers or slow-flowing streams, and even cordulegasterids and chloro-gomphids from mountain streams can be reared in still water conditions. Success will always be greater when natural conditions are reproduced and the maintenance of a good supply of oxygen and cold water temperature will be major factors in this respect. *Cordulegaster picta* has been observed to survive for several days in a totally frozen condition, becoming normally active upon thawing out. Unfortunately the aquaria were not so lucky!

Larvae of petalurids, which are predominantly burrowers, can be reared out using a

Aeshnids will devour water snails.

running water system such as above but, to replicate their environment, all but the lowest of the tank divisions, must be filled with a mixture of peat and sand to reproduce, as far as possible, natural burrow areas. Species such as *Tanypteryx hageni* and *T. pryeri* have been successfully reared over a two year period using these conditions; live food such as garden worms, spiders and woodlice were seized and dragged down into the burrow to be digested. Larvae can be induced to burrow next to the side of the container if sheets of material are placed around it to block out the light; these can be removed at intervals for observation

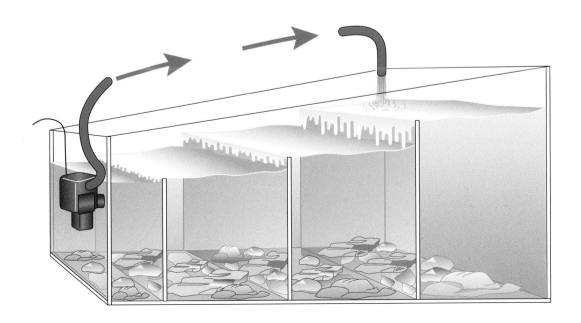

More complicated aquaria are required for species that breed in running water.

purposes. Similar methods need to be employed with other secretive species, such as the larvae of *Epiophlebia laidlawi* and *E. superstes*, both of which will seek out crevices in which they can hide and avoid any form of bright light.

Larvae can be transported for long distances with a minimum of equipment as long as they are kept cool and damp; water is only required as a medium for oxygen exchange and is counter productive in large amounts. Small containers such as 35 mm film canisters are ideal and should be packed with a damp material such as moss or tissue. These can then be placed inside a cool box lined with a supply of ice and will survive for periods longer than 24 hours. Tropical species such as *Pantala flavescens* will survive in these conditions too but, as a rule species from the more primitive families, such as Epiophlebiidae and Cordulegastridae appear able to survive longer in colder conditions and without food. (Keith Wilson tells me that fish are transported across the world but by using oxygen rather than air.)

Eggs can also be transported over long distances. For example, the eggs of *Tanypteryx hageni* have been sent successfully from the USA to the UK through the post. The eggs of tropical species should not be cooled too much in transit or they will probably not hatch; this has been experienced with eggs from *Orthetrum nitidinerve*, *Brachythemis leucosticta* and *Trithemis annulata*. Normally eggs from exophytic females (Gomphidae, Libellulidae or Corduliidae) are the more easily obtained but Cooper, Holland and Miller (1996) suggested that the females of endophytic species can be encouraged to oviposit into material such as chromatography paper, and Richard Rowe (1987) suggested blotting paper. A female *Aeshna multicolor* was observed to oviposit in the dry mesh of a butterfly breeding cage; its eggs were extracted and, some time later, hatched successfully.

Once the larvae are installed in their set-up and are ready to be fed, they should be divided into two sorts: those that need feeding frequently and those that do not. As a rule, the latter consist of those species which take longer to develop into adults, normally from more hostile environments, where food may be scarce and the climate produces a short or unreliable flying season. These include species from such families as Cordulegastridae, Petaluridae and Epiophlebiidae. According to A. Taketo (1971), larvae of the petalurid *Tanypteryx pryeri* have survived without food for four months. Starving them deliberately is one thing but overfeeding with live material, which also needs its own food supply, can be fatal without a system of regular monitoring. Tropical libellulid species are invariably voracious and need a regular food supply as they can rarely extend their life cycle by a further year and underfeeding will cause an inability to emerge successfully, or result in a miserable adult specimen.

Philip Corbet, in *Dragonflies* wrote that the percentage of losses in *Anax imperator* larvae emerging naturally was recorded at 8.5% in 1952 and 15% in 1953; artificially reared larvae can be expected to produce similarly fluctuating results. Disease, starvation, unsuitable conditions, overcrowding — or just a plain refusal to cooperate — will all conspire to cause mortality.

The exercise of rearing out, though demanding on time and effort if done on a large scale, not only has a scientific value but it is rewarding too and the thrill of obtaining a perfect specimen — rare or common, foreign or local — will compensate for the failures which will inevitably occur. When the object of all the care and attention finally emerges successfully, it is a wonderful experience and time to get out the camera!

12
Conservation

NORMAN MOORE

The overall objective of dragonfly conservation is to conserve as many species of dragonfly as possible; the maintenance of biodiversity is as important for dragonflies as it is for all other taxonomic groups. Having said that, we have to admit that some species are more special than others. Most would agree that the loss of one of the two surviving anisozygopterans or of *Hemiphlebia mirabilis* would matter much more than the loss of a species of *Sympetrum*, a genus which contains over 80 species. In addition to taxonomically isolated species, priority should also be given to species with unusual biology, such as *Megalagrion oahuense* with its terrestrial larva. Species in centres of endemism are of particular value for the study of evolution and should also be given priority. Notable centres of endemism occur in mainland South-East Asia (Cambodia, Laos, Myanmar, Thailand, Vietnam and south China) and in The Philippines and Indonesia; in New Guinea, New Caledonia, Australia and New Zealand; in the Ryu Kyu islands of Japan and in the Hawaiian islands; in Madagascar and the forested areas of West and Central Africa (notably Cameroon and Democratic Republic of Congo) and in

South Africa; in tropical South America (notably the eastern slopes of the Andes in Ecuador and Peru), Chile, Central America and the south-east of the USA. We conclude that the general objective to conserve as many species as possible should be supplemented by additional measures to conserve species of special interest.

The threat of extinctions demands a global perspective, but the necessary measures to prevent extinctions can only be achieved by national organisations. So, when a nation has performed its international obligations, it should take a national viewpoint so as to maintain biodiversity within its own borders. For example, *Lestes dryas* (see page 92) has an immense geographical range covering Europe, northern Asia and North America. It is certainly not threatened globally, but it is desirable to conserve its few British populations, both to maintain its presence on the edge of its range and to enable people in Britain to enjoy it and study it.

The basic problems of dragonfly conservation

The practical problems of conserving dragonflies worldwide are enormous. Over 6000 species have been described already but many await description, especially in the rainforests upon which so many dragonfly species depend. Outside Europe, North America, Japan, New Zealand and one or two other countries, very little is known about the distribution of many of the species which have been described, and even less about their habitat requirements. The important point is that the destruction of habitats, particularly rainforest, is happening much too quickly for us to acquire information about individual species in time to provide a detailed basis for their conservation. This crucial fact has to be faced if we are to make real headway in conserving dragonflies worldwide.

Many countries have legislation to prevent the collecting of rare (or even common!) dragonflies. Such legislation is almost irrelevant, since collecting very rarely affects populations; it can even be counterproductive since it obscures the fact that it is loss of habitat which really matters.

For centuries many species of dragonfly have been able to breed in human-built water bodies on farmland but, with the increasing industrialisation of farming, farmland becomes increasingly inimical to dragonflies. As a result, dragonflies depend proportionally more on unfarmed areas such as gravel pits, ornamental lakes and fishponds and, above all, on waters in protected areas where nature conservation is the primary land use. Protected Areas which are established to conserve their flora and fauna in perpetuity are extremely important since they will conserve their dragonflies whatever happens outside them. Also, they will provide bases from which the wider countryside can be colonised, if and when farming and commercial forestry methods can be modified to become more friendly to wildlife than they are now. Protected Areas have never been more important than they are

today. Their establishment is crucial for nature conservation, but how do we choose the places to make national parks and nature reserves when so little is known about dragonflies?

Great Britain — a laboratory for dragonfly conservation

Shortage of information and lack of time force us to develop a strategy based on what we know already. Experience in Great Britain shows a way forward.

Great Britain is an offshore island with an impoverished dragonfly fauna of 40 resident species. It is a densely populated country whose farming has been industrialised in the last 50 years. On the other hand, it has well-developed governmental conservation: notably a network of some 300 National Nature Reserves (NNR) and a system of Sites of Special Scientific Interest (SSSI) which cover about 6% of the country. There are numerous non-governmental conservation organisations, notably the Royal Society for the Protection of Birds (RSPB) and the county wildlife trusts. There is a growing number of farmers who integrate conservation with productive farming under the auspices of the Farming and Wildlife Advisory Group. There is a large naturalist public and a thriving society — the British Dragonfly Society — devoted to the study of dragonflies and their conservation. Much is known about the distribution of British dragonflies and at least something about their habitat requirements.

In the period 1953 to 1963, three species of Odonata became extinct in Britain: one as a result of pollution, one of agricultural change, and one of a natural disaster. Since 1963 most species have held their own, though there have been many local declines due to the intensification of agriculture and the lowering of water tables. Species which have been able to exploit the great increase in water-filled mineral workings have increased. However, an increasing number of species appear to depend on nature reserves or on farmland which is managed extensively as in Environmentally Sensitive Areas. The objective of the series of NNR is to conserve the best examples of all the main types of habitat in Great Britain. They are selected largely by using botanical criteria. None has been selected on odonatological grounds, yet populations of every British species but two are protected in one or more NNR. Similarly the national network of RSPB reserves, which are selected on ornithological grounds, also protects populations of virtually all British dragonflies. Nevertheless, some important localities for rare species remain outside NNRs and RSPB reserves. Some of these are protected by Wildlife Trusts and others receive some protection by SSSI designation. Special provisions of the SSSI system exist to enable SSSI to be designated specifically to protect populations of rare dragonfly species and exceptionally rich communities of dragonflies.

The main conclusions which can be drawn from the British experience are twofold. First, dragonflies can hold their own in a country with industrialised agriculture if there are numerous nature reserves, at least a large minority of farmers who attempt to integrate conservation with farming and at least some control of river pollution. Second, detailed studies on dragonfly distribution and habitat requirements, though highly desirable, are not necessary so long as there is a national network containing representative examples of all the main habitat types present in the country.

This last conclusion shows what can be done in countries where there is far less information about dragonflies than in Great Britain.

Dragonfly conservation throughout the world

Countries which have established networks of representative nature reserves are already doing much to conserve their dragonfly populations. Such countries tend to be those in the Holarctic region where there are relatively few species of dragonfly and where there are enough odonatologists to have odonatological societies, which publish journals and assist with the production of distribution maps. They include Belgium, France, Germany, the Netherlands, Japan, the United Kingdom and the USA. In these countries the success or failure of general conservation measures in conserving dragon-flies can be monitored to some extent.

Japan has a unique position in the field of dragonfly conservation. It is the only country where dragonflies are an important element in its culture. When it established the Dragonfly Kingdom at Nakamura in 1986, Japan became the first country to set up a nature reserve primarily for dragonflies. Since then 24 more such sanctuaries have been established in Japan. While there are still gaps in the coverage of

A Portuguese Prayer of the Woods in Bays Mountain Park, Tennessee, USA.

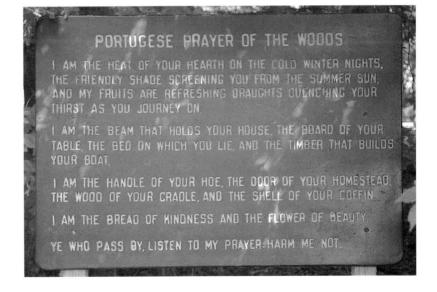

PORTUGESE PRAYER OF THE WOODS

I AM THE HEAT OF YOUR HEARTH ON THE COLD WINTER NIGHTS, THE FRIENDLY SHADE SCREENING YOU FROM THE SUMMER SUN, AND MY FRUITS ARE REFRESHING DRAUGHTS QUENCHING YOUR THIRST AS YOU JOURNEY ON.

I AM THE BEAM THAT HOLDS YOUR HOUSE, THE BOARD OF YOUR TABLE, THE BED ON WHICH YOU LIE, AND THE TIMBER THAT BUILDS YOUR BOAT.

I AM THE HANDLE OF YOUR HOE, THE DOOR OF YOUR HOMESTEAD, THE WOOD OF YOUR CRADLE, AND THE SHELL OF YOUR COFFIN.

I AM THE BREAD OF KINDNESS AND THE FLOWER OF BEAUTY.

YE WHO PASS BY, LISTEN TO MY PRAYER:HARM ME NOT.

protected habitats in the country, the dragonfly sanctuaries go a long way towards filling them.

Valuable conservation work is being done in a number of countries, notably Australia, India and South Africa, on local areas and specific problems, despite large gaps in knowledge about the distributions of species in those countries.

Cooperative measures in Europe under the Habitat Directive of the European Union will help conserve threatened dragonfly species. For example Special Areas for Conservation will be established for *Coenagrion mercuriale* (see page 109) throughout its range.

Unfortunately, many countries, including those with most endemic species, have few or no odonatologists. It is in these countries that the British experience is so important. If they could develop networks of representative Protected Areas, they could maintain most of their dragonfly species. To do this they require the support of the international community.

International support for national initiatives

Communication between odonatologists is maintained by the Worldwide Dragonfly Association (WDA) and its scientific journal *Pantala* and its newsletter AGRION, and Societas Internationalis Odonatologica Foundation (FSIO) and its journal *Odonatologica*. Both organisations hold biennial symposia in different countries. The Odonata Specialist Group of the Species Survival Commission of IUCN (World Conservation Union) acts as a forum for odonatologists concerned with conservation. It meets biennially on the occasion of the WDA symposia and publishes one or more Reports on dragonfly conservation matters each year. The Odonata Specialist Group gives international support to national conservation initiatives. It is developing a conservation data base for Odonata and has published *Dragonflies: Status Survey and Conservation Action Plan* (Moore N. W. (Compiler) 1997 IUCN/SSC Odonata Specialist Group. IUCN, Glund, Switzerland and Cambridge, UK. v + 28 pp). The principal recommendation of the Action Plan is to foster support for national networks of representative Protected Areas. These are not only essential for dragonflies but for all taxonomic groups. It is hoped that dragonflies can act as a flagship in supporting a concept which is fundamental to maintaining the world's biodiversity.

Glossary

andromorph a female with colour pattern closely resembling that of a male (cf. **heteromorph**)

antehumeral stripes stripes on top surface of thorax

anterior situated at the front of the body, e.g. the leading edge of the wing

apex, apical tip; e.g. that part of a wing that is furthest from the thorax

auricle a lateral projection on the second abdominal segment of some male Anisoptera

base, basal lowest part, or starting point; that part of a wing, leg, etc. that is closest to the thorax

bathymetry the art or method of taking deep soundings

bifid split partly into two

biotic pertaining to life

biotope 'living place'; a habitat or microhabitat type

calcareous containing or resembling calcium carbonate; chalky

catatonic involuntary immobility; 'playing possum'

caudal pertaining to the tail; caudal gills are situated at the rear of a damselfly's body

caudal lamellae plate-like structures acting as gills and/or a paddle for propulsion

cerci dorsal (superior) abdominal appendages at the tip of an odonate's body

chitin a substance (polysaccharide) that is the main structural component of the exoskeleton

clypeus the section of the face between the frons and the upper-lip

confluent running together, with a long area of contact, generally used when describing the degree of contact between the eyes of anisopterans

congeners other species within a certain genus

conspecific of or relating to the same species

costa the thickened vein at leading edge of all four wings

cryptic tending to conceal due to (e.g.) colour pattern

cuticle an impermeable layer of horny non-cellular material covering the epidermal cells

diapause a period of suspended growth or development

dimorphic having two distinct forms, especially of colour

discrete discontinuous

distal the part of a segment or appendage furthest from the centre of the body

dorsal upper surface of the body (cf. **ventral**)

ecdysis the periodic moulting of the 'skin' of a larva, between instars

ecosystem a biological community and the physical environment associated with it

endophytic describing a method of oviposition whereby ova are inserted into plant tissue or mud

epidermis the outermost layer of cells of the body of an animal; in invertebrates, it is normally only one cell thick and covered by an impermeable **cuticle**

epiphytic describing a method of oviposition whereby eggs are placed on the surface of floating plants

epiproct the single ventral abdominal appendage in dragonflies (cf. **paraproct**)

estivation passing the summer in a state of dormancy (cf. **hibernation**)

exophytic describing a method of oviposition whereby eggs are scattered into the water

exoskeleton the hard chitinous covering that protects and supports the bodies of all arthropods

exuvia (pl. **exuviae**) skin cast by an insect during a moult

falcate sickle-shaped

forcipate curved towards each other like the tips of forceps

fossil remains or traces of an organism that lived in the geological past

fossilisation petrifaction; the turning of an organism into stone

frons the 'forehead'

genus (pl. **genera**) taxonomic division grouping closely related species

haemolymph an insect's body fluid that is sometimes referred to as 'insect blood'

hamule or **hamulus** specialised, finger-like organ in the males of some species that plays a role in securing the female during sexual pairing

hawking flying backwards and forwards over an area searching for prey

heteromorph a female with a colour pattern different to that of males (cf. **andromorph**)

hibernation passing the winter in a state of dormancy (cf. **estivation**)

Holarctic region a combination of the Nearctic and Palaearctic regions (see **zoogeographical region**)

homology describing features of organisms that have the same evolutionary origin but have developed different functions (e.g. wings of a bat, flippers of a dolphin and arms of a man are homologous organs, having evolved from the paired pectoral fins of a fish ancestor)

hyaline clear, transparent (of wings)

imago the adult stage of an insect's life

inertia the state of being inactive

instar stage in the larval development, between two moults

intercalated describing extra cells in the wing venation

K/T line marks the boundary between the Mesozoic and Cenozoic eras (65 mya); i.e. between the Cretaceous and Tertiary periods

labium (pl. **labia**) or mask: the lower lip which is very large and specialised in odonate larvae.

lacustrine relating to lakes

lamella (pl. **lamellae**) see under 'caudal'

lamina a thin plate

lateral the side or from the side of the body

lithosphere the outer, rocky shell of the earth, the crust of the earth

marl a calcium carbonate sediment associated with calcareous wetlands and lakes

mask see under 'labium'

mesostigmal plate leaf-like structures at the front of the synthorax which are the only sure way to identify some female damselflies.

monotypic consisting of a single species within a genus, or a single genus within a family.

morphology relating to form and structure, particularly external.

moult (or **ecdysis**) the periodic splitting of the **exoskeleton** of one instar to allow the emergence of the next one; an essential part of the growth of all arthropods

occiput area of the head behind the eyes

orography the branch of physical geography pertaining to mountains and mountain systems

oval pertaining to ova (egg cells)

ovipositor organ at tip of abdomen of female insects through which eggs are laid

ovum (pl. **ova**) an egg cell; the mature reproductive cell of female animals, produced by the ovary

palp an elongated sensory organ, usually near the mouth, in many invertebrates

paraproct the pair of inferior abdominal appendages in damselflies (cf. **epiproct**)

perch place on which an active dragonfly settles (cf. **roost**)

percher a dragonfly (generally a libellulid) that spends much of its active time perched on an object

petiolate stemmed or stalked (used to describe the wings of some damselflies)

phylogenic evolutionary

phylogeny conjectural evolutionary history of a group of related organisms

phytotermata small bodies of water contained in or upon a plant (e.g. bamboo stems, treeholes)

polychromatic exhibiting more than one colour form

polymorphic having different forms, especially of colour

posterior situated at the rear of the body

prolarva the first larval stage of an odonate (and of several other types of insect)

prothorax the anterior segment of the thorax, bearing a pair of legs but no wings

proximal the part of a segment or appendage closest to the centre of the body

pruinescence a waxy bloom that develops on some species as they mature

pseudostigma a 'false' pterostigma

pterostigma a small, thickened area on the wing situated on the costal border near its apex, usually dark or differing in colour from the rest of the wing

refugium (pl. **refugia**) a geographical region that has remained unaltered by a climatic change affecting surrounding areas and that therefore forms a haven for relict fauna and flora

reticulation the network of veins or nervures on the wings

roost place on which an inactive dragonfly rests (cf. **perch**)

saccoid sack-like, referring to the shape of some damselfly larvae's caudal gills

secondary genitalia male organs situated ventrally on second and part of third abdominal segments

sedimentary rocks formed by the accumulation and consolidation of mineral and organic fragments that have been deposited by water, ice or wind

semivoltine completing one generation every two years

seta (pl. **setae**) a hair, bristle or thin spine generally with some sensory function

setose covered in long, fine setae

spiracles external openings leading to the **tracheae**; valve through which air enters an insect's respiratory system

strata (sing. **stratum**) the distinct layers into which sedimentary rocks are divided

sub-montane situated on or characteristic of lower slopes of a mountain

substrate underlying surface on which an animal or plant is positioned

subtending covering an area equivalent to a number of adjacent cells

sutures flexible zones between segments of the body which allow articulation in an exoskeleton

synthorax the posterior segment of the **thorax** that bears the two pairs of wings and the two posterior pairs of legs

taxon (pl. **taxa**) a named taxonomic group; thus, taxa Aeshnidae, Odonata, Insecta and Arthropoda are named examples of a family, order, class and phylum respectively

taxonomy study of theory, practice and rules of the classification of living and extinct organisms

tectonic distortion of the earth's crust due to forces within it

temperate pertaining to regions between the tropics and the latitudinal limit of trees and in which seasonal changes are from warm to cool

teneral the stage immediately following a moult, during which the exoskeleton is hardening; used to describe a newly-emerged imago

tepuis isolated tabletop mountains in the Guyana Highlands

thorax (pl. **thoraces**) the second segment of an insect's body which bears the wings and legs

tracheae tubes which conduct air from **spiracles** to tissues of the body

tracheal pertaining to tracheae

triquetral three-sided in cross section; referring to the shape of some damselfly gills

tropical pertaining to the region between latitudes 23°27' N and S and in which seasonal changes, if any, are from wet to dry

univoltine completing one generation per year

vagile having the ability to move about

venation the pattern of veins in the wings

ventral underside of the body (cf. **dorsal**)

vesicle any small sac or cavity

vulvar pertaining to the vagina

vulvar spine projection on ventral surface of some females' seventh abdominal segment

Wallace line hypothetical line dividing the Australasian region from the Oriental, running between Indonesian islands of Bali and Lombok, through Macassar Strait, and southeast of the Philippines; named after A. R. Wallace

zoogeography the branch of zoology concerned with the geographical distribution of animals

zoogeographical regions Six regions (sometimes referred to as Zones) into which the earth is divided, based on a system adopted by A. R. Wallace:

1. **Palaearctic** — Europe, temperate Asia, Africa north of the Sahara

2. **Ethiopian** — Africa south of Sahara, Madagascar

3. **Oriental** — India south of Himalayas, southern China, islands as far south as Philippines, Indonesia etc.;

4. **Australasian** — Australia, Papua New Guinea, Pacific islands including Lombock (New Zealand is considered a sub-region)

5. **Nearctic** — North America as far south as Mexico

6. **Neotropical** — central and South America, West Indies (see **Holarctic** above)

Dragonfly societies

Australian Dragonfly Society
Deniss Reeves
30 Bramston Terrace
Herston
Queensland 4006
Australia

**Belgische Libellenonderoekers-
Odonatologues Belges**
Geert de Knijf
Hofstraat 58
B-9000 Gent
Belgium

British Dragonfly Society
Dr W. H. Wain
The Haywain, Hollywater Road
Bordon, Hampshire GU15 0AD
United Kingdom

Dragonfly Society of Eastern Europe
Dr S. Gorb
Lab. Insect Physiol, Schmalhausen Inst. Zool.
Ukraine Acad. Sci.
B. Chmelnickogo 15
UKR-252601 Kiev
Ukraine

Dragonfly Society of the Americas
Dr and Mrs T. W. Donnelly
2091 Partridge Lane
Binghamton, NY 13903
USA

Gesellschaft deutschsprachiger Odonatologen
Ulrike Kruner
Gelderner Str. 39
D-41189 Monchengladbach
Germany

Groupement des Odonatologues de Suisse
C. Meier
Joggenweg 19
CH-8708 Mannedorf
Switzerland

Hokkaido Odonatological Society
Prof. Tomiyasu Koyama
2-7-516, Kitaa 1-jo,
Nishi 25-chome, Chuo-ku, Sapporo,
Hokkaido, 064-0821
Japan

Irish Odonata Recording Scheme
C. Ronayne
33 Dublin Road
Skerries, Co. Dublin
Ireland

Kansai Research Group of Odonatology
Mr Kozo Tani
Jizou-cho 129,
Nara-shi, Nara prefecture, 630
Japan

Nederlandse Libellenlonderzoekers
W. J. A. Hoeffnagel
Krekelmeent 72
NL-1218 ED Hilversum
The Netherlands

Nordic Odonatological Society
Dr H. Olsvik
N-6694 Foldfjorden
Norway

Odonata Research Society, Osaka
Mr Akio Muraki
4-2-309, Shigino-nishi 3 chome
Joto-ku, Osaka-shi,
Osaka prefecture, 536
Japan

Osterreichische Arbeitsgemeinschaft Libellen
Rainer Raab
Anton Brucknergasse 2/2
A-2232 Deutch-Wagram
Austria

S. I. O. Foundation
Editor of Odonatologica, Bastiaan Kiauta
PO Box 256
7520 AG Bilthoven
The Netherlands

Slovene Odonatological Society
Alja Pirnat
Vosnyakova 4/a
(Slovensko Odonatolsko Drustvo)
SL-1000 Ljubljana
Slovenia

Société Française d'Odonatologie
J-L. Dommanget
7 rue Lamartine
F-78390 Bois-d'Arcy
France

The Japan Society for Odonatology
Dr Shigeo Eda
Matsumoto Dental College Dept. of Oral
Pathology
1780 Gobara, Hirooka Shiojiri-shi
399-07
Japan

Tombo to Shizen wo kangaeru Kai
Mr Mitsutoshi Sugimura
Migiyama-Satsuki-machi,
9-7, Nakamura-shi,
Kochi Prefecture, 787
Japan

Worldwide Dragonfly Association
Jill Silsby
1 Haydn Avenue
Purley
Surrey, CR8 4AG
United Kingdom

Bibliography

In addition to back numbers of Pantala, Odonatologica, Folio Entomologica Mexicana, Journal of Bengal Natural History Society, Fauna of Saudi Arabia, Tombo, Kimminsia and WDA's AGRION, the following works are those that I have found of great value in the preparation of this book.

Asahina, S. 1993. A List of the Odonata from Thailand, ed. Br. Amnuay Pinratana (Soi Yoo Dee: Yannawa, Bangkok.)

Askew, R. R. 1988. 'The Dragonflies of Europe.' (Harley Books: Great Horkesley, Colchester.)

Cannings, R. A. & Stuart, K. M. 1997. The Dragonflies of British Columbia, British Columbia Provincial Museum Handbook No. 35.

Cooper, G., Holland, P.W.H. & Miller P.L. 1996. Captive breeding of *Ischnura elegans* (Van der Linden): observations on longevity, copulation and oviposition (Zygoptery; Coenagrionidae). *Odonatologica* 25(3): 261–273.

Corbet, P. S., Longfield, C. & Moore, N. W. 1960. 'Dragonflies.' (Collins: London.)

Corbet, P. S. 1983. 'A Biology of Dragonflies.' (Reprint of 1962 edition with replacement title page and verso.) (Classey: Faringdon.)

Davies, D. A. L. & Tobin, P. 1984. The dragonflies of the world: a systematic list of the extant species of Odonata. Volume 1 Zygoptera, Anisozygoptera. *Societas Internationalis Odonatologica Rapid Communications (Supplements)* 3, ixx+127.

Davies, D. A. L. & Tobin, P. 1985. The dragonflies of the world: A systematic list of the extant species of Odonata. Volume 2 Anisoptera. *Societas Internationalis Odonatologica Rapid Communications (Supplements)* 5, xi+151.

d'Aguilar, J., Dommanget, J-L, & Préchac, R. 1986. 'Field Guide to the Dragonflies of Britain, Europe and North Africa.' (Collins: London.)

Dumont, H. J. 1991. 'Odonata of the Levant.' (Israel Academy of Sciences and Humanities: Jerusalem.)

Dunkle, S. W. 1989. 'Dragonflies of the Florida Peninsula, Bermuda and the Bahamas.' (Scientific Publishers: Gainsville and Washington.)

Dunkle, S. W. 1990. 'Damselflies of Florida, Bermuda and the Bahamas.' (Scientific Publishers: Gainsville and Washington.)

Fraser, Lt-Col. I. M. S. 1933. 'The Fauna of British India.' (Today and Tomorrow's Printers and Publishers: New Delhi.)

Fraser, F. C. 1960. 'A Handbook of the Dragonflies of Australasia.' (Royal Zoological Society of New South Wales: Sydney.)

Holder, M. 1996. 'The Dragonflies and Damselflies of Algonquin Provincial Park.' (The Friends of Algonquin Park: Whitney.)

Martens, A. 1996. 'Die Federlibellen Europas.' (Neue Brehm-Bücherei Bd. 626, Westarp Wissenschaften, Magdeburg.)

Miller, P. L. 1995. Dragonflies, Naturalists' Handbooks 7 (The Richmond Publishing Co.: Slough.)

Needham, J. G. & Gyger, M. K. 1937. 'The Odonata of the Philippines.' (Bureau of Science, Dept. of Agriculture and Commerce: Manila.)

Pinhey, E. C. G. 1951. 'The Dragonflies of Southern Africa.' (Transvaal Museum: Pretoria.)

Pinhey, E. C. G. 1961. 'A Survey of the Dragonflies of Eastern Africa.' (Trustees of the British Museum: London.)

Polhemus, D. & Asquith, A. 1996. 'Hawaian Dragonflies.' (Bishop Museum Press: Honolulu.)

Rowe, R. 1987. 'The Dragonflies of New Zealand.' (Auckland University Press: Auckland.)

Tillyard, R. J. 1917. 'The Biology of Dragonflies.' (Cambridge University Press: Cambridge.)

Ubukata, H. 1993. 'Dragonflies of Kushiro Shitsugen.' (Japanese Society for Preservation of Birds: Kushiro, Japan.)

van Andel, T. H. 1985. 'New Views on an Old Planet.' (Cambridge University Press: Cambridge.)

Watson, J. A. L., Theischinger, G. & Abbey, H. M. 1991. 'The Australian Dragonflies.' (CSIRO: Canberra.)

Wilson, K. D. P. 1995. 'Hong Kong Dragonflies.' (Urban Council of Hong Kong.)

Interesting contributions to the literature, published in recent years:

Brooks, S. 1997. 'Field Guide to the Dragonflies and Damselflies of Great Britain and Ireland.' ed. S. Brooks (British Wildlife Publishing.)

Dunkle, S. W. 2000. Dragonflies through binoculars, a field guide to dragonflies of North America. Oxford University Press, New York, 266 pp., 383 color photos. ISBN 0-19-511268-7. Obtainable from IORI in Florida (e-mail: iori@afn.org).

Corbet, P. S. 1999. 'Dragonflies: Behaviour and Ecology of Odonates.' (Cornell University Press: New York and Harley Books, Great Horkesley, UK)

Hämäläinen, M. & Pinratana Bro. A. 1999. 'Atlas of the Dragonflies of Thailand.' (Chok Chai Creation Printing Group Co.: Bangkok, Thailand.)

Inoue, K. & Tani, K. 1999. 'All about Dragonflies.' (Tombow Publishing Co.: Osaka, Japan.)

Kotarac, M. 1997. 'Atlas of the Dragonflies (Odonata) of Slovenia.' (Centre for Cartography of Fauna and Flora, Miklavz na Dravskem polju: Slovenia.)

Merritt, R., Moore N. W. & Eversham, B. C. 1996. 'Atlas of the dragonflies of Britain and Ireland.' (Natural Environment Research Council, H. M. Stationery Office).

Needham, J. G., Westfall, M. J. Jr, & May, M. L. (2000). 'The Dragonflies of North America.' (IORI: Gainesville, Florida, USA.)

Nielsen, O. F. 1998. 'De danske guldsmede.' (Apollo Books: Stenstrup, Denmark) [In Danish]

Powell, D. 1999. 'A Guide to the Dragonflies of Great Britain.' (Arlequin Press: UK.)

Samways, M. J. & Whiteley, G. 1997. 'Dragonflies of the Natal Drakensberg.' (University of Natal Press: Pietermaritzburg.)

Westfall, M. J. Jr & May, M. L. 1996. 'Damselflies of North America.' (Scientific Publishers: Gainsville and Washington.)

Index of species

General index

METRIC CONVERSION TABLE
(approximate)

Length

10 mm	=	1 cm	=	⅖ in
100 mm	=	10 cm	=	4 in
1 m	=	3 ft 3 in		
1000 m	=	1 km	=	⅝ mile

Weight (mass)

100 g	=	3½ oz
1 kg	=	2⅕ lb

Temperature

0°C	=	32°F
20°C	=	68°F
40°C	=	104°F